AF608239

THE CATHOLIC UNIVERSITY OF AMERICA
CANON LAW STUDIES
No. 278.

THE TRANSFER OF RELIGIOUS TO ANOTHER COMMUNITY

AN HISTORICAL SYNOPSIS AND A COMMENTARY

BY THE

REV. JOSEPH G. KONRAD, A.B., J.C.L.
Priest of the Diocese of Brooklyn

A DISSERTATION

Submitted to the Faculty of the School of Canon Law of the Catholic University of America in Partial Fulfillment of the Requirements for the Degree of Doctor of Canon Law

THE CATHOLIC UNIVERSITY OF AMERICA PRESS
WASHINGTON, D. C.
1949

Nihil Obstat:

Hieronymus D. Hannan, A.M., LL.B., S.T.D., J.C.D.,
Censor Deputatus.

Vashingtonii, die 2 aprilis, 1949.

Imprimatur:

✠ Thomas Edmundus Molloy, S.T.D.,
Episcopus Bruklyniensis.

Bruklynii, die 11 aprilis, 1949.

COPYRIGHT, 1949
THE CATHOLIC UNIVERSITY OF AMERICA PRESS, INC.

Printed by
The Paulist Press
401 West 59th Street
New York 19, N. Y.
81

TABLE OF CONTENTS

FOREWORD

It is the purpose of this dissertation to examine the laws which govern the transfer of a religious or of a member of a society of the common life to another religious institute or society, or to another independent monastery of the same institute. It is beyond the scope of this work to consider the transfer of religious to another house or province of the same centralized institute.

The first section of the dissertation deals with the history of the legal regulation of transfer before the Code of Canon Law. The second section consists of a commentary on the laws of the Code. The subject matter of the first chapter concerns the legislation regulating transfer and is arranged, for the most part, in chronological order. The subject matter of the second chapter concerns the authoritative and doctrinal interpretation of the pre-Code legislation and is arranged according to a topical order. The content of the three articles which comprise the second chapter will correspond, in a general way, to the content of the three subsequent chapters. These last three chapters constitute the canonical commentary.

The writer must use this opportunity to express his deep gratitude to his Bishop, the Most Reverend Thomas E. Molloy, for assigning him to pursue advanced studies in Canon Law. It is His Excellency's kind generosity that has made possible the writing and the printing of this work. The writer wishes to thank also the Most Reverend Raymond A. Kearney, Auxiliary Bishop and Chancellor of the Diocese of Brooklyn, the Very Reverend Monsignor John J. Carberry, Officialis, the Very Reverend Monsignor John J. Heneghan and the Very Reverend Monsignor Vincent J. Baldwin, Vice Chancellors, and the other members of the Chancery Staff, for unfailing and kindly help and encouragement. He must express his gratitude to the members of the Faculty of the School of Canon Law for their constant guidance and assistance. In particular, he wishes to thank the Very Reverend Doctor Jerome D. Hannan for his valued direction and advice in the preparation of this dissertation, and the Very Reverend Doctor Clement V. Bastnagel for his generous expenditure of time and energy in checking the footnotes and the bibliography. Finally, he thanks all who in any way contributed to the completion of this work.

Part I

Synopsis of Early History

CHAPTER I

LEGISLATION CONCERNING THE TRANSFER OF RELIGIOUS

Article 1. Laws Concerning Transfer

1. From the Beginning to the Fifth Century

One of those perpetually renewed phenomena which are visible manifestations of the spiritual vitality of the Catholic Church has been the voluntary adoption by untold numbers of her children of a life dedicated not only to the keeping of God's commandments, but also to an ideal of perfection counselled by Christ and outlined in the inspired pages of the New Testament.

The monastic movement was a great, spontaneous mass movement among Christians toward the realization of this ideal. It began toward the end of the third century, and during the fourth and fifth spread swiftly to every corner of the Roman Empire. It was distinguished from the Christian asceticism which preceded it by the fact that it combined the ideals both of a contemplative life and that of the renunciation of family life and of earthly goods.[1] Monasticism developed in a double form: the first, from which its name was derived,[2] was the anchoretic life, that of the solitaries or hermits, who often lived together in the same place, but were not bound to-

[1] Rothenhäusler, "Ältestes Mönchtum und klösterliche Beständigkeit"—*Benedictinische Monatschrift* (Beuron, 1919—), IV (1922), 92.

[2] μονος = alone.

gether by a common rule and common exercises; the second form, which arose from the first by a natural evolution, was the coenobitic life, that of monks living in community in monasteries under the authority of superiors.[3] The two continued side by side for centuries, until a progressive realization that the eremitical life, difficult to control, had in it elements dangerous to the individual, to society and to religion, caused its absorption by coenobitism at the behest of ecclesiastical authority.

The problem of transfer to another religious community could of its very nature arise only in the coenobitic form of religious life. As far as is known, the earliest coenobitic communities had no restrictions on transfer. Thus the Rule of St. Pachomius contains nothing on the subject. In general, it can be said that in the early monasteries the bond which constrained monks to remain in the communities with which they had become affiliated was very weak, so that they were free to transfer from monastery to monastery, as well as from the eremitical to the monastic state or the reverse.[4]

But it was not long before the bond between the individual and his community began to be strengthened. Some of the early rules attributed to the Fathers declared that an abbot should not be permitted to receive a monk from elsewhere without the permission of his former abbot.[5] St. Basil (330-379), the Cappadocian Father who was called "The Great" even by his own contemporaries, was the author of "Rules" which exercised a decisive influence on the Monasticism of the East, and which were not without their effect in the West, though it must be understood that even in the East their influence was rather moral than juridic.[6]

St. Basil declared plainly that stability in the congregation with which the monk had become associated was strictly obligatory, since profession bound him spiritually to the fraternity. He com-

[3] Cayré, *Manual of Patrology,* tr. by H. Howitt (2 vols., Paris: Desclée & Co., 1936-1940), I, 502.

[4] Goyeneche, "De transitu ad aliam religionem,"—*Commentarium pro Religiosis* (Romae, 1920—), I (1920), 222 (hereafter cited *CpR.*).

[5] Rule of Sts. Serapion and Macarius, c. 13—Holstenius-Brockie, *Codex regularum monasticarum et canonicarum* (6 vols., Augustae-Vindelicorum, 1759), I, 13; Rule of the three holy Fathers, c. 14—*ibid.,* p. 18.

[6] Cayré, *op. cit.,* I, 412.

pared this spiritual bond to the bond which existed in marriage, and declared that it was a pact with the Holy Spirit, stronger therefore than any natural bond.[7]

He did, however, admit two reasons for transfer: danger to the salvation of the soul, because of the presence of evil brothers in the society, or a command of the Lord (ἐντολὴ τοῦ κυρίου). In the first case, there was to be an attempt to warn and to reform the brothers. If this was without effect, then the matter was to be laid before those capable of prudent judgment. As Rothenhäusler observes, St. Basil may well have meant here older and more experienced monks of the community, who were elsewhere called "spiritual fathers." If the majority of these voted for transfer, it was permissible to leave the community. Under the command of the Lord, as Rothenhäusler observes also, was meant always the command of the superior. A man who had left the community in contravention to the foregoing norms was impeded from being received into some other "fraternity." [8]

In the fifth century a growing realization of the need to strengthen the bond between the religious and his community became discernible. Praise of monastic stability and a warning of the danger of leaving the monastery even for the purpose of transfer to another monastic community is to be found in a sermon of Eucharius, in early life a cultured and refined Senator of Rome, later a monk at Lérins in France and Archbishop of Lyons (+424).[9] The legislation of this period also gives evidence of this trend.

The Ecumenical Council at Chalcedon (451), while it did not limit transfer directly, still attempted to prevent monks from leaving their monasteries and disturbing the public peace by subjecting them to the bishops where their houses were located, and by ordering that they should remain in the places that had been assigned to

[7] *Constitutiones Monasticae*, c. XXI—Migne, *Patrologiae Cursus Completus, Series Graeca* (161 vols., Paris, 1856-1866), XXXI, 1394-1402 (hereafter cited as *MPG*).

[8] *Regulae Fusius Tractatae*, c. XXXVI—*MPG*, XXXI, 1007-1010; Rothenhäusler, *art. cit.*, p. 226.

[9] Migne, *Patrologiae Cursus Completus, Series Latina* (221 vols., Paris, 1844-1864), L, 864 (hereafter to be cited as *MPL*).

them. Those who disobeyed were excommunicated.[10] Two years later, a synod of Angers (453) made the possession of letters of recommendation obligatory for traveling monks. Stern punishment was decreed for the monk who was outside the walls of his own monastery without such a letter, unless he could show that some serious business or other compelling reason was the cause of his journey. In 471 the Emperor Leo I (457-474), in the East, forbade monks to leave their monasteries for cities; necessary business was to be transacted through agents (*apocrisarii*), that is, through monks who took care of business matters of monasteries, who alone could come to town, and even then only for necessary matters. A synod at Vannes (465) in France forbade monks under pain of excommunication to remain outside of their monastery without letters of recommendation.[11]

II. From the Sixth Century to the Time of Gratian

The first few years of the sixth century witnessed the formation of a juridic concept of stability which directly restricted the right to transfer to another community, and which became a part of the monastic law and tradition of the West. Perhaps a most important rôle in laying the groundwork for this achievement was played by St. Caesarius of Arles (470-542). While abbot of the monastery of Lérins he wrote a rule for his monks, and as bishop of the city of Arles he wrote another for the sisters in the monastery he had founded for them there. In both these rules there was a definitive regulation that restricted the right to transfer. In his rule for monks the very first chapter declared that one who came to the monastery should be received on this condition, that he persevered there till death.[12] His rule for the sisters was even more

[10] C. 4—Mansi, *Sacrorum Conciliorum Nova et Amplissima Collectio* (53 vols. in 60, Paris: Arnhem-Leipzig, 1901-1927), VII, 395 (hereafter to be cited as Mansi); Hefele-Leclercq, *Histoire des Conciles* (10 vols. in 19, Paris: Librairie Letouzey et Ané, 1907-1938), Tom. II, Part II, p. 799 (hereafter to be cited as HL).

[11] C. 6—Bruns, H. Th., *Canones Apostolorum et Conciliorum Saecularum, IV, V, VI, VII* (2 vols., Berolini, 1839), II, 143 (hereafter to be cited as Bruns).

[12] *Regula ad Monachos*, c. 1—*MPL*, LXVII, 1107.

explicit. It provided that a woman who left her parents and wished to renounce the world and to enter the "sacred fold" ought not to leave the monastery until death.[13]

The Council of Agde in Gaul (506) was presided over by this same St. Caesarius. It had been called for all the bishops of the kingdom of the Visigoths. It prescribed that no abbot should presume to receive or to retain a monk unless he was transferring to another monastery with the permission or at the command of his abbot. Wherever he might be, he was to be recalled by his abbot by the authority of the canons.[14] Canon 38 of the same Council decreed that traveling monks had to bear letters of recommendation; unless they did so, they were to be forced to return to their monastery.[15]

At a national council at Orleans (511) attended by all the bishops subject to King Clovis I (481-511), a similar provision was adopted: an abbot who received a monk belonging to another monastery was to know that he would be guilty (of an infringement of the law).[16]

At a later council, again presided over by St. Caesarius of Arles, at Lerida in Tarragona (524) the previously mentioned provisions of the Councils of Agde (506) and of Orleans (511) were repeated and confirmed.[17]

At the very time that these Councils in Gaul were restricting transfer to another community, St. Benedict of Nursia in Italy (480-547) was at work writing for his monks the Rule which was to become the basic Rule for Monasticism in the West. It became

[13] *Regula ad Virgines,* c. 1—*MPL,* LXVII, 1099.

[14] C. 27—*MPL,* VIII, 331; Bruns, II, 151; HL, Tom. II, Part II, pp. 980, 981; c. 3, C. XX, q. 4—*Corpus Iuris Canonici* (ed. 2 curavit Friedberg, 2 vols., Lipsiae, 1879-1881) (hereafter all citations of the *Corpus Iuris Canonici* will be made from this edition).

[15] C. 38—*MPL,* VIII, 33; c. 3, C. XX, q. 4—HL, Tom. II, Part II, p. 97; Bruns, II, 153.

[16] C. 19: "Et reum se ille abbas futurum esse cognoscat qui . . . monachum susceperit alienum."—Bruns, I, 164; c. 16, C. XVIII, q. 2.

[17] C. 3: "De monachis vero id observari placuit, quod synodus Agathensis, vel Aurelianensis noscitur decrevisse"—*MPL,* VIII, 612; HL, Tom. II, Part II, p. 1064, V; c. 34, C. XVI, q. 1; Bruns, II, 21.

supreme in Italy before the end of the sixth century, in the countries which are now France and Germany after the era of Boniface, and in Spain after the ninth century. After the tenth century it was almost universally accepted throughout Christian Europe.

St. Benedict saw, evidently, the same evils which must have been apparent to the Fathers of the Councils above mentioned, and which they attempted to restrict in part by limiting the right to transfer from one community to another. A desire for change and motion had led bands of monks over the great roads of the Roman Empire, there to give themselves to all kinds of boisterous demonstrations. Under the name of Messalians, they wandered as gyrovagues from province to province, from cell to cell, remaining only three or four days in one place, always unstable, never at rest.[18] St. Benedict had only hard words for them in the first chapter of his Rule, concluding his brief denunciation of them with the statement that it was better to be silent than to speak of the most deplorable life which all of them led.[19]

In the Prologue of the Rule he announced his ideal of the monastic life, part of which was that by never departing from subjection to God and *by persevering in His teaching in the monastery until death* the monks should by patience become sharers in the sufferings of Christ.[20]

In the fourth chapter, which he entitled "The Instruments of Good Works," and which was an enumeration of the virtues which were proper to monks, he said that the workshops where they were to fulfill all these duties were the monastery enclosure and stability in the Congregation.[21] This last phrase, stability in the Congregation, *stabilitas in congregatione,* is very significant. The meaning attached by Benedict to the word stability was perseverance, not only in the general sense of perseverance in good or in the religious life, but in the precise sense of permanence in the

[18] Montalembert, *The Monks of the West* (6 vols., New York, 1897), I, 382.

[19] *Sancti Benedicti Regula Monachorum,* ed. by C. Butler (Friburgi-Brisgoviae, 1912), p. 11.

[20] *Ibid.*, p. 8.

[21] "Officina vero, ubi haec omnia diligenter operemur, claustra sunt monasterii et stabilitas in congregatione."—*ibid.*, p. 24.

supernatural family in which profession was made, of perseverance in the monastery.[22]

More important still, he made this ideal of stability binding on his monks not only as a purpose or a resolution, but by a solemn vow of perpetual perseverance. In the fifty-eighth chapter of the Rule it was required as one of the vows by which a novice became a professed member of the Congregation.[23]

But the problem of transfer itself was treated expressly in chapter sixty-one of the Rule. It dealt with the manner in which traveling monks were to be received in the monastery. If they came from distant provinces and wished to be received as guests, they could be received and stay as long as they wished, as long as they were quiet and peaceable and content with things and customs as they found them in the monastery.[24]

Indeed, if such a one, said St. Benedict, wished afterwards to confirm his stability, his request should not be refused, especially because during the time that he had been enjoying the hospitality of the monastery his life could be discerned for what it was.[25] St. Benedict went further still. A good monk should not only be received if he so wished, *but should be persuaded to stay*, so that others might be influenced by his good example, for everywhere it was the same Lord who was served, the same King under whom one fought.[26]

[22] Butler, *Benedictine Monasticism* (New York, 1919), p. 123; Delatte, *A Commentary on the Rule of St. Benedict* (New York: Benziger Brothers, 1921), 389; Williams, *Monastic Studies*, Historical Series No. LXXVI (Manchester, Manchester University Press, 1938), 69.

[23] "Suscipiendus autem in oratorio coram omnibus promittat de stabilitate sua et conversatione morum suorum et oboedientia coram Deo et Sanctis eius, ut si aliquando aliter fecerit, ab eo se damnandum sciat quem inridet."—*Sancti Benedicti Regula Monachorum*, p. 102.

[24] *Ibid.*, p. 106.

[25] "Si vero postea voluerit stabilitatem suam firmare, non renuatur talis voluntas, et maxime, quia tempore hospitalitatis potuit eius vita dignosci"—*ibid.*, p. 107.

[26] "Quod non si fuerit talis qui mereatur proici, non solum si petierit suscipiatur congregationi sociandus, verum etiam suadeatur ut stet, ut eius exemplo alii erudiantur, et quia in omni loco uni Domino servitur, uni Regi militatur."—*loc. cit.*

If the abbot should perceive that the new religious was a man of ability, he could even assign him a somewhat superior position in the monastery.

Finally, however, the abbot was to beware of receiving a monk from some other *known* monastery into the life of the community without the consent of his own abbot or without letters of recommendation, because it was written: Do not do to another what you would not wish to have done to you.[27]

It will have been noted that all of the foregoing provisions applied to transfer from some other monastery to the monastery for which St. Benedict had written his Rule. This was possible because there was no universal legislation against transfer, and because monasteries generally did not have rules that restricted transfer to other communities. The restrictions on accepting monks from elsewhere into the monastery was based on charity. But the vow of stability was an effective impediment that prevented a licit egress or transfer at will.[28]

It must be noted that in writing his Rule St. Benedict did not contemplate the growth of an "Order" in the modern understanding of the term. He was writing a Rule obligatory only on the monks of his own monastery. But this admirable document, because it was based on the best in a Monastic tradition that was by then several centuries old, and because it regulated all with the legal genius of a Roman and the wisdom of a Saint, soon became supreme in the Monasteries of the West; with it, stability as an ideal at least became an integral part of the framework of Western religious life.

In the sixth century also some civil legislation in the Eastern Empire restricted and regulated transfer to another community. In the year 535 Emperor Justinian (527-565), in one of his Novels, decreed that a monk who left his own monastery for another had to leave with the monastery the property that was his when he entered. The abbot of the monastery to which he desired to transfer was

[27] "Caveat autem abbas ne aliquando de alio noto monasterio monachum ad habitandum suscipiat sine consensu abbatis eius aut literis commendatitiis; quia scriptum est: Quod tibi non vis fieri, alio ne feceris."—*loc. cit.*

[28] Butler, *Benedictine Monasticism,* p. 125.

not to receive him. Bishops and archimandrites also were to prohibit transfer in order to preserve monastic virtue.[29] Another and later Novel likewise decreed that if a monk left his own monastery and transferred to another, all that he possessed at the time at which he left would belong to the former monastery.[30]

Pope Gregory I (590-604) had been, before his elevation to the Papacy, a monk of the monastery of St. Andrew in Rome. Throughout his reign he showed himself to be ever solicitous for the monastic state. The limitation of transfer for the good of the religious life was not excluded from his care. Thus in a letter which was later received into the Decretals of Gregory IX, and which had been written to a subdeacon in Sicily (April 22, 591), he ordered that certain monks there should no longer be allowed to transfer rashly from one monastery to another. If any should, nevertheless, presume to transfer, they were to be returned, for the punishment which was due them, to the former monastery and to the rule of the abbot from whom they had fled.[31]

In the same year (591), in a letter written to the same subdeacon he prescribed that priests, levites, monks, clerics, or any others who belonged to an ecclesiastical community, if they fell into serious sin (*si lapsi fuerint*), were to be sent to a monastery to do penance. In the case of monks, this could be understood as implying a transfer to another monastery, as it was by some of the glossators of the Middle Ages.[32]

[29] N(5.7).

[30] N(123.42).

[31] Ep. I, 40 (42)—*Monumenta Germaniae Historica*; *Epistolae* (Tom. I, 2. ed. Ewald et Hartmann, Berolini, 1887-1899), Tom. I, Pars I, p. 55 (hereafter to be cited as *MGH*); Jaffé, *Regesta Pontificum Romanorum ab condita Ecclesia ad annum post Christum natum MCXCVIII* (2. ed. by Kaltenbrunner [ad annum 590], Ewald [590-882], and Loewenfeld [882-1198], and so referred to as: JK, JE and JL, Lipsiae, 1885-1888), JE, n. 1110; Mansi, IX, 1058; *MPL*, LXXVII, 495; c. 5, X, *de regularibus et transeuntibus ad religionem*, III, 31. The subdeacon to whom the letter was addressed was a Roman cleric, present in Sicily as a *rector patrimonii*, and frequently entrusted by St. Gregory with special mandates.

[32] JE, n. 1112; c. 4(5), C. XVI, q. 6; *Decretum Gratiani Emendatum et Observationibus Illustratum una cum Glossis, Gregorii XIII Pont. Max. iussu*

In another letter, written in 593, Pope Gregory directed that a seduced nun be transferred to another and safer monastery.[33] A Council held in Rome (601) during his reign recognized another legitimate reason for transfer. It permitted monks, if they could not find a suitable candidate for the position of abbot in their own community to choose a monk from another monastery. The abbot-designate, however, could not assume his new office against the will of his own abbot.[34]

Toward the end of the seventh century, the Council of Hereford in England (673) forbade monks to migrate from place to place, that is, from monastery to monastery, *except by permission of their own abbot;* they were to persevere in that obedience which they had promised at the time of their conversion from the world.[35] The Council of Berghamsted in the same country (696) ordered that vagrant monks could be received as guests only once, unless they had permission to be away from their monastery.[36]

In the eighth century, a Council of the entire Frankish Church was convoked by King Pepin the Short (751-768) and held at Verneuil-sur-Oise in 755, shortly after the death of St. Boniface (672/73-754). It decreed that, if a monastery fell into the hands of the laity, monks who wished to transfer to other monasteries could do so, provided that they had the consent of the bishop and if they desired the transfer for God's sake and to save their souls.[37] In England, the Council of Cloveshoe (747) decreed that both those who had voluntarily left their monasteries and those who had been driven out by violence should be readmitted. If, however, they had

editum (Romae, 1582), *Glossa ordinaria* ad c. 4 (5), C. XIV, q. 6, *casus* (hereafter all citations from the *Glossa Ordinaria* will be taken from this edition).

[33] *Ep. X,* 3(8)—*MPL,* LXXVII, 1071, 1072; *MGH, Epistolae,* Tom. II, Pars II, p. 238; JE, n. 1281; c. 28, C. XXVII, q. 1.

[34] C. 25—HL, Tom. III, Part I, p. 329; about the same rule can be found in a letter of St. Gregory to the Abbot Maur (598)—JE, n. 1138; c. 5, C. XVIII, q. 4.

[35] C. 4—Mansi, XI, 129; Bruns, II, 310.

[36] C. 8—Mansi, XII, 112; Bruns, II, 312.

[37] C. 10—Mansi, XII, 582; VIIb, 172; *MGH, Leges in 4°*, Sect. II, *Capitularia,* Tom. I (ed. A. Boretius, Hannoverae, 1883), I, 38.

first transferred with permission to another monastery, they were to return to the latter.[38]

In this century, too, is to be found the only *universal* legislation that restricted transfer. The II Council of Nicaea (787) enacted that, if the purpose were that of transfer, no monks or virgins ought to leave the monastery to which they had become attached. If they were to do so nevertheless, it was necessary to receive them as guests, but not as members, ***except with the consent of the superior of their own monastery.***[39]

Almost at the end of the ninth century a Council at Tribur (895), not far removed from Mainz, decreed that, if any monk wished to transfer for the good of his soul or for the good of others (*pro lucro animae vel animarum*), he was permitted to do so, provided that he secured the consent of his bishop, of his abbot, and of his fellow monks. The Council significantly added the reason why it granted this permission: "because we read that many saints have done this." If, however, the monk transferred in order to escape from the regular discipline, he was to be forced to return and thereupon was to be punished. If he obstinately refused to return, he was subject to the same punishment that the Council of Chalcedon (451) had decreed for vagrant monks, namely, exclusion from communion with the faithful.[40]

In the tenth century, Odo, Archbishop of Canterbury (942-958), ordered in his "Constitutions" that monks were to remain in the churches (this term included monasteries) where they had taken their vows. They were not to be vagabonds, nor gyrovagues, who wanted to be called monks but spurned the obligations of this state of life.[41]

In the eleventh century the institute of the Canons Regular of St. Augustine arose from the collegiate chapters of canons, when Pope Nicholas II in a synod held at the Lateran (1059) decreed that these should be transformed into strictly religious institutes

[38] C. 29—Mansi, XII, 407.

[39] C. 21—Mansi, XIII, 755.

[40] C. 26—HL, Tom. IV, Part II, p. 701; Mansi, XVIIIa, 145; XVIIIa, 163; XIX, 577; cf. c. 1, C. XX, q. 4.

[41] C. 6—Mansi, XVIIIa, 396.

with the three substantial vows of religion, and that their members were to live in common under the so-called Rule of St. Augustine.[42]

In the rule written for them by Archbishop Anselm, of Havelberg, it was declared that no professed canon regular, unless he was a public sinner (*nisi . . . publice lapsus fuit*), could become a monk. Any who should disobey this prohibition had to return, and as a penance take the last place in choir and wear a special cowl.[43]

Pope Urban II (1088-1099), who had been schooled in the strictness of the Cluniac reform, in a letter to the abbot of the monastery of St. Rufinus decreed that no one who had been professed as a canon could leave the cloister without the permission of his superior and of the whole community, and this was obligatory even though he alleged as an excuse his desire for a stricter life. A professed canon regular could not be received by any bishop, abbot or group of monks, unless he had the necessary letters from his community.[44]

At a Council held at Autun (1094) a similar prohibition was levied against the transfer of canons regular to the monastic life.[45]

Since it happened occasionally that the obligation to remain within a community could be harmful to the individual, especially in communities which were far from their first fervor, a relaxation of this obligation was permitted. So, for example, some of the re-

[42] C. 4—Mansi, XIX, 897; HL, Tom. IV, Part II, pp. 1167, 1168; cf. Heimbucher, *Die Orden und Kongregationen der katholischen Kirche*, 2. ed., II, 7 (hereafter cited Heimbucher).

[43] *MPL*, CLXXXVIII, 1109, 1110; c. 2, C. XIX, q. 3. This canon was mistakenly attributed by Gratian to Pope Urban II.

[44] C. 3, C. XIX, q. 3; JL, n. 5763. Fagnanus (1598-1678) claimed that the oldest and best Codices of the text require, not the permission of the superior and of the whole community (*patris et totius congregationis permissione*), but simply the permission of the superior of the whole community, since the *et* is missing in the text (*patris totius congregationis permissione*)—*Commentaria in Quinque Libros Decretalium* (5 vols. in 3, Venetiis, 1719), lib. III, tit. 31, c. 18, n. 38 (hereafter cited Fagnanus). Friedberg (note 14 to this canon) reported that in four old manuscripts, three from the twelfth, the fourth more probably from the end of the twelfth but perhaps from the fourteenth century, the *et* is missing.

[45] HL, Tom. V, Part I, pp. 387-388; Mansi, XX, 799-802; c. 1, C. XIX, q. 3.

formed monasteries of the tenth century were given the privilege to receive monks from monasteries which had not been subjected to the reform.[46]

This privilege eventually found its way into the synodal law. As a privilege it was limited in time: once the monastery reformed its ways, the monk was to return. The synodal law made no such reservation. Thus the Council of Bourges in 1031 ordained that canons and monks ought not to transfer from the monasteries of which they were members except for a reasonable necessity, for the sanctification of their souls, or for the opportunity of a better observance of the religious life; they were not to transfer in order to obtain some position or dignity, or worldly office; and the consent of their bishop or of the abbot was required for the transfer.[47] At the Council of Limoges (1031) in the same year it was declared that monks whose monastery had fallen into the hands of a lay abbot could transfer to another where the regular discipline was observed, in fact, that to do so was praiseworthy and useful.[48]

By way of summary it may be stated that the entire period before Gratian shows three stages in the development of regulations for the transfer of religious to another community. In the beginning of

[46] John XI in 931 gave the Monastery of Cluny such a privilege: ". . . et quia sicut nimis compertum est, iam paene cuncta monasteria a suo proposito praevaricantur, concedimus, ut si quis monachus ex quolibet monasterio ad vestram conversationem solo duntaxat meliorandae vitae studio transmigrare voluerit, cui videlicet suus abbas regularem sumptum ad depellendam proprietatem habendi ministrare neglexerit, suscipere vobis liceat, quousque monasterii sui conversatio emendetur."—*MPL,* CXXXII, 1055; JL, n. 3584; the same privilege was given to the Monastery of Déols in the Archdiocese of Bourges (931)—JL, n. 3585, and to the Monastery of Fleury in the Diocese of Orleans (938)—JL, n. 3606.

[47] C. 25—"Ut canonici et monachi de monasteriis suis, ubi prius intitulati sunt, nisi causa rationabilis necessitatis, vel aedificationis animae, vel ordinem melius observandi, ad aliud monasterium non transeant propter adipiscendum aliquod monasterium vel honorem, vel occupationem terrenam, absque consensu episcopi sui vel abbatis."—HL, Tom. IV, Part II, p. 955; Mansi, XIX, 506.

[48] "Quibusdam vero sciscitantibus, si qui monachorum forte de eodem saeculari domo ad alium regularem migrare vellent, utrum eis liceat: eruditi qui aderant, recte sapere tales iudicabant. Tales, inquiunt, Deo placere student. Nam si perfectus est, qui inter malos bonus est: tamen bonorum consortium adipisci laudabile et perutile est. . . ."—Mansi, XIX, 537, 538; HL, IV-VI, 957.

coenobitism there was no restriction. Next, the need for stability began to be recognized, and stability came to be regarded as morally obligatory on the professed monk. Lastly, there was the gradual formation of a juridic bond between the religious and his community, forged by the legislative power of the Church and even of the State. Transfer was still possible, however, under certain conditions. Though St. Benedict's Rule was silent as to the possibility of transfer from his own monastery to others, the scattered legislation which has been cited shows that in general, the permission of the bishop and/or of the abbot, and sometimes of the community, or of all three was required for a transfer. One can also find mention of certain reasons considered as sufficient in justification of the transfer. It was upon this legislation, scattered as it was in various collections and compilations, that Gratian (+ ca. 1157) was to draw for the doctrine presented in his Decretum (ca. 1140), which in turn furnished the foundation upon which was built the structure of the Decretal law concerning transfer to another community.

III. The Decree of Gratian

Gratian treated the matter of transfer *ex professo* in two different sections. The first concerned transfer from one monastery to the other. A general restriction, however, against such transfer was asserted in a canon which Gratian had included under another section entirely. It was a canon taken from the I Council of Orleans (511), and the relevant passage stated that the abbot who received a monk belonging to another monastery was to know that he was guilty of an infringement of the law.[49]

In the twentieth cause of the second book Gratian introduced three canons, which concerned the most important principle of his teaching on transfer, namely, that monks were free to transfer to a monastery where the discipline was more strict than it was in the monastery with which they were affiliated. The first canon Gratian used in support of his doctrine was the 26th canon of the Council of Tribur (895), and was quoted as follows: "If sacred Virgins have proposed to transfer to another monastery for the profit of their

[49] C. 19, C. XVIII, q. 2; c. 19—Bruns, II, 164; see above, p. 5, note 16.

souls *by reason of the stricter life to be found there,* and have decided to remain there permanently, the synod hereby grants them permission to do so. If, however, they have sought to transfer in order to flee from discipline, they are to be forced to return." [50]

Gratian's text, at least according to recent opinions on the subject, is a redaction which differs somewhat from what seems to be the authentic reading.[51] The more acceptable text, which is that of the so-called "Vulgate" manuscripts, and which is given by Mansi (1692-1767) and by Hefele-Leclerq (1809-1893) in their collections, differs on two important items from the text received by Gratian. First, it refers not to nuns, but to monks. It is then a very odd circumstance that Gratian should use his own text in order to establish a rule by a sort of analogy for the transfer of monks.[52] It is also evidence for the fact that the rules for monks and nuns were applied interchangeably to either group. Secondly, nothing was said in the Vulgate text concerning a transfer to a stricter community. The conditions established there were rather that the monk could transfer if it was for the good of his own soul or that of others, and if he had the consent of his bishop, of his abbot, and of his fellow monks. This, of course, makes the legal authority of Gratian's fundamental principle somewhat doubtful.

The next two canons brought forward by Gratian were apparently out of harmony with the possibility of transfer to a more rigorous community, the doctrine of which he had just asserted, and hence had to be refuted by him. The first of these, purporting to be from St. Basil (329-379), but really coming from the Penitential of Theodore of Canterbury (602-640), stated that a monk could not make a vow without the consent of his abbot; if he did, his vow could be voided by the abbot. The second canon contained matter

[50] C. 1, C. XX, q. 4; Mansi, XVIIIa, 145; XVIIIa, 163; XIX, 577; HL, Tom. IV, Part II, p. 701. The italics and translations from the Latin are by the present writer. See above, p. 11, note 40.

[51] Cf. Krause, "Die Akten der Triburer Synode 895"—*Neues Archiv der Gesellschaft für ältere deutsche Geschichtekunde* (Hannover, 1876—); XVII (1892), 49-82, esp. p. 65; *ibid.*, pp. 281-326; *ibid.*, XVIII, 411-437; Seckel, *ibid.*, pp. 322-409.

[52] Dictum p. c. 1, C. XX, q. 4.

drawn from two canons of the Council of Agde (506).[53] This canon stated that no abbot should presume to receive or to retain a monk unless he was transferring to another monastery *with the permission or at the command of his abbot.* If this condition were missing *he was to be recalled by his abbot under the authority of the canons.*[54]

Gratian regarded the two canons as apparent objections to his main principle, namely that a monk could transfer to a stricter monastery than his own, and tried to reconcile them with it as follows: in the first canon, he declared, the prohibition against vows applied to special vows of abstinence or of some other ascetical practice which went beyond the general custom of the monks living in the same community; such vows could not be made without the abbot's permission, so that the other brothers might not be scandalized; the second canon, which demanded the permission or command of the abbot in order to make it possible for another abbot to receive or retain a monk in his community, was enacted for the purpose of restraining those who vowed to go on pilgrimages in order that they might evade the regular discipline; this, he continued, was forbidden both to monks and to clerics, so that they might have no occasion to return again to life in the world.[55] The *Glossa Ordinaria* had a different, and, it may be said, a more consistent explanation: transfer without permission or command of the abbot was forbidden, either when the monastery to which transfer was made was not a stricter one, or, if it was, when the monk transferred by reason of fickleness of mind *(causa levitatis).*[56] This was an argument by analogy from a canon regarding the transfer of canons regular, which will be considered a few pages further on.

Gratian included, in other parts of his "Decree," four canons which admitted other reasons for transfer to another monastery. Thus, in a canon which originated in a Council held in Rome (601), it was stated that, though ordinarily monks were not to choose as abbot a member of another monastery, they could do so if no one

[53] Cc. 27, 38—Bruns, II, 151, 153; c. 3, C. XX, q. 4; see p. 5, notes 14, 15.

[54] C. 2, C. XX, q. 4; Friedberg, note 12 to this canon. The italics are the present writer's.

[55] Dictum p. c. 3, C. XX, q. 4.

[56] Ad v. *Monasterium*; cf. c. 3, C. XIX, q. 3.

with the requisite qualities could be found in their own community. The abbot-designate, however, could not assume his new office against the will of his abbot.[57]

In another place, a canon ordered the transfer of nuns under certain circumstances. It provided that a lapsed nun was to be sent to another and safer monastery in order to do penance.[58] The case dealt really with the delict of adultery, and it is insinuated that some of the blame for the crime rested on the monastery. For this reason she was to be sent to a stricter monastery, and through her penance there give others "an example which would inspire fear." The *Glossa Ordinaria* declared that, if the first monastery was convicted of negligence, she was to be transferred, but that if it was not, she was to be brought back and not to be transferred elsewhere.[59] Another canon in the Decree of Gratian was taken from the *Novels* of Justinian as contained in the *Epitome* of Julian. It was declared that if any nun or other woman in the religious life or with the religious habit was carried off by force, or corrupted, or solicited, she should be sought for and transferred with her goods to a safer monastery.[60] Finally, there was an extract from another letter of Pope St. Gregory I (May 24, 591), written to Peter, his subdeacon in Sicily. It prescribed that priests, levites, monks, clerics, or any others who belonged to an ecclesiastical community, if they lapsed, were to be sent to a monastery for penance. Their goods, however, were not to be sent with them, though their expenses were to be taken care of lest they should be a burden to the place where they were doing penance.[61]

The other section in which Gratian treated the subject of transfer

[57] C. 25—HL, Tom. III, Part I, p. 239; c. 5, C. XVIII, q. 4; see above, p. 10, note 34.

[58] C. 28, C. XXVII, q. 1. This was a letter of Pope St. Gregory I to Ianuarius (and not to John, as the mistaken inscription of Gratian has it). It was written in 593. See above, p. 10, note 33.

[59] C. 28, C. XXVII, q. 1, ad v. *in aliud*.

[60] C. 30, C. XXVII, q. 1; Friedberg, note 403 to this canon.

[61] C. 4(5), C. XVI, q. 6. Cf. the *Glossa Ordinaria* on this text. The glossators disagreed concerning its application. Some thought it referred to the transfer of monks. Huguccio (+1210), however, understood it as referring to clerics who were in the service of some church. See also p. 9, note 32.

concerned the transfer of the Canons Regular of St. Augustine to monasteries of the Benedictine family. The Canons Regular, living according to the Rule of St. Augustine, arose as a strictly religious group with the three vows and a common life about a century before Gratian.[62] Gratian's first fundamental doctrine was that canons regular were forbidden to transfer to monasteries. The first canon adduced in support of this view was the only extant canon of a Council at Autun (1094) in the reign of Pope Urban II (1088-1099). Gratian mistakenly assigned it to an earlier Council of Autun (1077), in the reign of Pope Gregory VII (1073-1085). The canon stated that canons regular must not become monks. No abbot or monk should dare to induce canons regular to desert the purpose of their canonical profession, to receive the monastic habit, and so to become monks, as long as they could still find a church of their Order in which they could serve God in a canonical state of life and thus save their souls. If any should rashly attempt to do so, they were to fall prey to the Church's anathema.[63] Bernard of Pavia (+1213) later used this canon as support for his teaching that, though a canon regular could not transfer to a monastery, he could transfer to another church of his own Order, provided that it was stricter than the one he intended to leave.[64] The second canon reiterated this fundamental principle, but introduced the possibility of transfer under one condition. The canon declared that no professed canon regular, unless he had lapsed publicly *(nisi publice lapsus fuerit)*, could become a monk. It was ordered that any canon regular who transgressed this command had to return, and thereafter had to wear a special cowl and to take the last place in choir.[65]

Gratian immediately qualified this canon by observing that this was true only if the canon regular transferred without the permis-

[62] Heimbucher, II, 7; see above, p. 11.

[63] C. 1, C. XIX, q. 3; Mansi, XX, 799-802; HL, Tom. V, Part I, pp. 387-388.

[64] Bernardus Papiensis, *Summa Decretalium* (ed. by E. A. Th. Laspeyres, Ratisbon, 1860), lib. III, tit. XXVII, pp. 108-111.

[65] C. 2, C. XIX, q. 3; Friedberg, note 3 to this canon; Anselmus Havelbergensis, *De Ordine Canonicorum Regularium*, c. 25—*MPL*, CLXXXVIII, 1109, 1110; see above, p. 12, note 43.

sion of his superior *(nisi cum patris sui licentia religionis propositum induerit)*.[66] He supported this statement with a third canon, taken from a letter of Pope Urban II.[67] The canon decreed that no one who had been canonically professed could leave the cloister for any reason of levity or with the excuse of desiring a stricter institute, *unless* he had the permission of his superior and of the whole community. If he did leave, no abbot, monk, or bishop could receive him without the usual testimonial letters.

In summary, Gratian's doctrine was as follows:

1. A monk could transfer to another and stricter monastery even without permission, provided that he did so for the profit of his soul.

2. A canon regular could not transfer to a monastery, even though it was stricter than his own, without permission. Transfer to another community of his own Order was not forbidden.

3. A monk or canon regular could transfer to another community if he had the permission of his superior.

4. A canon regular who had lapsed could transfer to a monastery; lapsed monks and nuns were to be transferred to other monasteries for penance when their own monasteries were convicted of negligence.

5. Nuns could, in a case of danger to their souls, be transferred to safer monasteries.

6. If a monk was elected superior of another monastery, he could accept the election only with the consent of his own abbot.

IV. The Papal Decretals

The Decretals of Pope Gregory IX (1227-1241), which contained decretals drawn principally from the five ancient compilations of Papal decretals beginning with that of Bernard of Pavia, were

[66] Dictum p. c. 2, C. XIX, q. 3.

[67] C. 3, C. XIX, q. 3; JL, n. 5763 (1092-1098); Friedberg in note 13 to this canon designated it in the old edition of Jaffé by the number 4313; the number corresponding to this in the later edition is 5760, which however is not identical with the present canon. N. 5763, which *is* identical, is ascribed erroneously by JL to c. 2, C. XIX, q. 3; see above, p. 12, note 43.

edited and redacted at the behest of the Pope by St. Raymond of Pennafort, and promulgated with the Bull "*Rex pacificus*" on September 5, 1234. The collection was an authentic one, and the dispositive part of each decretal had the force of law through its inclusion in the collection.

Four of the five canons in the collection which dealt directly with the subject of transfer were drawn from the first ancient compilation, that made by Bernard of Pavia in 1191. The fifth, and most important of the five, was from the third compilation compiled at the order of Pope Innocent III and promulgated in an authentic collection in 1210.

The first canon was a letter of Pope St. Gregory I (590-604). It had been written in the year 591, but it was not included in the *Decree* of Gratian. As the *pars decisa* relates, it was occasioned by the fact that monks of the diocese of Sorrento, by deserting the rule of their abbots, were transferring as it pleased them from one monastery to the other. It was ordered that no monks could thenceforth transfer rashly from one monastery to the other. Those who did so had to be returned for punishment to the monastery in which they had lived from the beginning, and to the rule of the abbot from whom they had fled.[68]

The second was a decretal of Pope Alexander III (1159-1181). It had been sent to the ecclesiastical superiors of France, and concerned the Cistercians.[69] In the *pars decisa* of the decretal there is mention of the fact that by reason of the devotion and virtue of the Cistercian Order it had obtained a privilege in virtue of which members were forbidden to leave the enclosure without the permission of their abbots; those who did depart could not be received into other monasteries. The Holy Father wished to enforce this privilege and ordered that Cistercian monks or lay brothers *(conversi)* who had made their profession should not be received anywhere in France

[68] C. 5, X, *de regularibus et transeuntibus ad religionem*, III, 31; JE, n. 1110. See above, p. 9, note 31.

[69] The Cistercians were founded in 1098 by Robert, Abbot of Molesmes (+1110), at Citeaux, in France. Under St. Bernard (1090-1153), who joined the Order in 1113 and founded the celebrated monastery at Clairvaux, this very severe Order expanded enormously in numbers, in prestige and in influence.

without the permission of their own abbots. Those who had departed without permission had to be compelled to return.[70]

Next there was another decretal of Pope Alexander III, written at an undetermined period of his reign to the bishop of Hereford. It concerned the possibility of transfer for those who had been only implicitly professed, that is, those who were considered to have made their profession only by reason of their reception of the habit as it was wont to be worn by those who were professed. The Pope ruled that those clerics who had received the habit without as yet making express profession could not return to churches served by seculars, for they would in that way break the vow which they had made to God. But if they did not wish to observe the severe discipline of the Order in which they had taken the habit, they were to be forced to transfer to a community of less rigorous observance. He explicitly excluded from the effect of this decree those who were undergoing their probation and had not as yet received the habit, for these were free to return to the world if they so wished.[71]

For the sake of clarity, it may be helpful at this point to advert to several decretals of later collections which amplified and clarified the juridical concept of implicit profession. Thus a decretal of Pope Gregory IX, which was received into the *Liber Sextus,* indicated some very general norms requiring a distinction between the habits of novices and those of the professed. The habits could either be different altogether, or, if they were not, the habits of those who were professed could be distinguished from those of the novices if they had been blessed or if something else had been done to indicate that they were different.[72] In all but the Mendicant Orders implicit profession (the sources call it *professio tacita)* could be made during the year of probation through the assuming of the habit worn by the professed religious. Pope Boniface VIII (1294-1303) de-

[70] C. 7, X, *de regularibus et transeuntibus ad religionem*, III, 31; JL, n. 13849.

[71] C. 9, X, *de regularibus et transeuntibus ad religionem,* III, 31; JE, n. 13946.

[72] C. 1, *de regularibus et transeuntibus ad religionem,* III, 14, in VI°; the inscription attributes the decretal to Innocent IV, but Friedberg, in note (a), declared that it was issued by Gregory IX.

creed that in all Orders except those of the Mendicants, where a year of probation was obligatory, either explicit (then called express) or implicit (then called tacit) profession could be made during the first year which the applicant spent with the Order. This made profession possible without the completion of the novitiate. Explicit profession bound the member to the community in which profession was made. Implicit profession only obliged the one who was so professed to live as a member of some religious community in general, provided that he was of a sufficient age, acted knowingly and willingly, and perservered in his resolve for three days.[73] This meant that he could transfer at will to another community, though he could not return to the world.

Fourthly, another decretal of Pope Alexander III, written about 1159-1160, reversed the prohibition in the *Decree* of Gratian against the transfer of a canon regular to a monastic community.[74] The present decretal, in reference to a particular case, determined that a canon who had made his profession in one church, who had fled from it, and then had been received into a monastery as a monk, could be permitted to remain where he was with a good conscience if the community to which he had fled was more devout *(maioris religionis)* than the one he had left. If it was not, he was to be compelled to return. It will be of interest to note, by reason of a later controversy on the point, that the rubric of the decretal declared that a canon regular could become a monk if the community to which he transferred was *stricter* than his own, otherwise not *(si religio, ad quam transit, est strictior sua)*.[75]

The fifth of the laws on transfer in this title of the Decretals of Gregory IX was the all-important decretal of Pope Innocent III (1198-1216), taken from the third of the ancient compliations, and known as the decretal "Licet." It was issued in 1205.

The rubric declared that a religious could, out of zeal for a holier

[73] C. 3, *de regularibus et transeuntibus ad religionem*, III, 14, in VI°.

[74] See above, p. 18, note 63.

[75] C. 10, X, *de regularibus et transeuntibus ad religionem*, III, 31; JE, n. 11866. The rubric had no legal force, however, since it was of private origin, but had only doctrinal authority. The controversy will be treated in the section dealing with the interpretations of the decretalists and other commentators.

life *(zelo sanctioris vitae)*, transfer to a more rigorous community *(potest ad religionem transire strictiorem)*, provided that he had first asked the permission of his superior, even if the permission had not been obtained, and this even when the first monastery had a privilege that a religious could not transfer from it to the other, even if the latter was a stricter community *(ad illud etiam arctius transire non potest)*.[76]

The first part of the decretal summarized the general principles on which the ruling was based: if some monks, canons regulars, hospitallers,[77] and templars [78] had obtained indults from the Apostolic See to the effect that after profession their members could not transfer without the consent of their Orders to another community, even though transfer was made with the excuse that the religious life there was more rigorous *(arctioris religionis obtentu)*. These indults, declared Innocent III, had been given only for the purpose of preventing a rash and futile transfer made on the pretext of greater devotion *(maioris religionis)*, which resulted in loss and injury to the Order. If, however, a religious had asked for permission with humility and purity, with an unfeigned desire for a holier life, the Pope declared that it could not be denied. Two reasons were given for this ruling: the first, that the religious was absolved from obedience to the general and "public law" by a "private law," [79] and the second, that one who abused a privilege deserved to lose it. The decretal went on to extend to all who had such a privilege, the obligation of permitting transfer when the stated conditions had

[76] Cf. p. 22, note 75.

[77] The Knights Hospitallers of St. John, a Military Order, were here meant. Raymond of Puy drew up their body of statutes in 1118, and they were approved by Pope Innocent II (1130-1143).

[78] Another Military Order founded as a society of laymen in 1118, which in 1127 added the religious vows to the original vow to protect pilgrims.

[79] This was a principle first announced by Pope Urban II (1088-1099) in a fragment which had been included in the *Decree* of Gratian. The Pope formulated this principle in justification of the transfer of secular priests to the religious life. By the "public law" he meant the law of the canons, and by "private law" the inspiration of the Holy Spirit, which was therefore considered to be more noble and superior to the purely human law, which it was declared to supersede—C. 2, C. XIX, q. 2; JL, n. 5670; Mansi, XX, 714.

been met. Finally, it was declared, in case of a probable doubt as to the rightness of the motives of the one who wished to transfer, or as to whether the Order to which he wished to transfer was more or less rigorous *(ad ordinem arctiorem vel laxiorem)* than the one he was leaving, the judgment of a superior had to be sought. In this particular case, the monk who had transferred to the Cistercians was not to be molested, because he had transferred with a pure intention and a good conscience.[80]

The interpretations and disputes to which this canon gave rise will be discussed in another section (infra, pp. 41-44). It is easy, however, to see that the principle that a religious could transfer to a more rigorous community, provided that he had asked permission and even if it had not been obtained, was one that was sure to give rise to many difficulties and abuses in practice. Though this particular decretal was never abrogated by any contrary general law, the entire later history of the institute of transfer is replete with privileges, particular laws and finally decisions of the Sacred Congregations which made this decretal inapplicable in most instances.

Finally, in a decretal of Pope Honorius III (1216-1227), in another book of the decretals, it was declared that an abbot if elected from the members of another monastery could no longer vote in the elections of his former monastery, even when this right had been reserved to him by his former abbot and the community.[81]

A permission to transfer, which from the nature of the case was applicable only for a time, was included in a decree of the II General Council of Lyons (1274), and later incorporated in the *Liber Sextus,* which Pope Boniface VIII (1294-1303) promulgated as an authentic collection in 1298. The decree renewed the prohibition which Pope Innocent III had levied against the formation of new Orders at the IV General Council of the Lateran (1215).[82] The decree of the

[80] C. 18, X, *de regularibus et transeuntibus ad religionem,* III, 31; Potthast, *Regesta Pontificum Romanorum inde ab Anno post Christum Natum 1198 ad Annum 1304* (2 vols., Berolini, 1874-1875), n. 2763 (hereafter to be cited as Potthast).

[81] C. 47, X, *de electione et electi potestate,* I, 6; Potthast, n. 7717. This decretal is from the fifth ancient compilation, and was written somewhere between 1216 and 1227.

[82] C. 9, X, *de religiosis domibus,* III, 36; Mansi, XXII, 1002.

Council of Lyons affected new Mendicant Orders which had sprung up since the IV General Council of the Lateran and which had not been approved. The Dominicans, Franciscans, Hermits of St. Augustine and the Carmelites were specifically excepted from the effects of this ruling.

The decree forbade the condemned Orders to receive any more new members. General permission was granted to their members to transfer to other approved Orders. However, this was to be done individually; a whole Order or convent could not transfer itself and its house *in globo* to another Order or convent without the special permission of the Holy See.[83]

In the year 1281 Pope Martin IV (1281-1285) issued the decretal *Viam ambitiosae,* which was a prohibition against transfer from the Mendicant Orders to any other Orders, especially to the monastic Orders, for any reason, and even if permission had been given for such a transfer by the Pope's penitentiary, or by legates or nuncios of the Apostolic See, or by their own superiors. The only Order to which transfer could still be made, by reason of an express exception in this decretal, was that of the Carthusians. A transfer contrary to this provision was null and void, and both those who were received into an Order and those who received them incurred in the act an excommunication which was reserved to the Roman Pontiff except in the danger of death. Those who had already transferred to monastic Orders were to remain there. Those who, by using permission to transfer as a pretext, were wandering about with or without the habit were to be warned to return within fifteen days to the community which they had left. If they did not obey, they were excommunicated as notorious apostates.[84]

Finally, in the Clementine Constitutions, prepared in part at the Council of Vienne (1311-1312) under Pope Clement V (1305-1314), and promulgated in 1314, and given legal force by their transmission to the Universities at Orange and Paris in 1317 under John XXII (1316-1334), there was a canon which penalized the transfer of professed Mendicants to non-Mendicant Orders.

[83] C. un., *de religiosis domibus,* III, 17, in VI°; Potthast, n. 24675.

[84] C. 1, *de regularibus et transeuntibus ad religionem,* III, 8, in Extravag. com.; Potthast, n. 21773.

This new decree indicated that the practice of the Holy See had receded from the rigor of the decretal of Pope Martin IV, and that permissions for transfer were being granted by Rome. This seems clear from the fact that transfers from Mendicant to non-Mendicant Orders were penalized without being declared to be invalid.

The present decretal, which began with the words, "*Ut professores,*" was meant to discourage transfers from Mendicant to non-Mendicant Orders, which apparently were frequently made for unworthy motives. Even those Mendicants who thenceforth transferred to non-Mendicant Orders with the permission of the Apostolic See, were to be incapable of becoming priors, of exercising powers of administration, of holding offices, of exercising the care of souls, or of holding any kind of position of authority in the Orders to which they had transferred. An attempt to act in any way contrary to this decree, even if done in virtue of some privilege, left the act null and void. The constitution, however, made an express exception for those Mendicants who wished to transfer from Orders of Mendicants which, by decree of the Holy See, could no longer receive new candidates.[85]

V. The Tridentine and the Post-Tridentine Period

The transfer of religious to other communities was one of the matters considered by the Fathers of the great Council of Trent. The first decree concerning transfer was adopted at the fourteenth session, which took place on November 25, 1551. It was entitled, "Those transferred to another Order shall remain in the enclosure under obedience, and shall be disqualified to hold secular benefices." The text read as follows: "Since regulars, transferred from one order to another, usually obtain permission easily to remain out of the monastery, whereby occasion is given to wandering about and apostatizing, no prelate or superior of any order shall by virtue of any authority whatsoever, admit anyone to the habit and to profession, unless he remain in the order to which he was transferred and perpetually in the cloister under obedience to his superior, and one so transferred, even though he be a canon regular, shall be

[85] C. 1, *de regularibus et transeuntibus ad religionem,* III, 9, in Clem.

wholly disqualified to hold secular benefices, even with the *cura* annexed." [86] As Pirhing (1606-1679) and Schmalzgrueber (1663-1735) declared, this was a general provision which applied to all transfers, even to those which were made to more rigorous communities.[87]

This canon, as is evident from the text itself, was directed against what was an abuse of the time, by requiring that those who had transferred were not to be given permission to leave the monastery again and wander about the world. At the same time it meant to exclude the possibility of unworthy motives for transfer by requiring that those who had transferred could not hold secular benefices, even those which were connected with the care of souls. This last was identical with a provision penalizing the transfer of Mendicants to non-Mendicant Orders, as enacted in the Clementine Constitutions.[88]

Another great modification in the law was the prohibition which the Council of Trent also directed against transfer to less rigorous communities. In the twenty-fifth and final session of the Council (3-4th of November, 1563) it was provided that "no regular shall in virtue of any authority whatsoever be transferred to an Order less rigorous." [89] The Council did not modify the previous discipline with regard to transfer to a more or equally rigorous community.[90]

Another provision of the Council indirectly limited the freedom of nuns to transfer. It was a decree which enforced the enclosure of

[86] Conc. Trident., sess. XIV, *de ref.*, c. 11—Schroeder, *Canons and Decrees of the Council of Trent* (St. Louis: Herder, 1941), p. 113.

[87] Pirhing, *Ius Canonicum Nova Methodo Explicatum* (5 vols. in 4, Dilingae, 1674-1678), lib. III, tit. 31, n. 180 (hereafter cited Pirhing); Schmalzgrueber, *Ius Ecclesiasticum Universum* (5 vols. in 12, Romae, 1843-1845), lib. III, tit. 31, n. 240 (hereafter cited Schmalzgruebcr).

[88] C. 5, *de regularibus et transeuntibus ad religionem*, III, 31, in Clem. (promulgated in 1317); cf. p. 26, note 85.

[89] Sess. XXV, *de regularibus*, c. 19, ad finem—Schroeder, *op. cit.*, p. 229.

[90] Decisions of the S. C. of the Council—Pallottini, *Collectio Omnium Conclusionum et Resolutionum quae in Causis propositis apud Sacram Congregationem Cardinalium S. Concilii Interpretum prodierunt ab eius Institutione anno 1564 ad MDCCCLX* (18 vols., Romae, 1868-1895), "Regulares," I, nn. 44, 45 (hereafter cited as Pallottini).

nuns. It was ordered that "no nun shall after her profession be permitted to go out of the monastery, even for a brief period under any pretext whatever, except for a lawful reason to be approved by the bishop.[91] This of course made it impossible for nuns to transfer without first having obtained the permission of the bishop.

The ecclesiastical law limiting the enclosure of nuns was made even more stringent and universal under Pope St. Pius V (1566-1572). As is noted by Barry in his dissertation on the violation of the cloister,[92] some nuns refused to submit to the law of the Council of Trent which demanded the observance of the cloister. In view of this St. Pius renewed the decrees of Pope Boniface VIII and of the Council of Trent in his Constitution *Circa pastoralis*.[93] All nuns, whether or not there were immemorial customs or rules to the contrary, were to take solemn vows and to observe the strict enclosure. It was provided that the sustenance of these religious was to be taken care of by unprofessed lay sisters, or even by the professed, provided that they were over forty years of age. These could not, however, leave the house to collect alms without the permission of the bishop or of their superiors, nor could they enter the enclosure of other nuns except as permitted by their constitutions.

Four years later the Constitution *Decori* of the same Supreme Pontiff made the rule of enclosure more rigorous still. It provided that the religious could not leave the enclosure except in a case of leprosy, of an epidemic, or of an extensive fire. In case of an infirmity the judgment of the superior to whom the monastery was subject and of the bishop of the place had to be sought and their consent secured in writing. It was expressly declared that this applied to all Orders of nuns, and that those who violated the enclosure

[91] Sess. XXV, *de regularibus*; c. 5; Schroeder, *op. cit.*, p. 221. A somewhat lengthier but less stringent imposition of the enclosure is found in the decretal law (c. 1, *de statu regularium*, III, 16, in VI°).

[92] *Violation of the Cloister,* The Catholic University of America Canon Law Studies, n. 148 (Washington, D. C.: The Catholic University of America Press, 1942), p. 60.

[93] 29 maii, 1566—*Codicis Iuris Canonici Fontes,* cura Emi Petri Card. Gasparri editi (9 vols., Romae [postea Civitate Vaticana]: Typis Polyglottis Vaticanis, 1923-1939—Vols. VII, VIII et IX ed. cura et studio Emi Justiniani Card. Serédi), n. 112 (hereafter cited as *Fontes*).

either by leaving it, or by accompanying those who left, or by giving permission to another to leave, or by receiving those who left, incurred in the act a major excommunication reserved to the Roman Pontiff, except in danger of death. This, however, did not apply to those who offered help or hospitality from motives of urbanity, but to those only who co-operated in the crime.[94]

Even the provision of St. Pius V, which allowed certain of the professed nuns and extern sisters to leave the monastery in order to collect alms, was abrogated by Pope Gregory XIII (1572-1585) in his Constitution *Deo sacris,* issued on December 30, 1572.[95] In consequence of these constitutions the free use of the faculty to transfer to a more rigorous community in virtue of the decretal *Licet* was indirectly made illicit for all women religious with solemn vows, since they could not leave the enclosure for the purpose of transferring to another community.

However, the permission to transfer seems to have been given occasionally, for Pirhing taught that cloistered nuns had to ask permission for a transfer, not only from their abbess but also from the regular prelate to whom the nuns were subject; they had to ask permission also from the bishop or the ordinary of the place, at least if they were not exempt.[96] An undated decree of the Sacred Congregation of the Council perhaps confirmed this view when it declared that in virtue of the prohibition of Pope St. Pius V against the transfer of nuns to more rigorous communities such a transfer was to be permitted only with great circumspection.[97] Fagnanus (1598-1678), however, taught in virtue of the Constitution *Decori* the nuns who were subject to the papal cloister needed the special permission of the Holy See to leave the enclosure for the purpose of transferring to another and more rigorous community.[98]

The Tridentine prohibition against transfer to a less rigorous

[94] Const. *Decori,* 1 febr. 1570—*Fontes,* n. 133; Barry, *op. cit.,* pp. 61-63.

[95] *Fontes,* n. 143.

[96] Pirhing, lib. III, tit. 31, sect. 4, n. 162.

[97] Pallottini, "Regulares," I, n. 46. As noted above, the prohibition was only an indirect one. No explicit prohibition against the transfer of nuns it to be found in the decree "Decori."

[98] Fagnanus, lib. III, tit. XXXI, cap. XVIII, n. 62.

community was considerably sharpened by the Constitution *Licet sacra,* issued on February 13, 1726, by Pope Benedict XIII (1724-1730). Because of extant abuses in the granting of permission to transfer from Orders which had the enclosure to those which had not, the Holy Father forbade any such transfers in the future. He also forbade transfers to the Order of Hospitallers or to the Military Orders even if these observed the law of the enclosure. Quite a remarkable provision of this constitution was the abrogation of all faculties to grant such permissions held by all and sundry, all superiors of regulars, the Cardinal Papal Delegates, the Nuncios of the Apostolic See, the Vice Legate at Avignon, and the Sacred Congregations of the Council and of Bishops and Regulars. The faculty was reserved to the Roman Pontiff himself. All privileges and customs authorizing the granting of such permissions were also declared to be abolished.[99]

The Sacred Congregations mentioned in this constitution must soon have regained their faculties, for many decrees and indults were granted through them between this time and the Code.

The Major Penitentiary and the Office of the Penitentiary also enjoyed the faculty to grant transfers, as is evident from the Constitution *Pastor bonus* of the great canonist Pope Benedict XIV (1740-1748). This grant of faculties was very broad, in that permission could be given for transfer to less, equally or to more rigorous communities, provided that a just and grave reason, approved by the Major Penitentiary, was present. In order to insure the validity of the transfer, the Major Penitentiary was likewise given authority to derogate from all statutes and privileges granted by the Holy See if these were contrary to the permissions which he was empowered to grant.

The restrictions of the Constitution *Licet sacra* were still binding on the Major Penitentiary, however. He could not grant permission to transfer to Orders in which there was no enclosure or regular observance, nor to the Hospitallers or to Military Orders,

[99] Const. *Licet sacra,* 13 febr. 1726—Ferraris, *Prompta Bibliotheca Canonica, Juridica, Moralis, Theologica necnon Ascetica, Polemica, Rubristica, Historica* (8 vols., Parisiis, 1860-1863), "Regulares," n. 66 (hereafter to be cited as Ferraris).

except only the Order of St. John of God. This exception in favor of the Order of St. John of God is new, and cannot be found in the *Licet sacra.* Transfers to the Order of St. Benedict of the Primitive Observance or to similar congregations of any other Order were also forbidden.

The constitution also granted the Major Penitentiary the power to grant transfers from one monastery to the other, if these were situated beyond the Alps. There had to be a legitimate reason, to be discussed and approved by the Signatura. Finally, the permission had to be submitted to the local Ordinary, and issued with clauses making the grants dependent on the truth of the reasons alleged.[100]

Article 2. The Modification of the Law by Privilege

I. Privileges Concerning the Reception of Members from Other Orders

The influence of privileges on the development of the practice of the Roman Curia, and this in turn on the provision of the Code that the apostolic authority is required for all transfers from one institute or independent monastery to another, is a considerable one. Consideration will first be given, however, to a series of privileges which tended to counter this tendency, in that they favored the reception of transferring members into certain Orders.

The earliest of these privileges were in favor of monastic reform. So, for example, a number of reformed monasteries received in the tenth century permission to accept monks from unreformed monasteries until these latter should have returned to the observance of the obligations imposed by the monastic life.[101]

The Camaldolese, an austere branch of the Benedictine family, received in the thirteenth century the privilege to receive members of other congregations into their Order, provided that these should remain with them permanently.[102]

100 Const. *pastor bonus,* 13 apr. 1744—*Benedicti XIV Bullarium* (3 vols. in 4, Prati, 1845-1847), I, 360.

101 See above, p. 13, note 46.

102 Const. *Fervor,* 23 ian. 1227—*Magnum Bullarium Romanum* (19 vols., Luxemburgi, 1727-1758), I, 72.

About two centuries later this privilege was renewed, after the superior had complained to the Holy Father that the privilege had become useless by reason of later privileges granted to other institutes. It was now provided that the Camaldolese could receive both Mendicants and non-Mendicants, even Carthusians, as long as the transferring religious had asked permission from their own superiors for the transfer, even if it had not been obtained.[103] As is the case with most of these grants, the constitution closed with clauses derogating from all contrary laws and privileges. But usually these derogations were themselves abrogated by other and later privileges with derogating clauses granted to other institutes.

On the 28th of July, 1506, Pope Julius II (1503-1513) in a constitution gave to the Minims of St. Francis de Paula (1416-1507) the privilege to receive into their Order religious of Mendicant or other privileged Orders, provided that these had first asked for permission from their superiors, either verbally or in writing, either personally or through some intermediary, and even though the permission had not been granted.[104]

A general provision in a constitution of Pope Pius IV (1559-1565) provided that religious of both sexes who had entered monasteries of the Cistercian Order from other Orders either had to be ejected or had to make their profession within a year. Abbesses of the Cistercians were not to presume to receive nuns of other Orders unless the father superior to whom the monastery was immediately subject received their vows and administered the oath of abiding by the statutes of the said Order.[105]

These privileges which permitted the institutes that possessed them to receive religious of other Orders were revoked by Pope St. Pius V (1556-1572) in the Constitution *Quaecumque.* The superiors and prelates of religious orders had been receiving many apostates and members of various communities who had fled from them on

[103] Const. *Illa quae,* 24 nov. 1435—*Bullarum Diplomatum et Privilegiorum Sanctorum Romanorum Pontificum Taurinensis Editio* (24 tomes in 25 vols., Augustae Taurinorum-Neapoli, 1857-1872), IV, 328 (hereafter to be cited as *Bull. Rom. Taur.*).

[104] Const. *Dudum,* 28 iul. 1506—*Bull. Rom. Taur.,* V. 432.

[105] Const. *In eminenti,* 26 sept. 1563—*Bull. Rom. Taur.,* VIII, 260-265.

account of quarrels, contentions, levity, or crimes. Though the Council of Trent had ruled that those who transferred could be admitted to the reception of the habit and to profession only on condition that they would remain perpetually in the cloister, these superiors used the religious whom they had admitted from other Orders for the visiting of the sick and for carrying on the business and the administration of their houses. Some of these religious used the freedom thus granted them to curse the Orders from which they had fled, and to impugn their usages and customs.

St. Pius, therefore, revoked and abolished all privileges, faculties and indults, if they were not found in the common law, which permitted Orders to receive monks from other communities, even from less rigorous ones. Those who had in the past been received in virtue of such privileges were to be returned to their own Orders. Those who in contravention of this constitution admitted, received or retained religious of other Orders incurred in the act the loss of ecclesiastical dignities, of the rights of administration, of benefices, of offices, of trusts, and of pensions which perchance they held, and were furthermore to be incapable of holding such in the future.[106]

II. Privileges Concerning the Departure of Religious for Other Orders

The privileges just cited permitting the reception of religious who transferred from other Orders went beyond the common law. Another class of privileges, however, severely restricted the right of members of the communities to which the privileges were given to transfer to other Orders.

On the 4th of July, 1335, Pope Benedict XII (1334-1342) issued a constitution which prohibited the transfer of Mendicants to the Cistercians or the Benedictines. It was provided that Mendicants could no longer make such transfers even with the permission of their own superiors, *but would thenceforth require the permission of the Roman Pontiff.* The reason advanced was that many professed of the Mendicant Orders were wont to transfer to these com-

[106] Const. *Quaecumque,* 14 oct. 1569—*Bull. Rom. Taur.,* VII, 783-785.

munities, and that experience taught plainly that this had caused many disturbances, vexations, losses and scandals.[107]

Four years later, Pope Eugene IV (1431-1447) issued a constitution which forbade the Cistercians to transfer to any other Order at all except to the Carthusians, even on the excuse that they had letters from the Major Papal Penitentiary to this effect, and even if in the same there should be express mention of the present prohibition.

The reason for this restriction was, so the constitution declared, that according to the petition addressed to the Holy See by the abbot of the Cistercians, monks were trying to obtain permission from the Apostolic See to transfer to other Orders of Regulars, or to remain there, some on the fictitious pretense of leading a holier life *(ficto colore sanctioris vitae)*, some in order to flee from the yoke of obedience and the salutary medicine of discipline.

The constitution provided that those who disobeyed were to be subject to punishment by the said abbot and by the said Order, and that those who transferred as well as the abbots who gave them permission to transfer were by that very fact excommunicated.[108]

Pope Callistus III (1455-1458) issued a constitution in favor of the Order of the Blessed Virgin for the Ransom of Captives *(Ordo Beatae Mariae de Mercede Redemptionis Captivorum)* on the 31st of October, 1457. It decreed that solemnly professed members of this Order could not transfer to any other Order *without the permission of the Apostolic See.* The reason for this decree was as follows: anyone who had with fickleness *(leviter)* transferred to an Order less rigorous had to be returned to the Order at his first obedience. By reason of the vow which the members of the Order of the Blessed Virgin for the Ransom of Captives took, namely, of being ready to go into captivity and even to undergo torture and death in order to redeem the captives of pagans, it was declared that there was no stricter order. Therefore, no member of the Order could transfer to houses or to monasteries of Mendicants or of any other Orders. Those

[107] Const. *Regularem*, 4 iul. 1335—*Bull. Rom. Taur.*, IV, 328.

[108] Const. *Regularem*, 14 febr. 1439—*Bull. Rom. Taur.*, V, 39.

who transferred, even though they did so with the permission of their superiors, were to be sought for and returned.[109]

A series of privileges were granted to the Society of Jesus in the course of the sixteen century. These had the effect of considerably restricting the freedom of its members to transfer.

Thus Pope Paul III (1534-1549) decreed that no professed member, scholar, or coadjutor of the Society of Jesus could transfer to any other order, excepting only the Carthusians, ***without the express permission of either his superior general or of the Holy See.*** The superior general as well as inferior superiors of the Society were given power to excommunicate, arrest, and imprison those who violated this provision, in whatever place they might be found, and to call upon the help of the secular arm for this purpose.[110] Pirhing made mention of a controversy as to whether this privilege was communicated to other Orders.[111] Sanchez held that all Mendicants enjoyed this privilege through the juridical agency of the communication of privilege, while Fagnanus held that the application of this juridical factor did not extend to privileges which the Holy See granted only rarely and with reluctance. He based his opinion on declarations of the Sacred Congregation of the Council and on a decision of the Rota.[112]

The provisions of the constitution of Paul III were repeated and somewhat extended by Pope Gregory XIII in the Constitution *Decet Romanum Pontificem* issued on October 24, 1579. It was provided that those who transferred to the Carthusians had to enter that Order within three months after they had left the Society of Jesus, and that those who left (with permission, of course) for other Orders were to enter these within the time fixed by the superior general of the Jesuits. Those who did not wish to remain or could not remain in the Order to which transfer had been made had to return to the Society under pain of excommunication.

109 Const. *Super gregem,* 31 oct. 1457—*Bull. Rom. Taur.,* V, 141.

110 Const. *Licet debitum,* 18 oct. 1549, n. 11—*Bull. Rom. Taur.,* VI, 396.

111 Pirhing, lib. III, tit. 31, n. 168.

112 Sanchez, *Opus Morale in Praecepta Decalogi* (2 vols., Parmae, 1723), lib. VI, c. 7, n. 12 (hereafter cited Sanchez); Fagnanus, lib. III, tit. 31, c. 18, n. 22.

It had been alleged in some quarters, so the constitution stated, that Jesuits were free to transfer to more rigorous Orders, especially to the Mendicants, and that those who transferred were not subject to the bond of excommunication which apostates incurred, since they had not returned to the world, but had entered another Order of Regulars. It was now provided that Jesuits who had transferred to more rigorous Orders had to return to the Society of Jesus after having been warned of their obligation to do so.

For those who had transferred to the Carthusians, and who still were in a privileged position with regard to transfer, another modification was introduced in this constitution. Some of the members of the Society who were in the missions had alleged that they wished to transfer to the Carthusians and then had left their posts without permission. It was therefore provided, since there were no houses of the said Order outside of Europe, that Jesuits there who wished to transfer to them had to have the permission of the superior general in writing. If they transferred without this permission, they incurred the penalties imposed on apostasy or infamy, and an excommunication which was reserved to the Holy Father, to the superior general of the Order, or to a delegate of the latter. It was ordered that the Carthusians must not receive Jesuits from outside Europe without testimonial letters from the superior general.[113]

In the Constitution *Ascendente Domino,* issued by Pope Gregory XIII (1572-1585), it was further determined that not only professed Jesuits and so-called "formed coadjutors," but also all who had finished two years of probation and had taken the three substantial vows of the religious life, even if these were only simple vows, were forbidden to transfer to any Order but the Carthusians without the express permission of the Society of Jesus. They could not transfer even with the purpose of leading a life of greater perfection. Those who contravened the decree incurred the penalties imposed on apostasy and of excommunication from which they could be absolved only by the superior general.[114]

Transfer between Orders which had a common origin was also

[113] Const. *Decet Romanum Pontificem—Bull. Rom. Taur.,* VIII, 320-327.

[114] 25 maii 1584, § 14—*Fontes,* n. 153.

interdicted, as is evident, for example, from a series of constitutions which forbade Observants of the Franciscan Order to become Capuchins, and Capuchins from becoming Observants.[115]

St. Pius V (1566-1572) in 1567 forbade transfer from the Capuchins to the Minims of St. Francis de Paula, because of the disturbances and the bad example given by brothers who had transferred, sometimes even without permission of their superior, from one to the other. Subsequent transfers were to be null and void, even though they had been made with permission of the superiors and with a just reason.[116]

In 1582 Pope Gregory XIII issued a constitution which contained a great concession against the law in favor of the Society of Jesus. The constitution began with the words, *Cum alias,* and provided that the superior general of the Society could dismiss whomever he wished, and that the dismissed religious, with his permission, could transfer not only to the Carthusians, but to any other Order, whether it was of an equally rigorous, more rigorous, or less rigorous observance than the Society. The institute to which transfer was to be made was to be prescribed by the superior general himself, with the concomitant consent, however, of the superiors of that institute. The religious who had so transferred could make profession in the new institute, wear the habit of that Order, and live under its discipline.

The privilege was, however, limited in that it could not be

[115] The following constitutions forbade Observants to become Capuchins: Clemens VIII, *Cum sicut accepimus,* 27 maii 1530—Waddingus, *Annales Minorum seu Trium Ordinum a S. Francisco Institutorum* (3. ed., 27 vols., Quaracchi, Ad Claras Aquas: 1932-1934), XVI, 336-338; Clemens VII, *Alias postquam,* 2 dec. 1531—*ibid.,* pp. 347-350; Paulus III, *Accepimus,* 18 dec. 1534—*ibid.,* p. 440. The Constitution *Accepimus* was revoked by another Constitution of the same Pope, *Nuper accepto* 12 ian. 1535—*ibid,* pp. 463-465. Another Constitution of the same Pope, *Pastoralis officii cura,* 14 aug. 1535, revoked the Constitution *Nuper accepto—ibid.,* pp. 459-461, to be again recalled within the same year by the Constitution *Dudum postquam,* 19 aug. 1535—*ibid.,* pp. 473-474. A final Constitution in this series forbade transfer from either Order to the other—Paulus III, const. *Regimini universalis ecclesiae,* 4 ian. 1537—*ibid.,* pp. 487-489.

[116] Constitution *Sedis Apostolicae,* 6 oct. 1567—*Bull. Rom. Taur.,* VII, 617.

shared with any other Order by way of the intercommunication of privileges.[117] It had not been abrogated at the time of the promulgation of the Code.

In 1628 Pope Urban VIII (1623-1644) issued a constitution in favor of the Capuchins. As was seen earlier in this chapter, St. Pius V (1566-1572) in the Constitution *Sedis Apostolicae* had forbidden Capuchins to transfer to the Minims of St. Francis de Paula, or the latter to transfer to the Capuchins. Now it was decreed that Capuchins could not transfer to a less rigorous community without the permission of the Apostolic See, or to a more rigorous community *without special permission in writing from the minister of the Order.* All transfers, even to privileged communities, were indicated as comprehended by this constitution. Those who contravened its prohibition incurred in the very act the penalties attached to apostasy from a religious institute: perpetual infamy, excommunication and deprivation of both the right to vote and the right to be elected in the community.[118]

In 1680 a French Congregation of Canons Regular of St. Augustine asked for a prohibition against transfer by its members even to more rigorous communities, but especially to that of the monastery of La Trappe, except with express permission in writing of the superior general of the congregation or of the Sacred Congregation of Bishops and Regulars. It was stated that to the detriment of the obedience due to their superiors and to regular discipline, some of the canons, under the pretext of a more rigorous life, were transferring to that monastery either without having asked permission or at least without having obtained it. The abbot of the monastery, besides, was admitting or dismissing these religious with equal facility after they had worn the habit for several months, against the provisions of the law.[119]

The privilege was granted. In the grant there was contained mention of a similar privilege of unknown date which had been granted by Pope Clement X (1670-1676) to the Congregation of the Benedictines of St. Maur, also of France. One of the motives

[117] Const. *Cum alias,* 22 sept. 1582—*Bull. Rom. Taur.,* VIII, 398.
[118] Const. *Iniuncti nobis,* 9 aug. 1628—*Bull. Rom. Taur.,* XIV, 1, 2.
[119] Cf. c. 9, C. XIX, q. 3.

for the grant was the support of a reform within the Order, which reform this congregation then had introduced.[120]

In a later decree of the Sacred Congregation of Bishops and Regulars mention was made of the same concession of Pope Clement X, by which the Congregation of the Benedictines of St. Maur were granted the privilege that no religious of the Order could transfer to any other Order, even to the Carthusians, except with the express permission of the superior general of the Congregation of St. Maur. Now a dispute had arisen with regard to a monk who had transferred to the Camaldolese, and it was referred to Rome. The Sacred Congregation of Bishops and Regulars first gave instructions that both sides should be given a hearing, and that an inquiry should be made whether the religious who had transferred had obtained permission to do so. There was then sent to Rome, a new petition in which it was requested both that the Sacred Congregation state explicitly that the Minims of St. Francis de Paula, the Camaldolese and every other institute worthy of special mention be included with that of the Carthusians, and that the religious who had transferred be obliged to return even though the use of the censures which were provided for by the constitution of Clement X. Both requests were granted.[121]

So numerous did the grants of privileges which prohibited transfer except with papal permission become, that Reiffenstuel (1642-1703) reported that in his day almost all religious institutes, with a few exceptions, had privileges by which their professed members were forbidden to transfer to another institute without the special permission of the Pope. He therefore warned the religious superior against the reception of the professed members of other Orders into his own, even though they had been given permission to do so by their superiors, lest this should be done against prescriptions enacted by the Apostolic See.[122] Such privileges, therefore, made

[120] 20, sept. 1680—*Analecta Ecclesiastica* (Romae, 1893-1911), X (1902), 28, n. 180.

[121] 30 iul. 1683—*Analecta Ecclesiastica,* XI (1903), 179.

[122] Reiffenstuel, *Ius Canonicum Universum* (5 vols. in 7, Parisiis, 1864-1870) —lib. III, tit. 31, nn. 9, 261 (hereafter cited Reiffenstuel).

the common law of the Decretals almost a dead letter, and gave occasion to the practice of appeal to Rome for permission to transfer. The Council of Trent had already forbidden transfers to less rigorous communities. A universal prohibition against all transfers without the permission of Rome became part of the general law through the promulgation of the Code.

CHAPTER II

THE AUTHORITATIVE AND DOCTRINAL INTERPRETATION OF THE LAW BY THE SACRED ROMAN CONGREGATIONS AND BY CANONICAL COMMENTATORS

Article 1. The Permission and Conditions Required for Transfer

I. Transfer To a More Rigorous Community

The source on which the authors based their commentary concerning transfer to a more rigorous community was first and foremost the principal font of the law, the celebrated decretal *Licet* in the Decretals of Pope Gregory IX.[1] The Council of Trent had introduced no innovations concerning the laws affecting this kind of transfer, as was authoritatively declared by two undated decrees of the Sacred Congregation of the Council.[2]

The authors postulated several conditions for transfer to a more rigorous community.

1. The first condition for such a transfer was quite obviously that the community to which transfer was being made should be superior to the community which the religious was leaving. It was not quite so obvious, however, in precisely what the nature of this superiority was to consist.

St. Thomas Aquinas[3] and Suarez (1548-1617).[4] followed by

[1] See above, pp. 22-24.

[2] Both are entitled *In Dubium ad Cap. 19, sess. 25, de Reg.*, and are cited by Pallottini, "Regulares," nn. 44, 45.

[3] "Excellentia . . . non attenditur secundum solam arctitudinem; sed principaliter secundum id ad quod religio ordinatur; secundario vero secundum discretionem observantiarum debito fini proportionatarum."—*Opera Omnia Iussu Impensaque Leonis XIII P.M. edita* (15 vols., Romae, 1882)—*Summa Theologica*, IIa-IIae, q. 189, a. 8.

[4] Commentarii in I-I, *De Religione*, tract. VIII, lib. III, cap. 9, nn. 9, 10—

other theologians, held that the superiority of the receiving Order was to be measured by its perfection. The perfection, in turn, was to be judged not only by the strictness and rigor of the community, but also, and principally, by the end to which the community was ordained; secondarily, according to the aptness of the means and observances used in the community to attain that end. This opinion, however, if it had been the common one, would have led to innumerable difficulties. It was not easy to determine which Order had a more perfect end, and which used means more perfectly adapted to the attaining of that end.[5]

Partly for this reason, but principally by reason of the very text of the law, the common opinion of canonists was against the opinion of the theologians. Thus Ioannes Andreae, (1271-1348), after a long digression on the norms for measuring the perfection of differing types of religious communities, which he drew largely from St. Thomas, stated plainly that canonists did not concern themselves with such subtleties, but considered only whether the manner of life of the community was more rigorous *(arctior)*, stricter *(districtior)*, more difficult *(durior)*, or whether it required greater courage *(fortior)*.[6] Pirhing agreed, stating that it was not the perfection of the aim or end of the community, nor the adequacy of the means used there for the attaining of that end, but the greater austerity, rigor and strictness of the religious life which served as a standard for discrimination between two communities as to the justification of transfer. One had especially to attend to such factors as silence and solitude. He stated that this was the more probable and the more common opinion, especially among canonists.[7]

Reiffenstuel also defined a more rigorous order as one the observances of which were more contrary to nature by reason of continual or frequent fasting, of insufficiency of clothing, of silence,

Opera Omnia (28 vols., Parisiis, 1856-1861), Vol. XVI, pt. 1 (hereafter cited Suarez, *De Religione*).

[5] Cf. *Summa Theologica*, IIa-IIae, q. 188, aa. 6, 7, 8; Ioannes Andreae, *In Sex Decretalium Libros Novella Commentaria* (6 vols. in 5, Venetiis, 1581), lib. III, tit. 31, cap. 10, nn. 2-9 (hereafter cited Ioannes Andreae).

[6] Lib. III, tit. XXXI, cap. 10, nn. 2-9.

[7] Pirhing, lib. III, tit. 31, n. 159.

of vigils, of solitude, of bodily mortifications, etc. He held that the more probable opinion and the one which seemed to him more conformable to law was that an order in which life was more difficult and more austere was the one to which transfer was permitted under the law, and not the Order which absolutely considered was the more perfect.

His reasons were: (1) that in the decretal *Licet* one finds the word *arctior* used; (2) that in c. 1, C. XX, q. 4, of the Decree of Gratian are found the words, *propter districtiorem vitam;* (3) that in the decretal *Viam ambitiosae* (c. 1, *de regularibus et transeuntibus ad religionem,* III, 8, in Extravag. com.) Mendicants, though forbidden to transfer to other Orders, were permitted to make a transfer to the Carthusians, not because this Order was more perfect (since those Orders which practiced both the active and the contemplative life were the more perfect), but because it was held to be more strict by reason of the perpetual facts, solitude, silence, etc.; (4) that, if greater perfection were the condition required for transfer, this could almost never take place without controversy, since each institute contended that it was equally or more perfect than others, even if not more rigorous; and (5) that the reason why the Church conceded the making of a transfer to such a community was the greater security for the leading of the religious life there, and that this was ordinarily due to the greater austerities.[8]

All agreed that the Carthusians were the most rigorous of all religious Orders, though it seemed unwarranted to call them the most perfect Order, if one followed the opinion of St. Thomas, who held that the most perfect expression of the religious life was a mixture of the contemplative and the active life.[9]

Another point on which all seemed to agree was that the greater rigor was not to be measured only by the rule which was followed in the community, nor even by the constitutions by which the rule

[8] Reiffenstuel, lib. III, tit. 31, n. 263.

[9] Bouix, *Tractatus de Jure Regularium* (2 vols., Parisiis, 1857), II, 529, 530 (hereafter to be cited as Bouix); Petra, *Commentaria ad Constitutiones Apostolicas* (5 vols. in 2, Venetiis, 1729), IV, in const. 8 Eugenii III, n. 3 (hereafter to be cited as Petra).

had been modified, but principally by the actual manner of life of any particular community at the time at which transfer was made.[10]

2. A second condition for transfer was that the motives of the transferring religious had to be right and good. According to the *Glossa Ordinaria* this was to be presumed, unless the contrary was proved.[11] Reiffenstuel advanced a number of examples of grave reasons for transfer: (1) an extraordinary zeal for tending toward greater perfection, when the religious saw that there were more numerous and efficacious means to obtain it in another community than in his own; (2) the departure of a community from the perfection which it ought to possess, as when the regular discipline was only partially or not at all observed, or when those who wished to live piously and according to the institutes of the Order, and to tend toward perfection, suffered persecution or ridicule, were ill thought of, and in other ways were deterred or impeded from their purpose; (3) the manifestation of hatred against the religious by his confrères, or his suffering of ill and unworthy treatment from them, unless the religious himself wickedly gave cause for such treatment. In practice, so Reiffenstuel held, it was sufficient to say that his motive was one of acquiring greater perfection; if he had one of the other reasons, he could, if he wished, manifest it to the superior of the community which he was leaving, but he was not to manifest it to the superior of the community to which he was transferring, lest he cause loss of reputation to the first community.[12]

3. Thirdly, no serious harm or loss of reputation should result for the community by reason of the transfer. Thus Ioannes Andreae taught that, if the first community was enormously harmed or defamed by reason of the transfer, the transfer should not be made;

[10] Reiffenstuel, lib. III, tit. 31, n. 264; Pirhing, lib. III, tit. 31, n. 159; Ioannes Andreae, lib. III, tit. 31, c. 10, n. 3; Hostiensis (Henricus de Segusio), *Commentaria in Quinque Libros Decretalium* (5 vols. in 3, Venetiis, 1581)—lib. III, tit. 31, c. 10, s. v. *ubi nunc* (hereafter cited Hostiensis); Panormitanus, (Nicholas de Tudeschis), *Commentaria in Quinque Libros Decretalium* (5 vols. in 7, Venetiis, 1578), lib. III, tit. 31, c. 10, s. v. *permittas,* n. 2 (hereafter cited as Panormitanus).

[11] S. v. *corde puro,* ad c. 18, X, *de regularibus et transeuntibus ad religionem,* 31.

[12] Reiffenstuel, lib. III, tit. 31, n. 276.

if it was made, the superior could seek to have the religious returned.[13] Panormitanus held the same opinion.[14] Some reasons for this condition were given by Reiffenstuel: (1) the common good was to be preferred to the good of an individual; (2) a worthy transfer was an act of the virtue of charity; but not to harm another was an act of the virtue of justice; justice had to be acknowledged precedence over charity.[15]

4. Fourthly, the religious must at least have asked for permission to transfer, even if it had not been obtained.

A decree of the Sacred Congregation of Bishops and Regulars, issued August 7, 1654, declared that this provision of the general law bound under pain of the invalidity of the transfer. The ruling was issued on the occasion of complaints by Mendicant Orders that their subjects were transferring to the Carthusians without their knowledge and without having requested the permission of their superiors, on the pretext of entrenched custom or privilege. This sometimes worked injustice, since some of the religious involved were guilty of various crimes.

The Sacred Congregation declared that, though the Carthusians were excepted in the law itself from the provisions that invalidated the transfers from the Mendicants to other Orders, they were still bound by the provisions of the general law as found in the *Decree* of Gratian and in the Decretals,[16] which required that the permission be at least requested, even if it was not granted. Privileges to the contrary were abrogated by the decree. This decree was confirmed one year later by a constitution of Pope Alexander VII (1655-1667), who cited its provisions, and stated that there should be absolutely no exceptions.[17]

Which superior was to be asked to give this permission? The more common and the more probable opinion was that the immediate

[13] Lib. III, tit. 31, c. 18, n. 22.

[14] Lib. III, tit. 31, c. 18, n. 12.

[15] Reiffenstuel, lib. III, tit. 31, n. 266.

[16] C. 3, C. XIX, q. 3 (cf. *supra*, p. 19, note 67), and c. 18, X, *de regularibus et transeuntibus ad religionem*, III, 31 (cf. *supra*, p. 24, note 80).

[17] Const. *Emanavit*, 12 iul. 1655—*Bull. Rom. Taur.*, XIV, 34, 35.

or local superior was the one to be asked. The reasons, as given by Reiffenstuel, were that the decretal *Licet* required the permission of the "prelate;" this could also be the local superior. In a case of doubt, the superior to whom appeal was to be made was the major superior; therefore, the superior whose permission was to be sought was the local or the immediate superior. Pirhing agreed that not only the superior general, or the provincial, but also the local superior could give the permission which had to be sought.[18]

A religious superior who had no superior within an Order and who wished to transfer had to *seek* the permission of the Holy Father. The common opinion of the authors was that, if the Holy Father neither denied nor answered the petition, the religious could transfer. Some authors, however, maintained that such superiors must not only have sought but also have received permission from the Holy See.[19]

Permission to transfer to another institute had to be sought, not after the transfer, but before.[20] After permission had been sought, transfer was not to be made immediately, but the religious had to wait a reasonable time for an answer.[21] If the superior refused permission, if the reason for his refusal was obviously false or unjust, or if he denied permission without any reason, the religious could transfer.[22]

In this connection Reiffenstuel pointed out that, as a matter of good procedure, the superior ought to ask the religious what his reasons were, and that the religious in turn was bound to manifest them, so that the superior might know whether he could give permission or whether he should deny it. If the reason was a just one,

18 Reiffenstuel, *ibid.*, n. 270; Pirhing, *ibid.*, n. 162.

19 Cf. Piatus, *Praelectiones Iuris Regularis* (Parisiis, 1888), I, 178 (hereafter cited Piatus); Pirhing, *ibid.*, n. 163.

20 Panormitanus, *ibid.*, c. 18; Reiffenstuel, *ibid.*, n. 267; Schmalzgrueber, lib. III, tit. 31, n. 233.

21 Schmalzgrueber, *ibid.*, n. 234; Reiffenstuel, *ibid.*, n. 267.

22 Ioannes Andreae, *ibid.*, n. 7; Schmalzgrueber, *ibid.*, n. 234; Reiffenstuel, *ibid.*, n. 268; Pirhing, *ibid.*, n. 161.

the superior was bound to give permission without making any difficulties.[23]

In a case of doubt regarding the motives for which the religious wished to transfer, or regarding the more rigorous character of the community to which he wished to transfer, the judgment of a superior had to be sought. There was a dispute as to who this superior should be. One opinion held that the superior was the one to whom the religious would ordinarily appeal when he had some complaint, that is, to a superior within the community. It was not the superior who had denied the permission, for he would in that event be a judge in his own case.[24] Another opinion was that the superior ought not to be one from that monastery or institute, since he, too, would act as a judge in his own case. It should rather be that superior who was competent to settle a controversy between the two communities involved in the transfer.[25]

Pope Benedict XIV affirmed in a letter that the second of these two opinions was more in accord with the policy of the Holy See.[26]

In the case of an appeal to the higher superior, his permission had actually to be obtained if the transfer was to be made possible.[27]

5. The fifth condition which was required for transfer by the commentators was that the transferring religious have letters of dismissal. This requirement was based on one of the canons of the *Decree* of Gratian (c. 3, C. XIX, q. 3). If there were none, the superior of the receiving order was to ask the superior of the dismissing order for them. If the latter stated that the monk had permission, or if he declared that permission had been denied, but the reasons assigned for the denial were plainly false, the religious could be received. If, however, the reason as given was just, or

[23] *Ibid.*, n. 269; Ioannes Andreae, *ibid.*, n. 3; Hostiensis, *ibid.*, s. v. *teneri*, et *quia sicut*.

[24] Reiffenstuel, *ibid.*, n. 270; Panormitanus, lib. III, tit. 31, c. 18, n. 1; Petra, IV, in Const. 3 Benedicti XII, n. 12.

[25] Schmalzgrueber, *ibid.*, n. 235; Hostiensis, lib. III, tit. 31, c. 18, s. v. *Superioris*.

[26] Ep. *Ex quo*, 14 ian. 1747, § 14—*Fontes*, n. 374. Cf. Vermeersch, *De Religiosis institutis et personis* (2 vols., Brugis, 1902), II, 262 (hereafter cited *De Religiosis*); Bouix, II, 526.

[27] Panormitanus, lib. III, tit. 31, c. 18, n. 1.

probably just, the religious had to be returned even if he offered to prove his side of the controversy.[28]

6. A sixth condition was that the institute from which the transfer was being made did not have a privilege that forbade the transfer unless the permission of the superiors had been obtained.[29] A difficulty arose from the fact that the law itself (the celebrated decretal *Licet* in the Decretals of Gregory IX) had declared that a religious could transfer to a more rigorous institute without having obtained the permission of his superiors, even if the institute had obtained a privilege to the effect that such a transfer could not be made if they were unwilling.

The authors believed, however, that this law applied only in the case in which the privilege stated in general terms that the religious could not transfer if the superiors were unwilling. If it was granted after the promulgation of the law, and if it stated specifically that permission had not only to be asked, but had also to be obtained, even in the case of transfer to a more rigorous institute, they held that the privilege derogated from the general law.[30]

The arguments were, first, that otherwise many privileges granted after the enactment of the law of the decretal *Licet* would have been entirely useless, since they would have allowed no more than was permitted by the law itself; and second, that a decree of the Sacred Congregation of the Council had declared the vow of a religious to transfer to a more rigorous institute invalid by reason of the fact that the constitutions of his own community forbade transfer without the permission of the superiors of the dismissing institute.[31]

7. Before the religious could leave, however, and even before permission to transfer had been given, the superior had to be certain that some more rigorous community was prepared to receive the

[28] Ioannes Andreae, *ibid.*, n. 13; Pirhing, *ibid.*, n. 161. Reiffenstuel, *ibid.*, n. 273; Hostiensis, lib. III, tit. 31, c. 18, s. v. *iudicium requirendum.*

[29] Pirhing, lib. III, tit. 31, n. 168; Reiffenstuel, lib. III, tit. 31, n. 270.

[30] Fagnanus, lib. III, tit. 31, nn. 22, 23; Petra, IV, in const. 8 Eugenii IV, n. 5; Ioannes Andreae, lib. III, tit. 31, cap. 18, n. 2; Sanchez, lib. VI, cap. 7, nn. 10, 12.

[31] Petra, *loc. cit.*; Bouix, II, 531, 532. The decision in question, cited by Petra, is also found in Pallottini, "Regulares," I, n. 48 (S.C.C. decr., 17 ian. 1693, *in Dubium Validitatis Voti*).

religious who wished to make the transfer. This was an innovation introduced by the Sacred Congregation of the Council in 1624.[32] Reiffenstuel held this to be the common opinion, but Pirhing stated that a superior could give his subject permission to leave the monastery in such a way that while seeking a stricter community he was to remain under obedience.[33]

The question was asked, with regard to the conditions which were postulated for a transfer to a more rigorous community, whether a transfer was valid when they were disregarded. Schmalzgrueber (1663-1735) held that as long as the transfer had been made to a more rigorous community, and as long as the transfer was not forbidden by a privilege to the contrary, or by the decretal *Viam ambitiosae* of Martin IV, which forbade Mendicants to transfer to Orders of non-Mendicants, the profession was not invalid simply in consequence of the fact that permission had not been sought or as a result of some similar defect in the requisite conditions, even though the transfer was gravely sinful. The religious could be recalled if he had not yet made profession: if he had already made profession, then suitable punishments could be inflicted.[34]

It is strange that there should have been question concerning the invalidity of a transfer when permission had not even been asked, since this had been authoritatively decided, as was seen above, by the Sacred Congregation of Bishops and Regulars in a decree confirmed by Pope Alexander VII.[35] Nevertheless, there was a controversy among the authors on the point, though the more common opinion was that a disregard of this provision of the law invalidated the transfer.[36]

When indults to transfer to more rigorous communities were granted by the Sacred Congregation of the Council, it appears that the indult presupposed that the superiors of the Order had been consulted concerning the motives for the transfer. Apparently the

[32] Decr., 21 sept. 1624, n. 3—*Fontes*, n. 2454; cf. Benedictus XIV, *De Synodo Dioecesana* (2. ed., 2 vols., Parmae, 1764), lib. XIII, c. 11, n. 4.

[33] Reiffenstuel, *ibid.*, n. 272; Pirhing, *ibid.*, n. 161.

[34] *Ibid.*, nn. 227-229.

[35] Cf. *supra*, p. 45.

[36] Bouix, II, 525; Petra, IV, in const. 1 Benedicti XII, n. 14.

indult sometimes was given before a particular community had been determined on, but its use was made subject to the condition that the religious find a community which would receive him.[87]

The practice of seeking the permission of the Holy See for transfer to a more rigorous community seems to have had its origin mainly in the many privileges which had been granted with a view to limiting the operation of the general law on this point, which privileges, as was seen in the preceding chapter, were obtained either directly or through the agency of the intercommunication of privileges as it existed for most of the religious institutes. Even when a religious had the permission of his own superior, it could not easily be established with certainty that his community did not have a privilege which would invalidate the transfer.[88] A convenient way to eliminate all doubt was to seek an apostolic indult, which would derogate from any contrary privilege possessed by the original community. Another factor in the development of this practice of seeking the permission of the Holy See was that the law itself could be applied only with difficulty to individual cases because of the inherent complexity of the problem of determining which community was more rigorous than the other. The law itself provided that in case of a doubt on this point, or on the point whether namely the motives of the religious were right and good, the judgment of the superior had to be sought. As pointed out above, this had resulted in a further controversy among the authors as to which superior was the competent one to make the decision. To obviate controversies and delays, as Pope Benedict XIV stated, it was the practice to seek the permission of the Holy See for the transfer. Religious, after they had explained the reasons for their desire to transfer to a more rigorous community, and had proved them, were readily given permission for the transfer by the Roman Pontiff. Included in the permission was a derogation from the necessity of having the consent of the

[87] S. C. C., Decr., aug. 28, 1649, *in Bisuntina*: "Concessa hinc fuit, annuente Sanctissimo, licentia Religioso transeundi ad strictiorem Religionem, auditis Superioribus suae Religionis super motivo transeundi, an sit fervore devotionis, et dummodo benevoles inveniat Receptores."—Pallottini, "Regulares," I, 47.

[88] Reiffenstuel, lib. III, tit. 31, nn. 9, 261.

superior of the community which the religious was about to leave.[39] Several authors of the seventeenth and eighteenth century stated that the transfer of professed religious even to a more or equally rigorous Order could not take place without a consultation of the Holy See. The reason given was the *praxis et stylus curiae.*[40] This opinion was not however entirely unanimous.[41]

This difference of opinion continued to the time of the promulgation of the Code of Canon Law. Some authors believed that by reason of the *stylus et praxis curiae* the permission of the Holy See was necessary for transfers to more rigorous institutes,[42] while other authors held that they could not see how one could maintain that the decretal *Licet* had been abrogated, since there was no general law that was contrary to its provisions.[43] Bouix pointed out that it was even more important to heed this point in his own time (the nineteenth century), since there were many religious congregations which did not enjoy the privileges which had been granted in this matter to most of the Orders, and whose members could take advantage of the general law when transferring to more rigorous communities.[44] It appears to the writer, however, that this author was not mindful of a decision of the Sacred Congregation of Bishops and Regulars, dated April 22, 1796, which required the permission of

39 Ep. *Ex quo,* 14 ian. 1747, § 14—*Fontes,* n. 374. Cf. Vermeersch, *De Religiosis,* II, 262.

40 Ferraris (+ ca. 1763), "Transitus," n. 1; Monacelli (+1715), *Formularium Legale Practicum* (3. ed., 3 vols., Romae, 1844), Pars II, tit. XVI, form. 3, n. 18. Mattheucci (+1722), *Officialis Curiae* (cited by De Angelis (+1881), *Praelectiones Iuris Canonici* [2. ed., 5 vols., Romae, 1908], II, 117, cap. 41, n. 25; De Luca (+1683), *Theatrum Veritatis et Iustitiae* (16 vols. in 9, Coloniae Agrippinae, 1706), Tom III, Pars I, *De regularibus,* discursus 35, n. 35; discursus 37, n. 3.

41 Petra (1662-1747) disagreed, and held that the decretal *Licet* was not entirely abrogated.—IV in const. 1 Benedicti XII, n. 28.

42 Nervegna, *De Jure Practico Regularium* (Romae, 1900), pp. 209-210; Bachofen, *Compendium Iuris Regularium* (New York, 1903), 348-349; Piatus, I, 180; Sebastianelli, *Praelectiones Iuris Canonici* (3 vols., 2. ed., Romae, 1905), *De Personis,* p. 429 (hereafter cited *De Personis*).

43 Bouix, II, 532; Vermeersch, *De Religiosis,* I, 186, 187, note 1.

44 Bouix, II, 533.

the Holy See for a transfer from one congregation to another. Closer study will be given to this decision in Section V below.

II. Transfer To An Equally Rigorous Community

There was no special or explicit provision in the general law concerning transfer to an equally rigorous community.[45] Nor did the Council of Trent introduce any innovations.[46] Canonists, however, drew their doctrine by way of deduction from implicit references to such transfers in the law, for example, from several passages in the Decretal legislation.[47] It was held that religious could not transfer licitly or validly to an Order of merely equal rigor without the permission of the superior or of the Holy See. The reasons offered were, first, that the commutation of the vows involved in such a transfer was not a *"commutatio in melius,"* and, secondly, that the bond between the religious and the community which they had effected could later be broken only by an external authority, not by the religious himself.[48]

It was the common opinion that the transfer could be permitted by the superior when a good reason was present, but not otherwise.[49]

Hostiensis (+1271) had taught that an abbot could grant permission to transfer to an equally rigorous community if there was a reason for the dispensation.[50] The *Glossa Ordinaria* contained the same doctrine.[51] Panormitanus later cited Innocent III as holding the opinion that a dispensation had also to be sought from the bishop. He, himself, believed, however, that if there was no reason for the dispensation, even the bishop could not permit the transfer. If there was a reason Panormitanus taught that the permission of

45 Bouix, I, 527; Petra, IV, in const. 8 Eugenii IV, nn. 12, 13.

46 S. C. C., decr., *in Dubium ad cap. 19, Sess. 25, de Reg.*—Pallottini, "Regulares," I, 45.

47 E.g., cc. 5, 7, 10, X, *de regularibus et transeuntibus ad religionem,* III, 31; cf. above, pp. 20-22.

48 Bouix, II, 527; Sebastianelli, *De Personis,* p. 428.

49 Petra, IV, in const. 8 Eugenii IV, nn. 13, 14; Bouix, II, 527.

50 Ad c. 7, X, *de regularibus et transeuntibus ad religionem,* III, 31, s. v. *sine licentia.*

51 Ad c. 7, X, *de regularibus et transeuntibus ad religionem,* III, 31, s. v. *permittatis.*

the abbot sufficed, though the safer course was to seek a dispensation from the bishop, too.[52]

This doctrine was slightly amplified by post-Tridentine authors. Both Schmalzgrueber and Pirhing taught that if the order was exempt, and if the superior of the community was subject to another by means of an intermediary superior, such as a provincial or a general, one of these latter had to give the consent. The reason, as given by Pirhing, was that in an exempt Order, the whole Order, or at least the province, had acquired a right to the religious by reason of his profession. In non-exempt communities the permission of the bishop was required. In both cases the following conditions had to be observed: (1) there had to be a just reason: without it, even the Pope could not dispense, because the institute had an acquired right to the religious of which it could not be deprived; (2) if the bishop gave permission, the consent of the religious superior was also required; the reason was that c. 7, X, *de regularibus et transeuntibus ad religionem,* III, 31, required the permission of the abbot for the transfer; and (3) the community or the chapter had also to give its consent to the transfer.[53]

However, in opposition to the doctrine of Schmalzgrueber it was the common opinion of the commentators that the Pope could dispense without a justifying cause, and that such a dispensation was both licit and valid. The reason given was that all religious were subject to the Holy Father, and that he could use this power over religious to transfer them, especially when the first community would not be harmed by the loss of this member.[54]

III. Transfer To a Less Rigorous Community

The pre-Tridentine commentators, basing their view on the decretal *Sane,*[55] maintained that ordinarily a transfer to a less rigor-

[52] Lib. III, tit. 31, c. 7, n. 6.

[53] Schmalzgrueber, lib. III, tit. 31, n. 237; Pirhing, lib. III, tit. 31, n. 165.

[54] Petra, *ibid.*, n. 15; Bouix, II, 527; Lombardi, *Iuris Canonici Privati Institutiones* (2. ed., 3 vols., Romae, 1901), I, 444 (hereafter to be cited as Lombardi); Sebastianelli, *De Personis,* p. 428.

[55] C. 10, X, *de regularibus et transeuntibus ad religionem,* III, 31; see above, p. 20.

ous community was forbidden. The *Glossa Ordinaria* declared that the abbot, however, could dispense, so that a religious could transfer to a less rigorous community.[56] Hostiensis also declared that, though some denied this, a religious could transfer for a good reason *(ex causa)* even to a less rigorous community if he had the permission of his abbot.[57] Innocent III held that the religious should seek also for a dispensation from the bishop, but Panormitanus favored the opinion that the permission of the abbot sufficed. It was acknowledged as the safer procedure, however, to obtain a dispensation also from the bishop.[58]

The Council of Trent forbade transfer of any Regular in virtue of any authority to a less rigorous Order.[59] But so deeply entrenched was the doctrine that superiors of religious could grant permission to transfer to a less rigorous community that despite this prohibition canonists continued to teach for some time that it applied only to an illegitimate transfer, that is, to one granted when there was no just reason, or when there had been no sufficient investigation. Schmalzgrueber held that not only the Pope, but more probably other superiors also who were inferior to the Pope, such as the provincial, or at least the general, of an Order, if it was exempt, and the bishop, if the Order was not exempt, could also grant permission for this transfer. This doctrine was identical with his teaching on the transfer to equally rigorous Orders. He noted that the privileges of individual Orders had to be inspected in a particular case, for some superiors had been given the right to grant such a transfer.[60]

Pirhing taught that besides the general and the provincial of an Order any exempt prelate, if he was subject only to the Pope and had *quasi-episcopal authority* over his subjects, likewise had the power to grant this permission. It was safer, however, so Pirhing held, to

[56] C. 7, X, *de regularibus et transeuntibus ad religionem,* III, 31, s. v. *permittatis.*

[57] C. 7, X, *de regularibus et transeuntibus ad religionem,* III, 31, s. v. *sine licentia.*

[58] Panormitanus, lib. III, tit. 31, cap. 7, n. 6.

[59] See above, p. 27.

[60] Lib. III, tit. 31, n. 238.

approach the Holy See if there was no danger in delay. If, however, there was no just reason for the transfer to a less rigorous community, he held that only the Pope himself could dispense, and even this did not excuse the religious in the forum of conscience, since even the Pope could not licitly relax a law without a just reason.[61]

Certain other authors also favored this mild interpretation of the Tridentine prohibition.[62] Certain others, however, denied this, for they claimed that after the Council of Trent, only the Holy See could give permission for making a transfer to another Order.[63] The decisions of the Sacred Congregations settled the matter in favor of the more rigorous opinion. Though there is record of permissions which were granted as well as of permissions which were refused by the Sacred Congregations, the doctrine became quite explicit that any transfer to a less rigorous community was reserved to the Holy See.

On the 19th of May, 1668, the Sacred Congregation of Bishops and Regulars denied a request for a transfer from the Olivetans to the Hierosolymites, the latter an Order of Hospitallers which, together with the Military Orders, seems to have been the least rigorous of all the Orders. For this reason any transfer to them was greatly discouraged.[64] This tendency toward restriction of the permission for transferring to this Order had, however, found occasional reversals, for Cardinal Petra reported that many indults for transfer from Mendicant Orders to the Hierosolymites were granted during the reign of Pope Sixtus V (1585-1590).[65]

A decree which was regarded as definitive in the matter by

[61] Lib. III, tit. 31, nn. 166, 167.

[62] Lessius, *De Iustitia et Iure Caeterisque Virtutibus Cardinalibus* (Lovanii, 1605), lib. II, cap. 41, n. 104; Sanchez, *Opus Morale in Praecepto Decalogi,* lib. VI, cap. 7, n. 65 ff. Krimer, *Quaestiones Canonici in V libros Decretalium* (5 vols., Augustae Vindelicorum, 1706-1709), n. 2792.

[63] Fagnanus, lib. III, tit. 31, nn. 27, 35; Petra, IV, in const. 8 Eugenii IV, nn. 19, 20.

[64] Decree reported by Perta, IV, in const. 8 Eugenii IV, n. 26. This decree, as many others on this matter, is not to be found in the standard collections, and hence is cited from the indirect source provided by Petra.

[65] *Loc. cit.*

Cardinal Petra was issued by the Sacred Congregation of the Council on January 26, 1675. It decided that religious superiors could not with a safe conscience permit any of their religious subjects to transfer from an institute in which the eating of meat was forbidden to a less rigorous one in which the use of meat was permitted, even if the superiors feared that the religious whose request for transfer was denied would defect from the faith.[66] Later decrees confirmed this.

Two years later the Sacred Congregation of Bishops and Regulars refused the petition of a religious to transfer from the Carmelites to the Benedictines despite the fact that both superiors had agreed to the transfer. In a footnote to the decree it was declared that first of all a transfer to a less rigorous institute was not possible. A second reason for the rejection of the petition was that ill health was declared to be an insufficient reason for transfer; the transfer would also be unfair, as it would burden a community which the religious had not served in time of health.[67]

In 1680 a decree of the Sacred Congregation of Bishops and Regulars refused to grant a petition for a transfer on the grounds of ill health. A priest confessor and preacher of the Minor Recollects of St. Francis wished to transfer to the Benedictines, and a well-known doctor testified that the religious involved could not endure the austerity of his own Order without endangering his life. The Order to which he wished to transfer was one in which there was a due observance not only of the regular discipline but also of the enclosure. Cardinal Casanate (1620-1700), probably the secretary of the Congregation, added that the superiors of his Order were to treat him with kindness.

The rigor of the Sacred Congregation of Bishops and Regulars at that time is shown by another refusal of a petition for transfer two years later. A religious of the Fathers of the Reformed Minors Observants wished to transfer, for a just reason and because of most serious infirmities, to the Canons Regular of the Lateran. He had the consent of the superiors of the two institutes, and his petition

[66] Decree reported in Pallottini, "*Regulares,*" I, n. 43; Petra, IV, in const. 8 Eugenii IV, n. 19.

[67] 12 mart. 1677—*Analecta Ecclesiastica,* XI (1903), 265.

was seconded by an archbishop. The response was in the negative. The reason given by the Sacred Congregation was that a transfer to a less rigorous community could not take place.[68]

Toward the end of the century, however, there was issued a general indult which permitted apostates from a religious institute to transfer to a less rigorous institute if the enclosure and the regular observance was practiced in this institute.[69] On the 30th of August, 1698, Pope Innocent XII (1691-1700) approved the opinion of the Sacred Congregation of the Council that the religious of the Holy Spirit, an Order of Hospitallers, could not receive religious who transferred in virtue of this indult.[70] Just after the end of the century a religious used this indult in transferring to the Canons Regular of St. Anthony of Vienne. He apparently did not meet the requirements of the indult, since the Sacred Congregation of the Council ordered him to return to his institute under pain of incurring the penalties decreed against apostates in the aforesaid indult.[71]

Apparently at that time, that is, at the end of the seventeenth century, there was a slight relaxation of the strictness that had prevailed some years earlier, since Cardinal Petra noted that even though apostates were permitted by indult to transfer only to Orders in which the enclosure and the regular observance were practiced, nevertheless at the time just indicated permission to transfer to religious institutes without the enclosure was given in special cases by the Holy See to those religious who had been resident for a long time among heretics.[72]

With this exception the constitution *Licet sacra*,[73] was rigidly enforced in reference to transfer to less rigorous communities. In a letter to the Bishop of Sao Paolo in Brazil, written on the 27th of May, 1746, Pope Benedict XIV gave a clear picture of the practice of the Roman Curia of that day. The Pope declared that no one,

[68] 26 iun. 1682—*Analecta Ecclesiastica*, VI (1897), 495.

[69] Mentioned in Pallottini, "*Regulares*," I, n. 41; no exact date is given for this indult.

[70] Cited by Cardinal Petra, IV, in const. 8 Eugenii IV, n. 25.

[71] 24 mart. 1703—Pallottini, "*Regulares*," I, n. 41.

[72] Cardinal Petra, IV, in const. 8 Eugenii IV, n. 26.

[73] See above, pp. 29-31.

according to the rules that had been enacted, could be transferred from one community to another, unless in the second there was the practice of the enclosure and the regular observance; a transfer could not be made to an Order of Hospitallers or to a Military Order. He wished the bishop to know that if he should hear that some religious had been so dispensed by the Apostolic See as to be authorized to transfer to another community in which there was no enclosure or regular observance, that this happened most rarely, and only for most grave and reasonable causes.[74]

Several decrees illustrate this adherence to the provisions of the Council of Trent and of the Constitution *Licet sacra* which forbade a transfer to Orders in which there was not the practice of the enclosure and the regular observance. In 1748 the Sacred Congregation of Bishops and Regulars gave the Apostolic Nuncio of Paris the faculty to permit a religious who had apostatized from his Order to enter another Order if he could find one to receive him. This Order, however, had to be one in which there was the practice of the regular observance and the enclosure, and could not be a Military Order or a congregation. If he found an Order to receive him, he was to repeat his year of probation. If he could not within a year find an Order to receive him, he was to return to the enclosure of his own Order, which was enjoined to receive him and to treat him kindly.[75]

In 1776, a letter of reproval was sent by the same Sacred Congregation to the Vice-Legate at Avignon for granting a transfer in which the conditions enacted in the Constitution *Licet sacra* had not been observed. A religious, after obtaining permission to transfer, had transferred to a monastery where there was no regular observance. He had not gone even there, but had lived in a secular dwelling in the garb of a priest, and had made his novitiate and profession for the Benedictine Order in an Augustinian monastery. It was declared that the provisions of the said Constitution had been violated, and that a religious who transferred had to take the

[74] Litt. ap. *Pontificia commendatione,* 27 maii, 1746—in Vermeersch, *De Religiosis,* II, 61.

[75] 21 ian. 1748—*Analecta Juris Pontificii* (Romae, 1855-1869; Parisiis, 1872-1891), XIV (1875), p. 847, n. 1305.

habit, complete the novitiate and make profession, under pain of the invalidity of the transfer, in the Order to which he had transferred.[76]

A third decree concerned a Franciscan who had transferred, contrary to the Constitution *Licet sacra,* to a community of Benedictines where there was neither the regular observance nor the enclosure. The Sacred Congregation of Bishops and Regulars did not wish to approve of this irregular transfer even indirectly, and therefore refused the petition of this religious, though made twenty-two years after the irregular transfer, to leave money to a hospital and to his indigent parents, something which it was possible to do under the rules of the community to which he had transferred.[77]

The law which forbade the transfer to a less rigorous community, as constituted by the Council of Trent, is truly the forerunner of the present law, which forbids all transfers except with the permission of the Holy See. This is amply demonstrated by the fact that it is the only previous law cited by Cardinal Gasparri (1852-1934) in his footnotes to the canons which in the Code of Canon Law treat the question of transfer.

IV. The Transfer of Nuns

Until the time of the promulgation of the Constitution *Decori* by Pope Pius V,[78] it seems that nuns were subjected to the same laws as regulars in the matter of transfer. In general, the laws applying to Regulars were used *mutatis mutandis* as norms for the women religious of those times. The Constitution *Decori,* however, limited the right of nuns to leave the cloister to very great emergencies only. This was interpreted as severely inhibiting for nuns the right at least theoretically enjoyed by male religious, namely to transfer to more rigorous Orders under the norms and conditions specified by law. Thus this Constitution was declared by the Sacred Congregation of the Council to inhibit the right to make a transfer. It was

[76] 15 dec. 1776—*Analecta Juris Pontificii,* XVI (1877), p. 618, n. 1387.

[77] 11 aug. 1786—*Analecta Juris Pontifici,* XVI (1877), pp. 633-634, n. 1410.

[78] Cf. *supra,* pp. 28, 29.

declared that a transfer could, therefore, be permitted to a nun only wih great circumspection.[79]

Who could give this permission? Pope Benedict XIV, in his work on the diocesan synod, revealed that a nun could obtain both from the Sacred Penitentiary and from the Sacred Congregation of Bishops and Regulars the permission to make a transfer. There had to be precautions to protect the law of the enclosure: it would be incongruous to permit a transfer from a monastery bound by the cloister to one where there was no obligation of this kind.[80] A number of authors asserted that in view of the Constitution *Decori* nuns could no longer transfer without the permission of the Holy See,[81] but there are also to be found a number of authors who still believed that these religious could transfer, provided that they had the permission of the abbess, of the Prelate of Regulars to whom the monastery was subject, and, at least if they were not exempt, of the bishop of the place.[82] The bishops of the Netherlands had obtained by custom the authority to grant this permission to women religious of monasteries in their territories who had been subjected to them because of the circumstances of the times, but this privilege was declared to obtain no longer after the promulgation of the Code.[83]

Examples of the transfer of nuns were those which were granted by the Sacred Congregation of Bishops and Regulars when the reason was the bad health of the religious. Somewhere between 1677 and 1690 a nun was permitted by the Sacred Congregation to transfer with her servant from one community to another because of her bad health, but a second petition to transfer back again was refused.[84]

79 S. C. C., decr. *in Dubium ad cap. 19, sess. 25 de Reg.*—Pallottini, "Regulares," n. I, n. 46.

80 *De Synodo Dioecesana,* lib. XIII, c. 12, n. 29.

81 Cf. Piatus, I, 177; Santi-Leitner, *Praelectiones Juris Canonici* (4. ed., 5 vols. in 2, Ratisbon, 1903-1905), lib. III, tit. 31, n. 40.

82 Cf. Piatus, I, 177; Pirhing, lib. III, tit. 31, n. 162.

83 Cf. Mothon, *Traité sur l'État Religieux* (Paris, 1922), p. 63, nota 2 (hereafter cited as Mothon); S. C. de Religiosis, resp., 9 nov. 1926—*Acta Apostolicae Sedis* (Romae, 1909-), XVIII (1926), 90 (hereafter cited *AAS*).

84 *Analecta Ecclesiastica,* XI (1903), 131. This is one of a series of decrees

The Sacred Congregation, on another occasion, refused a petition for the transfer of a Carmelite nun from one monastery to another because of ill health brought on by the climatic conditions of the place where her monastery was located. The nun was in fact so ill that for the major part of the year she was unable to assist at the common religious exercises of her Order. In the petition it was stated that she would leave to the monastery she wished to leave the dowry she had already furnished and would give a new dowry to the monastery she wished to enter. The petition was refused.[85]

Another and similar petition, made two years later, was apparently granted, but only with some reluctance. The Sacred Congregation wrote first to the bishop of the diocese where the monastery was situated, and it was only after he answered to the effect that the nun was truly ill, as claimed, that she could not be cured in the monastery where she then lived, and that she had the consent of the nuns to whose monastery she wished to transfer, that permission was given.[86]

V. Transfer To a Congregation

It appears that congregations were classed among the less rigorous communities, so that transfer to them from an Order of Regulars was forbidden except with the permission of the Holy See, which probably was quite hard to obtain. So, for example, a decree of the Sacred Congregation of Bishops and Regulars, dated January 21, 1748, and mentioned earlier in this chapter, forbade an apostate religious who had been given permission to transfer to another Order to make a transfer to a congregation.[87]

A decree of the Sacred Congregation of Bishops and Regulars as issued in 1796 declared that it was permitted to transfer from one house of a congregation to another of the same congregation with the permission of the superior of the latter house. But an apostolic indult was required for transfer to another congregation,

reported in *Analecta Ecclesiastica* without a more exact specification of the date of issue.

85 15 mart. 1685—*Analecta Ecclesiastica,* IX (1901), 82.

86 21 febr. 1687—*Analecta Ecclesiastica,* X (1902), 135.

87 See above, p. 58.

even though it followed the same rule, in this case the rule of St. Augustine.[88]

The authors held that the Decretal *Licet* applied to transfer from a congregation to an Order, unless there were a privilege to the contrary. [89] For transfer from one congregation to another, however, Vermeersch (1858-1936) believed that only the consent of the superior was necessary, since this removed what he believed to be the only obstacle to the transfer, the acquired right of the community to which the religious first belonged.[90] It is hard to see how the view can be reconciled with the decision of the Sacred Congregation of Bishops and Regulars of 1796 cited just above.[90a]

The *Normae,* moreover, issued for congregations of simple vows in 1901 for the purpose of outlining the procedure required for their approval, confirmed the practice of requiring a dispensation of the Holy See for transfer from one congregation to another. It was provided that those who had taken either perpetual or temporal vows in an institute could not be admitted into another institute without a dispensation of the Holy See as long as these vows still endured.[91] From this time on, at least, a congregation could no longer receive transferring members from other institutes without an apostolic authorization to do so.

[88] S. C. Ep. et Reg., *Plurium,* 22 apr. 1796, ad 6: "Transire de domo ad domum eiusdem congregationis licere cum beneplacito superioris ad quem; transire ad aliam congregationem, licet sub eadem regula S. Augustini, non licere nisi cum dispensatione apostolica."—*Analecta Juris Pontificii,* XVI (1876), p. 733, n. 1427. See also S. C. Ep. et Reg., 20 aug. 1897, ad 11, cited by Wernz-Vidal, *Jus Canonicum* (7 vols. in 9, Romae: Universitas Gregoriana, 1923-1938), Vol. III, *De Religiosis* (1933), p. 452, note 11 (hereafter cited *De Religiosis*). This last decree is not available to the writer, but applies plainly to sisters with simple vows.

[89] Vermeersch, *De Religiosis,* II, 32; Bouix, II, 533.

[90] *Loc. cit.*

[90a] See Wernz-Vidal *De Religiosis,* p. 451, p. 452, note (11).

[91] Art. 61, 5°. "Sine dispensatione S. Sedis admitti non possunt in Institutum . . . qui in alio Instituto vota perpetua, sive etiam temporaria emiserunt, its perdurantibus."—*Normae secundum quas S. Cong. Episcoporum et Regularium procedere solet in approbandis novis institutis votorum simplicium* (Romae, 1901).

VI. Testimonial Letters

Testimonial letters for aspirants to religious institutes date from about the middle of the nineteenth century. The decree *Romani Pontifices* enacted this requirement in 1848. The testimonials were to be sought from the ordinary of the place of origin and from the ordinary of every place where the aspirants had dwelt for more than a year after the completion of their fifteenth year of age.[92] This requirement was declared to be, not for the validity of the admission to the novitiate and of profession, but for licitness only.[93]

To settle a doubt concerning this requirement as to its application to postulants, novices, and professed religious coming from other communities, it was declared that novices, postulants and secularized religious had to secure the testimonials from their ordinaries. Professed religious who were still with their own communities were to seek the letters not from their ordinaries but from their religious superiors. The superiors were determined as the general or provincial superiors, or the local superiors if there were no provincial superiors in the said Order. If the religious had been in several different communities, the superior of the last was the one who was to give the testimonials. The superiors were obliged to make a diligent inquiry concerning the character of the religious before giving these testimonials.[94]

Letters of dismissal, indicating that the religious had received permission to leave his own community, had been recognized from ancient times, as was seen above.[95]

Article 2. The Renewal of the Novitiate and of Profession

The Decretal legislation had nothing to say concerning the renewal of the novitiate in the receiving community on the part of the transferring religious, but it had been imposed on them from

[92] S. C. super statu Regularium, decr. *Romani Pontifices,* 25 ian. 1848—*Fontes,* n. 4375.

[93] S. C. super Statu Regularium, declar., 1 maii, 1851, ad 8, 9—*Fontes,* n. 4377.

[94] S. C. super Statu Regularium, declar., 19 mart. 1857—*Fontes,* n. 4381; declar., 29 maii, 1857, ad 3—*Fontes,* n. 4382.

[95] See above, pp. 12, 47.

ancient times in virtue simply of the fact that it was required of all new members of a community.[96] This was explicitly confirmed as far as transfer to a stricter Order was concerned, by the Sacred Congregation of the Council in 1633 when it decreed that a religious who transferred from a less to a more rigorous community was obliged to undergo a year of probation.[97] An indult, already cited above as granting an apostate religious the permission to seek an Order which would receive him, declared that he was to repeat his year of probation.[98]

Another decree, also cited earlier in this chapter, and issued in 1776 by the Sacred Congregation of Bishops and Regulars, seems to have required the renewal of the novitiate for the validity of the transfer to a less rigorous community.[99]

The authors, therefore, held that a novitiate of one year was necessary, even if the transfer was made to a less rigorous institute of the same Order. The profession of vows had then to be made. If it was not, the religious was obliged to return to his original community.[100]

Cardinal Nervegna was witness for the fact that at the beginning of the twentieth century transfers were granted by the Sacred Congregation of Bishops and Regulars on condition that the transferring religious be placed in the novitiate and there repeat the entire period of probation. This was true whether the transfer was to a more; equally or less rigorous community. Ordinarily there was no dispen-

96 Cf. Goyeneche, "De Transitu ad aliam religionem"—*CpR,* I (1920), 226; c. 1, C. XVII, q. 2; c. 16, X, *de regularibus et transeuntibus ad religionem,* III, 31; c. 2, *de regularibus et transeuntibus ad religionem,* III in VI° 14; Conc. Trident., sess. XXV, *de regularibus,* c. 15; sess. XIV, *de ref.,* c. 11.

97 S. C. C., 30 aug. 1633—Pallottini, *"Regulares,"* I, 49.

98 S. C. Ep. et Reg., 21 ian. 1748—*Analecta Juris Pontificii,* XIV (1875), p. 847, n. 1305; see above, p. 58.

99 See above, p. 58.

100 Cf. Ferraris, s. v. "Transitus," n. 2. He cited a declaration of the Sacred Congregation of the Council as requiring a year of probation for a religious who transferred with the permission of the Apostolic See to a less rigorous institute even if it belonged to the same Order: "Transeuntem de licentia Sedis Apostolicae ad laxiorem religionem etiam eiusdem Ordinis, teneri in secunda religione secundum annual probationis peragere." Suarez, *De Religione,* tract. VIII, lib. III, cap. 15, n. 1.

sation from this requirement.[101] The only exception which he noted concerned transfer to a community which had a common origin with the one which was being left, as was the case, for example, with the several branches of the Benedictines or of the Cistercians. In that case no new novitiate, but only thirty days of spiritual exercises performed in the new community before the religious became enrolled by the superior as a member of the community were demanded by the Sacred Congregation.[102]

A new profession was also required in order to complete the transfer to another religious institute. The transferring religious, under penalty of the invalidity of the transfer, had to make this profession in the Order to which he was transferring.[103]

Pirhing stated that a new profession was required when the religious transferred to another institute. This profession could be either explicit or implicit. It was by reason of the fact that his election and confirmation as superior of a different community than his own was equivalent to implicit profession that the superior could no longer return to his original community in case he lost his position. The monastery to which he first belonged lost its right over him by his transfer. The same, said Pirhing, was true of simple monks or of professed religious.[104] Hence, once the new profession was made, the bond which united the religious to the dismissing institute was entirely severed, and he was incorporated as a member in the receiving institute or monastery.[105]

According to Cardinal Nervegna, the ordinary practice of the Sacred Congregation was to require that the transferring religious make a new profession, but return to the Order which he had left in case that he did not do so. A simple profession before the solemn profession was strongly urged in the case of those communities in

101 Cf. also Vermeersch, *De Religiosis*, II, 188; Sebastianelli († 1920) on the contrary, stated that the Holy See usually dispensed from the novitiate, except for a brief period, unless the receiving institute was much more austere than the dismissing one (*De personis*, p. 429).

102 Nervegna, *De Jure Practico Regularium*. Cardinal Nervegna was probably speaking of transfer to another independent monastery.

103 See above, p. 59.

104 Lib. III, tit. 31, n. 181.

105 Lombardi, I, 444; Sebastianelli, *De Personis*, p. 429.

which this was the rule. No new profession was required when there was a transfer from one community to another which had a common origin with the first. The religious was simply enrolled as a member of the community by the superior after his declaration that he would abide by its rules and assume its obligations.[106]

Article 3. The Effects of Transfer

1. *The Rights and the Obligations of the Religious in the New Community*

With regard to prerogatives and privileges enjoyed by the religious in the community to which he formerly belonged, those which were founded upon profession in that particular institute, precedence, for example, and upon its rule, did not follow him but were lost once the transfer was completed.[107] Others, however, which by their very nature belonged to him in virtue of his being in the religious state, were not lost in consequence of the transfer.[108] Doctoral degrees could still be retained, but if these were not given in the receiving institute they could not be used there.[109] If the degrees of Lector or Master were like the doctoral degree, they came under the same rule. If, however, they signified something proper to one particular institute, they were lost when the religious left that institute by way of transfer.[110]

The same was true of the obligations of the community to which the religious formerly belonged. Special vows, for example, which were proper to the dismissing community, but not found in the receiving community, ceased once the transfer had been made.[111]

[106] *De Jure Practico Regularium*, pp. 215-216.

[107] Suarez, *De Religione*, tract. VIII, lib. III, cap. 15, n. 1. Precedence was not lost when there was a transfer from one monastery to another of the same Order.—*ibid.*, n. 14.

[108] *Ibid.*, n. 15.

[109] Suarez, *loc. cit.*

[110] *Ibid.*, n. 114.

[111] Pirhing, III, tit. 31, n. 182; Passerini, *De Hominum Statibus et Officiis* (3 vols., Lucae, 1732), I, q. 189, art. 8, n. 170 (hereafter cited Passerini); Lezana, *Summa Questionum Regularium* (Lugduni, 1655), tract. I, cap. 22, n. 19; Tamburini, *De Iure Abbatum* (Lugduni, 1640), disp. VII, q. VI, n. 6.

The single exception was the vow taken by certain regulars in the presence of their superiors either before, after, or in the very act of profession, not to accept any dignity, or prelacy, or position of authority outside their own institute, unless forced or obliged to do so by the precept of one who had such power under the law. This vow, because of a special constitution of Pope Urban VIII, still bound these religious after their transfer to a community where such a vow was not taken.[112]

With regard to the rights and the privileges of the members of the receiving community, all rights and prerogatives which were enjoyed by other members were enjoyed also by the member who had transferred to it from another community, unless this was specifically forbidden by the law. Suarez offered as his reasons for this assertion that, since all rights and privileges enjoyed in the community to which the religious had previously belonged had been lost by his new profession, the religious ought to have those of the receiving community; secondly, because of his new profession, he was bound by the same vows as the other members of the community, and therefore ought also to have the same advantages, for example, as to precedence based on the date of profession, and as to vote and elegibility for office.[113]

The law, however, provided for exceptions to this general rule. For instance, the Clementine law forbade Mendicants who transferred to non-Mendicant Orders, except only the Carthusians, to become superiors or to have a vote in the chapters. This was repeated by the authors practically verbatim, so that it need not be treated at length here.[114]

One relevant commentary respecting it, however, was that this constitution extended not only to the four older Mendicant Orders, but also to those which arose later and received the designation of Mendicant Orders from the Holy See: to the Minims of St. Francis

[112] Const. *"Honorum dignitatumque,"* 24 febr. 1643—*Bull. Rom. Taur.*, XV, 240-243; Vermeersch, *De Religiosis*, I, 188.

[113] Suarez, *De Religione*, tract. VIII, lib. III, cap. 15, n. 2.

[114] For the content of the law, see above, p. 26; Vermeersch, *De Religiosis*, I, 188.

de Paula, for example, and to the Jesuits.[115] The prohibition extended to the holding of any administrative position in the new community, but did not prohibit teaching or preaching.[116]

The Council of Trent had decreed that Regulars who transferred to another Order should be admitted to profession only on condition that they should remain in the Order to which they had transferred, and persevere perpetually in the cloister under obedience to their superiors, and that they should be wholly disqualified to hold secular benefices, even with the charge of souls attached.[117] This restriction, however, did not mean that they could not be given permission to leave the cloister like other religious of the community. According to the mind of Suarez, at least, the Council of Trent meant only to forbid transfer made with the purpose of having the institute acquire only a right over the religious without the concomitant duty of supporting him, while the religious would then be given permission to live outside the cloister and to seek means of support for himself. This, however, would not be the case if in the matter of permission to leave the cloister he were treated just as other religious were.[118] Because the Council of Trent spoke of transfer to another distinct Order, the authors did not extend this law to a transfer from one monastery to another. In such a case, neither the precedence of the religious, based on the date of his profession, nor other prerogatives common to the order as a whole, were lost by transfer.[119]

When was the community to which the transfer was made to be considered as another distinct institute? This question became important when the transfer was made between branches of the same Order which did not have the same superior general, for example, between the branches of the Benedictine Order in Portugal, in Castile, and in Italy; between the less strict and the discalced Carmelites; and between the Conventuals, the Observants, and the

[115] Schmalzgrueber, lib. III, tit. 31, n. 239; Suarez, *ibid.*, n. 3.

[116] Suarez, *loc. cit.*

[117] Sess. XIV, *de ref.*, c. 11.

[118] Suarez, *ibid.*, nn. 17, 18.

[119] Suarez, *ibid.*, n. 14.

Capuchins within the Order of St. Francis.[120] The doubt arose because in these and similar cases there seemed to be some unity among the branches, since there was a similarity in the rule and an identity in their first founder, so that one could consider them as one community; on the other hand, they seemed distinct because they had different superiors general, and the unity of a religious institute was the unity of a political body, which did not seem possible if there were not but one head.[121] In the opinion of Suarez, there was sufficient unity, even though they did not have the same superior general, to evade the application of the restriction provisions of the Council of Trent to transfers between the communities mentioned. This was certain when the diversity was only material, in that it was due simply to a difference of nationality, while the substantial means, ceremonies, rule, enclosure, and habit remained the same—even if there was a slight difference in the privilege of apostolic exemption. There was some doubt in Suarez' mind on this point if there was also a difference between the groups as to rigor of life, as to the observance of the rule, and to some degree in the habit also. But he held that in practice one could count them as one Order, since they were such in the common estimation of men, and since the substantial character of the religious life remained the same.[122]

II. The Property and the Dowry of the Religious

The doctrine on the transfer of property accompanying the transfer of the religious seems to have been drawn originally from the Roman Law only, and that not until the post-Tridentine period, Schmalzgrueber[123] distinguished the goods that came to the religious before his transfer, or after his profession in the receiving

[120] Cf. Suarez, tract. VIII, lib. III, cap. 15, n. 15.

[121] "In his enim et similibus est specialis ratio dubitandi (an sit distinctus ordo eo ipso cum habet distinctum Generalem) quia, licet propter convenientiam in regula et primo fundatore, censeantur una religio, tamen simpliciter videntur distinctae, quia unitas religionis est unitas corporis politici, quae sine uno capite non videtur esse posse."—Suarez, *loc. cit.*

[122] *Loc. cit.*

[123] *Ius Ecclesiasticum Universum,* lib. III, tit. 31, n. 243.

community, or during the period of probation in the receiving community but before his profession.

(1) Goods which the religious acquired before his transfer belonged to the dismissing community. The reason for the conclusion was that by virtue of the profession of the religious the dismissing community acquired an absolute right to all the goods which were owned by the religious at that time. This last principle was drawn from two texts in Roman Law. The first, from the Code of Justinian, concerned the form to be used by nuns in making their wills; the second, more pertinent, from the Novels, provided that one who entered a monastery ceased to be the owner of the goods which had been his; they all belonged to the monastery, with exception made as to part of the property so as to provide for the children who were necessary heirs, and also as to that part which belonged to the wife's dowry, in the case of a married man.[124] So a decree of the Sacred Congregation of Bishops and Regulars determined that a monk or nun who transferred to another monastery with the required permission could not transfer his or her goods to the receiving monastery.[125] (2) If the goods came to the religious after his transfer and profession in the receiving community, they belonged to this community if it was capable of acquiring title to them; otherwise they belonged to his intestate heirs. The reason for this conclusion was that by his profession the religious was absolved of his subjection to the dismissing and made subject to the receiving community.

3. There was a controversy as to which institute received the property which came into the possession of the transferring religious while he was in the novitiate of the receiving institute. Some believed that the dismissing institute acquired this property. The reasons given were that until his profession the transferring religious remained incorporated in this original religious family, and that the property acquired by a religious is acquired by his religious family

[124] C(1.2), 12; N(5.5); cf. pp. 8-9.

[125] Decr. (issued somewhere in the period between 1677-1690), *Analecta Ecclesiastica*, VII (1899), 165.

or monastery. The bond wth this family was not broken by the novitiate, but only by the new profession.[126]

Others disagreed. They inclined to the opinion that the property should belong to the receiving institute, at least if and when the religious should make his new profession there. The argument advanced for this view was that the religious who transferred should, during the novitiate, be considered as a member of the receiving, and not of the dismissing, institute. An axiom of Roman law was used in support of this principle: "*proxime accingendus pro accinto habetur*." Just as a secular who becomes a novice is said to belong rather to religion than to the world, so a religious who transfers to another institute should be said rather to belong to the receiving than to the dismissing institute. Furthermore, so it was argued, it was only right that since the receiving institute had to support the religious while in the novitiate, it should also profit from him by acquiring the property which came to the religious during this period.[127] According to Nervegna, the Sacred Congregation of Bishops and Regulars at the end of the nineteenth century usually left the matter to be decided by amicable agreement between the two superiors involved, since it was considered a matter of internal administration.[128]

Another question can be raised regarding the effect of transfer on certain goods in the possession of the religious. The question relates, first of all, to manuscripts. There was a controversy of long standing on the point whether manuscripts were part of the remote matter of the vow of poverty. Differing views on the effect of transfer on the ownership of manuscripts followed as a logical consequence of the three different opinions concerning the ownership of the manuscripts themselves. (1) Some believed that manuscripts were not part of the remote matter of the vow of poverty, but were completely subject to ownership by the religious. (2) Others believed that all manuscripts, except only those which were no longer useful, belonged to the institute or the monastery.

126 Passerini, I, q. 189, art. 8, n. 185; Sanchez, *Opus Morale in Praecepta Decalogi*, lib. VII, cap. 32, n. 9.

127 Schmalzgrueber, lib. III, tit. 31, n. 243.

128 Nervegna, *De Jure Practico Regularium*, p. 212.

(3) A third group of authors made a distinction between the right of ownership and the right of use. Manuscripts belonged to the community with respect to the right of ownership, but belonged irrevocably to the religious with respect to the right of use.

The first of these three opinions was the more common one.[129] This meant of course that the religious could take the manuscripts with him in case he went to another institute. They did not have to be restored to the releasing community after his death.[130] He could also alienate or destroy them. This opinion was enshrined by custom, and continued as a very widespread opinion down to the twentieth century.[131] St. Alphonsus (1696-1787) in his day thought it was the more probable opinion.[132]

The reasons given for this opinion were that manuscripts were spiritual goods in the sense that they were aids to the memory, thoughts and meditations written on paper, products of one's own talent, almost a part of one's knowledge. Spiritual "property" was not part of the remote matter of the vow of poverty. It was held that these manuscripts came under the rule for spiritual property in accordance with the maxim, "Accessorium sequitur principale." [133] An important factor was that until fairly recently manuscripts had no monetary or sales value. The author would receive nothing for them, and indeed either the religious or his friends had to pay the expenses of printing them in order to have them published. The custom of not considering them as a part of the remote matter of the vow of poverty continued, even though conditions had changed.[134] As was pointed out by Lehmkuhl (1834-1918) before

[129] Cf. Turner, *The Vow of Poverty,* The Catholic University of America Canon Law Studies, n. 54 (Washington, D. C.: The Catholic University of America, 1929), p. 93 (hereafter to be referred to as Turner); Ferreres, "Anno-taciones"—*Razón y Fe* (Madrid, 1900), XXXVII (1913), 244.

[130] Rotarius, *Theologia Moralis Regularium* (3 vols. in 2, Venetiis, 1735), I, lib. III, cap. 3, n. 10; Salmanticenses, *Cursus Theologiae Moralis* (6 vols. in 4, Venetiis, 1724-1728), Tom. III, *De Restitutione,* tract. 22, cap. 2, n. 195.

[131] Turner, p. 93.

[132] St. Alphonsus de Liguori, *Theologia Moralis* (4 vols. in 2, Augustae Taurinorum, 1825-1828), lib. IV, n. 14.

[133] Authors cited in note 129.

[134] Turner, p. 96.

the beginning of the twentieth century, if someone now produces a manuscript which becomes a profitable investment or could easily become so if given to a printer, it is certain that this manuscript is commonly thought to have money value.[135]

Some of the ancient writers had extended the ownership which they believed religious had over manuscripts to manuscripts given them by others.[136] There was, however, no serious doubt that the manuscripts given them by others belonged to the institute like other temporal goods.[137]

The second opinion was that all manuscripts, except only those without any use, belonged to the institute or the monastery. Whether they had been composed by the religious who possessed them or by another made no difference, as long as they had been produced in the institute. The reason given was that they were a product of the industry of the religious, and therefore could not be taken elsewhere.[138]

Suarez admitted that this opinion was the safer of the two opinions, but maintained nevertheless that it was doubtful, because writings seemed to be as it were a part of a person's knowledge and learning, since they were helps to the memory on which knowledge to a great extent was dependent.[139]

A third opinion in the field made a distinction between the right of ownership and the right of use. Manuscripts belonged to the community with respect to the right of ownership, but belonged irrevocably to the religious with respect to the right of use. The ownership remained with the institute, at least if the manuscript had money value. But it was argued that the use of books by their own author could not have money value, and hence abstracted from the factor of price, since it was intrinsically related to the use of

135 Lehmkuhl, *Theologia Moralis* (4. ed., 2 vols., Friburgi-Brisgoviae, 1887), I, n. 523.

136 Cf. Piatus, I, q. 272; Ferreres, *ibid.*, p. 245.

137 Ferreres, *ibid.*, p. 246.

138 Cf. Suarez, *De Religione*, tract. VIII, lib. III, cap. 13, n. 10—*Opera Omnia*, XVI, pt. 1.

139 Suarez, *Religione*, tract, VIII, lib. III, cap. 13, n. 10—*Opera Omnia*, XVI, pt. 1.

his knowledge. Hence the religious could not alienate the manuscripts, or destroy them, since this would be to exercise an act of of ownership of which he was not capable. He could, however, take them with him, even without permission, when transferring from one religious house to another.[140] Several modern theologians made this theory their own, and held that it was more probable than the other.[141]

A decision of the Sacred Congregation of Religious which was issued in 1913 upheld this third opinion at least in part. It denied that religious of simple or of solemn vows who had written a manuscript while they were under vows had ownership of it, so that they could give it away or alienate it under any title.[142]

The wording of this decree is not entirely without ambiguity. It was not interpreted as a certain denial of ownership of the manuscript on the part of the religious, but merely as a denial of the right to exercise ownership through alienation or donation of the manuscript. Salsmans (1873-1944) and Ferreres (1861-1936) ex-

140 Passerini (I, q. 189, art. VIII, n. 184): "Manuscripta propria, et a religioso composita quantum ad dominium sunt religionis sed quantum ad usum proprium sunt religiosi irrevocabiliter, quia usus talium librorum respectu auctoris non est res pretio aestimabilis, sed supra omne pretium, nam est quid intrinsece spectans ad usum scientiae"; Suarez, tract. VIII, lib. III, cap. 13, n. 10; Petra, IV, in const. 6 Eugenii IV, sect. un., n. 3.

141 Fine, *Jus regularis tum communis tum particularis quo regitur societas Iesu declaratio* (Prati, 1909), p. 341; Prümmer, *Manuale Juris Ecclesiastici* (2 vols., Friburgi-Brisgoviae, 1907), Tom. II, q. 74, pp. 85, 86; Gennari, *Il Monitore Ecclesiastico,* series 3, V (1913), 264-165. The last named taught clearly that the monastery acquired the right of ownership because the manuscript was a fruit of industry, and appealed to the *Normae* of 1900, to support his statement that the fruit of industry belonged to the institute.

142 This decision was a sequel to another decision, according to which religious of simple vows could not publish their manuscripts without the *imprimatur* of their superior; if the *imprimatur* was refused, they could not give it to a printer to have it published anonymously with the *imprimatur* of the local ordinary (S. C. de Religiosis, decr. 2 iun. 1911—*AAS,* III (1911), 270. It was now decided as follows: "Nunc autem rursum ab Ea (*Congregatione*) quaesitum est: 'An religiosi tum votorum solemnium, tum votorum simplicium, qui aliquid manuscriptum durantibus votis exaraverunt, eiusdem dominium habeant, ita ut illud donare aut quocumque titulo alienare valeant." Resp.: "Negative" (11 jul. 1913). Confirm. a Pio X (13 jul. 1913)—*AAS,* V (1913), 366.

pressly declared that it could not be argued from the decree that a religious would sin against either justice or his vow of poverty, if he refused to give his manuscript to the superior, if he sent it to the press, or if he simply destroyed it.[143] It was also held that this decree had not settled the problem of whether or not a religious could take manuscripts with him when transferring to another community. Ferreres and Salsmans held that the view that it was possible for a religious to do so could still be maintained.[144]

Salsmans taught that, if the religious transferred to another monastery of the same Order, he could take his manuscripts with him with at least the tacit consent of his superior; if the manuscript was published, at least part of the profit could be given to the dismissing monastery. If, on the other hand, he transferred to another Order or was secularized, Salsmans believed that it was still most equitable to permit him to take his manuscripts with him. The community, however, could require compensation for the expenses incurred in the writing of the manuscript, and could take precautions against the publication of secrets of the Order.[145]

It is quite evident that the decree in question dealt with manuscripts which could be printed and published, and which for that reason acquired the character of a temporal thing which could be priced and which had commercial and sales value. It did not deal with purely personal writings, such as brief notes made from books read, brief summaries of doctrine, or outlines or points for preaching. This latter type of manuscript, by universal admission, was not included as matter of the vow of poverty.[146]

143 Salsmans, "Annotationes,"—*Periodica de Religiosis et Missionariis,* 8 vols., Brugis, 1905-1919 (Vol. I: 1905, 2. ed., 1911; II and III: 1907, 2. ed., 1911; IV: 1909, 2. ed., 1913; V: 1911, 2. ed., 1913; VI: 1912; VII: 1912-1914; VIII: 1919); from 1920: *Periodica de Re Canonica et Morali utilia praesertim Religiosis et Missionariis,* 7 vols., Brugis, 1920-1927 (Vol. IX: 1920; X and XI: 1922-1923; XII: 1923-1924; XIII: 1924-1925; XIV: 1925-1926; XV: 1926-1927); from 1927: *Periodica de Re Morali, Canonica, Liturgica,* Brugis (1927-1936) at Romae (1937—); Vol. XVI, 1927—, VII (1914), 167 (hereafter cited *Periodica*); Ferreres, "Annotaciones,"—*Razón y Fe,* XXXVII (1913), 246-247.

144 Ferreres, *ibid.,* p. 246; Salsmans, *loc. cit.*

145 Salsmans, *loc. cit.*

146 Cf. Wernz-Vidal, *De Religiosis,* p. 349, note 54.

Another type of property which must be considered with regard to transfer to another religious community consists of pensions, life incomes, and other annual or other periodic payments, which are acquired by the community to which the religious belong by reason of their coming to the religious himself.[147]

If the religious was in simple vows, and the income came to him in his private capacity, there was of course no problem. The income became part of his estate, whose radical ownership remained with him. If, however, he had been solemnly professed, and thereupon transferred to another community, then in the opinion of all the authors who mentioned the matter the income followed the religious to the receiving Order or monastery.[148]

The reasons given are as follows: first, that while these payments are owed to the person in whose favor they are made, this is not true of the capital sum, and therefore they are not acquired until given.[149] Vermeersch and Piat likewise numbered these payments among things over which no one has acquired any rights, and concluded that they must be given to a religious after his secularization even when a renunciation or positive donation of them was rightly made prior to solemn profession.[150] This was not in conflict with the general statement of other authors that property which the religious brought to the monastery or which had already come to the community by reason of the presence of the religious within it were acquired by the dismissing monastery and could not be transferred to the receiving community. Future payments of this sort had not as yet been acquired.[151] Lopez therefore concluded that the constant and common opinion of the authors was on the side of the payment of future installments to the receiving community after the transfer of the religious. The authors did not discuss to whom

[147] These are called by the authors "legatum redituum vel annui reditus, annuae praestationes, item ususfructus annuus, legatum successivum, annua pensio, census, livellum, vitalitium"; cf. Lopez, "Cuinam debeatur legatum annui reditus Monacho relictum, ipso post sollemnem professionem in aliud Monasterium definitive translato,"—*CpR,* IX (1928), 220.

[148] Lopez, *art. cit.,* pp. 221 ff.

[149] Lopez, *art. cit.,* p. 226.

[150] Vermeersch, *De Religiosis,* I, nn. 204, 278, 322; Piatus, I, 144.

[151] Lopez, *art. cit.,* p. 227.

this particular type of property accrued while the transferring religious was making a novitiate in the new community.

There is however a decree which the Sacred Congregation of the Council issued on December 10, 1633, and which provided that one who had been professed in an Order which was incapable of ownership could not, after transferring to another Order capable of ownership, receive interest from property which he had expressly renounced.[152]

The dowry for women religious, through analogy with the dowry required for women given in marriage, began to be required after the Council of Trent.[153] It was commonly defined as a certain sum of money, determined by the legitimate superior, which was given to a monastery for the support of a nun who was making her profession there.[154]

A distinction has to be made between women religious of solemn vows and those of simple vows. With regard to the former, the common teaching was that by profession the dowry was irrevocably required by the community when the solemn profession was made.[155]

The ordinary rule, was therefore, as the Sacred Congregation of the Council decided, that nuns who had been professed in one monastery and were transferring to another could not bring the dowry with them, but had to leave it with the monastery to which it had first been given.[156] A controversy in the nineteenth century concerning the dowry of a nun who had received an indult to transfer to another monastery because of her health was settled as follows: The Sacred Congregation of Bishops and Regulars ruled that the

152 Decr. *in Nullius,* 10 dec. 1633—Pallottini, "Regulares," I, n. 50.

153 Cf. Kealy, *Dowry of Women Religious,* The Catholic University of America Canon Law Studies, n. 134 (Washington, D. C.: The Catholic University of America Press, 1941), pp. 17 ff.

154 Pellizarius, *Tractatio de Monialibus* (Venetiis, 1651), c. III, sect. III, n. 39; Bouix, I, 660.

155 Pellizarius, *Tractatio De Monialibus,* c. III, sect. II, nn. 69, 70; Pignatelli, *Consultationis Canonicae* (11 vols. in 4, Coloniae Allobrogarum, 1700), I, consult. 432, nn. 1-13; Verani, *Juris Canonici Universi Commentarius Paratitlaris* (5 vols., Monachii, 1703-1708), lib. III, tit. 31, c. VIII, nn. 46-49; Petra, III, in const. 16 Eugenii XV (*Regularem*), sect. I, nn. 12-16; Goyeneche, "Consultationes"—*CpR,* V (1924), 390-393.

156 27 iun. 1637—Pallottini, "Monialium," I, n. 13.

dowry should remain with the dismissing monastery, but that as long as it kept the principal, which amounted to five hundred ducats, it was to pay six ducats a month to the receiving community for her support. It could free itself of this burden by transferring the entire dowry to the second monastery.[157] The practice of the Sacred Congregation of Bishops and Regulars, as it seems, was to hold that, if the monastery had not given cause for the transfer of the nun to another institute, it was not bound to give back the dowry or to support the religious, unless perhaps out of charity, when the nun did not have the means to give a new dowry. If, however, the monastery had given occasion for the transfer, it was obliged to restore the dowry.[158]

With the lapse of time, the jurisprudence of the Sacred Congregation of Bishops and Regulars showed an increasing tendency to restore the dowry to nuns leaving the monastery.[159] Vermeersch, at the turn of the century, stated that the Sacred Congregation was accustomed to order the restoration of the dowry when the nun transferred to another religious institute.[160]

With regard to sisters in simple vows, the practice was always to return the dowry to the sister when she transferred. This is quite clearly demonstrated in a case decided by the Sacred Congregation of the Council in 1792.[161]

[157] 30 maii 1856—Bizzarri, *Collectanea in usum Secretariae Sacrae Congregationis Episcoporum et Regularium edita* (2. ed., Romae: ex Typographia Polyglotta S. C. de Propaganda Fide, 1885), pp. 645-648; cf. Piatus, I, c. 1, q. 96.

[158] Petra, in const. 16 Eugenii IV, sect. un., n. 16; Bachofen, *Compendium Iuris Regularium*, pp. 351-352; Monacelli *Formularium*, pars II, tit. XIV, tom. V, nn. 21-22; De Luca, *Theatrum Veritatis et Institiae*, tom. VII, *De Dote*, discursus 167, n. 28; S. C. C., 27 iun. 1637—Pallottini, "Monialibus," I, n. 13; S. C. C., *Civitatis Castellanae*, 3 mart. 1792—*Fontes*, n. 3875; S. C. Ep. et Reg., *Ferrarien.*, 17 febr. 1702—Monacelli, *ibid.*, n. 21; S. C. Ep. et Reg., *Valentina*, 13 febr. 1699—Petra, *ibid.*, n. 16.

[159] Goyeneche, "Consultationes"—*CpR*, V (1924), 391-392.

[160] *De Religiosis*, tom. I, n. 181.

[161] S. C. C., *Civitatis Castellanae*, 3 mart. 1792—*Fontes*, n. 3875.

Part II

Canonical Commentary

CHAPTER III

THE PRELIMINARIES OF TRANSFER

Can. 632. Religiosus nequit ad aliam religionem, etiam strictiorem, vel e monasterio sui iuris ad aliud transire sine auctoritate Apostolicae Sedis.

Can. 681. Praeter proprias cuiusque societatis constitutiones, circa transitum ad aliam societatem vel ad aliquam religionem . . . serventur, congrua congruis referendo, praescripta can. 632-635.

Article 1. The Notion of Transfer

Canon 632 of the Code of Canon Law declares that a religious cannot transfer to another religious institute, even though it be a stricter one, or from one independent monastery to another, without the permission of the Apostolic See. Canon 681 extends this rule to the transfer from one society of the common life to another such society or to a religious institute.

The primary concern of this article will be to define the nature of transfer to another reigious community. Several different types of transfer must be distinguished from one another. First of all, one must distinguish between the permanent transfer to another community and the temporary transfer. The canons with which this dissertation professedly deals are concerned only with the permanent transfer to another community, and consequently the word *transfer,* when used by this writer, will always signify a permanent transfer unless the contrary is explicitly stated. The three principal types of transfer may be defined as follows:

1. *Transfer to another religious institute* [1] is the process by which a religious properly so called is freed of the juridical bond which incorporates him in a stable way in one religious institute, and is subjected simultaneously to a new juridical bond which incorporates him in a stable way in another religious institute.[2]

2. *Transfer to another independent monastery* [3] may be defined as the process by which a religious properly so called loses the juridical bond which incorporates him in a stable way in one independent monastery, and is subjected simultaneously to a new juridical bond which incorporates him in a stable way in another independent monastery.[4]

3. *Transfer to another society of the common life* [5] may be de-

[1] *Religious institute,* or simply, *institute* will be the term used throughout this dissertation for the type of community to which the Code applies the name "*religio.*" It is defined by can. 488, 1°, as a society approved by legitimate ecclesiastical authority, the members of which strive after evangelical perfection according to the laws proper to their society, by the profession of public vows, either perpetual or temporary, the latter to be renewed after fixed intervals of time.

[2] Cf. Goyeneche, "De transitu ad aliam religionem,"—*CpR,* I (1920), 219; Schaefer, *De Religiosis* (3. ed., Romae: Herder, 1940), p. 928, n. 516 (hereafter to be cited as Schaefer); Wernz-Vidal, III, p. 449, n. 418; Berutti, *Institutiones Iuris Canonici,* Vol. III, *De Religiosis* (Taurini-Romae: Marietti, 1936), p. 318 (hereafter to be cited as Berutti); Coronata, *Institutiones Iuris Canonici,* Vol. I, 2. ed., Taurini: Marietti, 1939), p. 848, n. 636 (hereafter to be cited as Coronata).

[3] The term *independent monastery* or *autonomous monastery* is used by the present writer for the term "*monasterium sui iuris*" as used by the Code. The Code does not define this term. It may be briefly described as a monastery which is self-ruling in its internal government—Larraona, "Commentarium Codicis"—*CpR,* III (1922), 133. A more detailed exposition of this concept will be undertaken in the second article of this chapter.

[4] See the works cited above, note 2.

[5] The term *society of the common life,* or *society,* will be used by this writer for the type of association which is dealt with in Title XVII of the second book of the Code. It is described by canon 673, and is composed of those

fined as the progress by which a duly incorporated member of such a society loses the bond which incorporates him in a stable way in the society, and is subjected simultaneously to a new bond which incorporates him in a stable way in another society.[6]

Other types of transfer, however, are possible. The Code specifically contemplates, in canon 681, the possibility of a transfer from a religious society to a religious institute. Furthermore, a transfer from a religious institute to a society cannot be said to be impossible.[7] In order to avoid a multiplication of definitions, therefore, one may conveniently phrase a definition which will apply to any and every type of transfer:

> TRANSFER IS THE PROCESS BY WHICH A DULY INCORPORATED MEMBER OF A RELIGIOUS INSTITUTE, OF AN INDEPENDENT MONASTERY, OR OF A SOCIETY OF THE COMMON LIFE, LOSES THE JURIDICAL BOND WHICH INCORPORATES HIM IN A STABLE WAY IN THAT COMMUNITY, AND BECOMES SUBJECT SIMULTANEOUSLY TO A NEW JURIDICAL BOND WHICH INCORPORATES HIM IN ANOTHER COMMUNITY.

This definition requires explanation: 1. It refers only to *a duly incorporated member* of a religious institute, independent monastery or society of the common life. Therefore the term *transfer* is not applicable to those who have not as yet made their profession or been incorporated in a community, nor to those who have lost their membership, as can happen in some cases by voluntary egress or dismissal, or whenever a decree of secularization has been obtained.[8]

2. It distinguishes transfer from a mere change of residence or a physical passage from one community to the other. The term

who imitate the religious life by living in common under the authority of superiors according to constitutions approved by ecclesiastical authority, but either without any vows, or at least without public vows. Such a society is not properly a religious institute, nor can its members be properly called religious.

[6] See Wernz-Vidal, III, p. 500, n. 458, VI.

[7] Cf. Goyeneche, *art. cit.*—*CpR*, I (1920), 362.

[8] See below, pp. 88-90.

transfer implies not a mere change of place, but a juridical change in the status of the individual concerned. The bond of juridical obligations and rights which incorporates him in one community is replaced by a new and similar juridical bond which unites him to another.[9]

The nature of this juridical bond differs somewhat in the various types of transfer. In the case of religious who are members of a centralized religious institute, it binds the religious to persevere in the institute, though not in any particular house or province of that institute. It arises from the act of profession. Profession in its strict sense is the public reception of the three vows of poverty, chastity and obedience in a religious institute approved by the Church. It has two distinct but inseparable elements: the first is the reception of the vows; the second is the offering of himself made by the religious to the institute, and the acceptance of that offering by the institute.[10]

It is from the second of these elements that the juridical bond between the religious and his institute arises. It is the almost unanimous opinion of post-Code authors that profession is a contract between the religious and the institute.[11] It is a bilateral contract in a proper but less strict sense, inasmuch as the obligations to which it gives rise are binding not in commutative but in legal or distributive justice.[12] The religious binds himself to obey the superiors and the constitutions of the institute. He gives the institute the right to the legitimate use of the faculties of his body and of his soul. The institute on its part is obliged to direct the religious in spiritual affairs, and is bound to provide him with food, clothing and dwelling: to admit him to the communion of all the goods of the institute and to community life with other religious: to keep him perpetually, if he is making perpetual profession, or temporarily, if temporary

[9] Cf. Schaefer, p. 928, n. 516, note 24; Berutti, III, 318.

[10] Schaefer, p. 566, n. 263.

[11] For a list of the authors who maintain this view see O'Neill, *The Dismissal of Religious in Temporary Vows,* The Catholic University of America Canon Law Studies, n. 166 (Washington, D. C.: The Catholic University of America Press, 1942), p. 72, note 32.

[12] O'Neill, *op. cit.,* pp. 72-73.

profession, unless he prove a harmful member: finally, to treat him as a son. It is a juridical bond between the religious and the institute, inasmuch as it is given sanction by the Church and produces juridic effects.[13] Consequently, the obligations to which it gives rise, in particular the obligation with which this dissertaton is especially interested, namely the obligation to persevere in the community, are also juridic.

In the case of transfer from one independent monastery to another, the case is somewhat different. Independent monasteries are characteristic especially of those religious families which are in the monastic tradition which in the West stems from St. Benedict (ca. 480—ca. 550). Here, too, as in the case of the religious who belong to centralized communities the bond arises from the act of profession. But the juridical bond is not so much a bond which binds the professed religious to the institute, but one which binds him to the particular family, the independent monastery in which he was professed. This bond is commonly known by the term *filiation*. This bond would be severed even in the case of a transfer to another independent monastery in the same monastic congregation. It has an intimate connection with the vow of stability, which is a part of the Benedictine formula of profession.[14]

The case of members of a society of the common life is decidedly different from the case of religious in that the bond between the members and the society does not arise necessarily from the taking of vows. In some cases, as with the Congregation of the Missions and of the Daughters of Charity, the bond arises from a profession in which private vows are taken. In other cases, an obligation to persevere in the community may arise from a promissory oath, or from a special promise. In some communities the bond between the member and the society arises from the act of his incorporation by the superior after a period of probation, and may be severed by the member himself at his own discretion without recourse to ecclesiastical authority.

This is true, for instance, of Sulpicians and of the members of

[13] Schaefer, p. 567, n. 263.

[14] See above, pp. 6-8.

the Oratory of St. Philip Neri.[15] But in every case, in order that a true transfer may be said to be possible, there must have been a juridical bond of incorporation in the society. This incorporation consists, like the contractual element of religious profession, in the offering of himself to the society on the part of the candidate, and in the acceptance of this offering on the part of the society.[16] There is no reason for denying that this incorporation is a contract in the sense in which religious profession is a contract, provided that it gives rise to a bond of mutual rights and obligations between the candidate and the society which are binding in legal and distributive justice. It is this bond which is broken by a transfer.

The bond may be temporary, as is the case of those who have taken only temporary vows, or it may be perpetual, as in the case with those who have made final profession.

3. Transfer implies a change in the juridical incorporation of the individual in his community. It does not inherently, however, imply any change of state.[17] This is most evident in the case of a transfer to another institute or to another independent monastery. There is a distinction between the religious state and a religious institute. The religious state is described in the Code of Canon Law as a stable manner of life in community in which the faithful, by making vows of poverty, chastity and obedience, undertake to observe the evangelical counsels in addition to the precepts which are obligatory for all.[18] A religious institute, on the other hand, is a particular association of the faithful in which this kind of life

[15] Cf. Stanton, *De Societatibus sive Virorum sive Mulierum in Communi Viventium sine Votis* (Halifaxiae: Apud Custodiam Librariam Maioris Seminarii a Sanctissimo Corde B. M. V., 1936), pp. 161, 162 (hereafter to be cited as Stanton).

[16] Cf. Stanton, p. 100.

[17] Goyeneche, *art. cit.*, *CpR,* I (1920), 219. There is an exception to this rule, transfer from a society of the common life to a religious institute, or from a religious institute to a society—see *infra,* pp. 85-86.

[18] Can. 487. "Status religiosus seu stabilis in communi vivendi modus quo fideles, praeter communia praecepta, evangelica quoque consilia servanda per vota obedientiae, castitatis et paupertatis suscipiunt. . . ."

is lived, in which the abstract notion is particularized and becomes a part of the concrete world of reality.[19]

It is evident, therefore, that in exchanging his affiliation with a particular institute or monastery for affiliation with another such community the religious does not abandon his state, but merely one particular form of it for another form of the same state. This is also true of a transfer from one society of the common life to another. A society of the common life embodies the religious state only in a wide and improper sense, however, and not in the strict and limited sense of canon 487.

The very definition of a religious society in canon 673 makes this quite plain by stating that a society in which the members *imitate* the manner of life proper to religious by living in common under the rule of superiors according to approved constitutions, but are not bound by the three usual and public vows, is not properly a religious institute, nor can its members properly be designated by the name of religious.[20] Strictly taken, a change as between a society and an institute implies a change of state, since the members of such societies are truly seculars, though they are seculars who are in a special way dedicated to the pursuit of perfection by the practice of the evangelical counsels. Some authors do not hesitate to say, however, that they have embraced the religious state as understood in a wide or improper sense, inasmuch as their life imitates that of religious to a greater or a lesser degree.[21]

[19] The religious state, in today's law at least, cannot exist apart from particular religious communities. The Church no longer gives juridical recognition to the religious state as found in the life of hermits. It gives juridical recognition only to the religious state as concretized by life in an approved religious institute. Cf. Schaefer, p. 64, n. 35.

[20] Can. 673, § 1. "Societas sive virorum sive mulierum, in quo sodales vivendi rationem religiosorum imitantur in communi degentes sub regimine Superiorum secundum probates constitutiones, sed tribus consuetis votis publicis non obstringuntur, non est proprie religio, nec eius Sodales nomine religiosorum proprie designantur."

[21] This is implied by can. 673, in that it states that these societies cannot *properly* be called religious institutes, and that their members cannot *properly* be designated as religious (Goyeneche, *art. cit.—CpR,* I [1920], 297).

Accordingly, a member of such a society who transfers to another society does not change his state. It must be noted, however, that a religious who transfers to a society of the common life, or a member of a society who transfers to a religious institute, can be said not to have changed his state only if the religious state is understood in a wide and improper sense.

4. Finally, the definition clearly distinguishes the term *transfer* from a process which seems to be very similar, but is really distinct: namely, egress from one community followed by ingress into another. For in the case of transfer as considered by the canons which are the subject of this dissertion, there is no single point of time at which the transferred person has been without affiliation with one or the other community. Egress from one community followed by ingress into another, on the other hand, implies a distinct period of time during which the person involved in not affiliated with any religious community. This may occur, for example, in the case of a religious who has voluntarily left his community upon the expiration of temporary vows,[22] or who has secured an indult of secularization,[23] and who subsequently secures an apostolic indult in order to enter another institute or a society of the common life.[24] This is not a transfer in its strict and proper sense, as it is outlined by canons 632 to 636 and canon 681, and the term *transfer* will not be used for this process in the course of this canonical commentary.[25]

Cf. Schaefer, p. 56: "Status religiosus sumi potest in sensu proprio seu stricto et in sensu improprio seu latiore. In sensu proprio definitur Status religiosus in can. 487. In sensu improprio seu latiore est Status religiosus societas sive virorum sive mulierum in communi viventium since votis (cf. can. 673)."

[22] Cf. can. 637.

[23] Cf. can. 640.

[24] There is one possible exception to the principle that the concept of transfer does not imply a period of time during which the member is without juridical affiliation with any community. This is the case of a transferring religious whose vows expire while he is in the novitiate. This case will be discussed below, pp. 170-173 (see can. 633, § 2).

[25] Cf. Wernz-Vidal, III, 500; Vermeersch-Creusen, *Epitome Iuris Canonici* (3 vols., Vol. I, 6. ed., Mechliniae-Romae: Dessain, 1937), I. p. 584, n. 790 (732) (hereafter to be cited as *Epitome*); Chelodi, *Ius Canonicum de Personis* (3. ed., ed. P. Ciprotti, Trento: Libreria Moderna Editrice, 1942), p. 285, note 2 (hereafter to be cited as *Chelodi*).

ARTICLE 2. THE REQUIRED PERMISSION

I. The Extension and the Force of Canon 632

A. Transfers Which Require the Authority of the Apostolic See.

1. The Transfer of Religious from a Religious Institute to Another Religious Institute or to a Society of the Common Life.

(a) Canon 632 applies to all religious—

Canon 632 states that a religious cannot transfer to another religious institute, even to a more rigorous one, without the permission of the Apostolic See. This norm is a universal one, in that no distinction is made between the various types of religious. Therefore, *every* religious must have the permission of the Apostolic See in order to be able to transfer to *any* religious institute which is distinct from his own. The reason for this is that where the Code does not distinguish, but uses the general term *religious,* the interpreter may not distinguish either.

All religious are therefore put now on an equal plane. It does not matter whether they belong to institutes of pontifical or of diocesan approval,[26] or whether they have taken vows which are simple or solemn, temporary or perpetual.[27] All are equally subject to the law of canon 632.

[26] Augustine, *A Commentary on the New Code of Canon Law* (8 vols., Vol. III, 3. ed., St. Louis; Herder, 1922), III, 365 (hereafter this work will be cited as Augustine); Bastien, *Directoire canonique à l'usage des congrégations à voeux simples* (4. ed., Bruges: Beyaert, 1933), p. 431, n. 608, 2 (hereafter to be cited as Bastien); Coronata, I, p. 849, n. 636, 2°

[27] Cf. Berutti, III, 317; Goyeneche, *art. cit., CpR,* I (1920); *Epitome,* I, 584-585, n. 790 (732); Wernz-Vidal, III, 453, note (14). The last named authors point out that it is clear from the wording of can 633, § 2, that those in temporary vows are comprehended by the canons which concern transfer—"nisi interim votorum tempus exspiraverit"—and likewise from can. 634. They say that it may be advisable for one in temporary vows to secure a transfer, since it may happen that the reason for the transfer is so urgent that one cannot wait until the vows have expired. A second reason given is that it may be easier to obtain an indult to transfer than an indult to enter another institute after having left the institute of first profession, inasmuch as a transfer is treated

Apostolic permission to transfer is necessary for those who have been dismissed while bound by perpetual vows if they wish to enter some other community. This applies both when the dismissal was effected according to the legitimate procedure prescribed in the Code,[28] or when, as is provided for in the case of several very grave crimes, the dismissal resulted from the automatic operation of the law.[29] The reason why dismissed religious who have taken perpetual vows need an indult of transfer to enter any other community is that the Code declares that such religious remain bound by their vows. An exception to this rule exists only when it is provided through the constitutions of the institute or by means of a special indult that the dismissed person is freed of his former vows, but in this case a dispensation from the invalidating impediment of former profession, mentioned in canon 542, must be obtained to make possible his or her entrance into the novitiate of any other community.[30]

The apostolic permission for transfer to another community is needed also if those who have physically left their own communities but who are still bound by the obligations of their vows intend to enter another institute rather than return to their own. In this category are apostates and fugitives, [31] and those who have obtained an indult of exclaustration.[32]

The apostolic permission is not necessary, however, for the transfer of those who cannot as yet be reckoned as religious, nor for the transfer of those who can no longer be reckoned as religious.

by the law as something licit once permission has been obtained, while previous profession is treated as an invalidating impediment to entrance into the novitiate (can. 542, 1°).

[28] Cans. 649-668.

[29] Can. 646.

[30] Can. 669. A confirmatory argument establishing the fact that persons dismissed while in perpetual vows are still truly religious is that they are denominated as such by one of the headings of the Code (Book II, Title XVI, Caput IV: "De religiosis dimissis qui vota perpetua nuncuparunt."—Goyeneche, *art. cit.*, *CpR.*, I (1920) 297.

[31] "Apostata et fugitivus ab obligatione regulae et votorum minime solvuntur et debent sine mora ad religionem redire."—Can. 645, § 1.

[32] "Qui indultum exclaustrationis ab Apostolica Sede impetravit, votis ceterisque suae professionis obligationibus, quae cum suo statu componi possunt, manet obstrictus."—Can. 639.

Those who are not as yet religious, namely aspirants, postulants and novices, do not need apostolic permission for a transfer to another community.[33] Novices and, *a fortiori*, aspirants or postulants are free to leave a religious institute at any time. They can also be dismissed by the superiors or by the chapter, as directed by the constitutions, for a just cause.[34] Furthermore, the law of the Code places no obstacle to hinder their entrance into some other religious community. They will be obliged, however, to secure a testimonial letter from the major superior of the community into whose novitiate or postulancy they had been admitted, if they seek to enter the novitiate of another community.[35] They will of course be obliged there to repeat their novitiate.[36]

[33] Beste, *Introductio in Codicem* (2. ed., Collegeville: St. John's Abbey Press, 1944), p. 428 (hereafter cited Beste); Chelodi, p. 452, note 2; Coronata, I, p. 848, n. 636; Schaefer, p. 928, n. 517.

[34] Cf. can. 571, § 1.

[35] Can. 544, § 3; Larraona, "Commentarium Codicis"—*CpRM,* XIX (1938), 257. A joint decree of the Sacred Congregation for Religious and of the Sacred Congregation for Seminaries and Universities issued July 25, 1941, declared that recourse must be had to the Sacred Congregation for Seminaries and Universities for the admission to a seminary of a student who belonged by any title to a religious family, and recourse to the Sacred Congregation for Religious for the admission to a religious family of a person who for any reason had left a seminary—*AAS,* XXXIII (1941), p. 371. A private reply dated May 11, 1942, declared that this decree did not include those who leave a seminary or college in order to embrace a life of perfection in some religious institute, as sufficient provision is made for them in can. 544, § 3. This reply is reproduced in Bouscaren, *The Canon Law Digest* (2 vols., Milwaukee: Bruce, 1934-1943), II, 166.

[36] Hofmeister, "Der Übertritt in eine andere religiöse Genossenschaft"—Archiv für katholisches Kirchenrecht (Innsbruck, 1857-1861, Mainz, 1862—), CVIII (1928), 441 (hereafter cited *AKKR*). This canonist believes that an exception to this rule may be made in the case of a transfer by a novice from one independent monastery to another. He will not be required to repeat the novitiate, at least if the two monasteries belong to the same monastic congregation. Hofmeister believes this is implicit in the wording of canon 556, § 4, which declares that, if a novice is transferred by the superiors into another novitiate house of the same institute, the novitiate is not interrupted. Such a transfer would require the permission of the superiors of both monasteries. The admission into the novitiate would have to be made by the major superior

Canon 632 likewise does not apply to those who have been freed of their vows, and in consequence thereof can no longer be called religious. Such are they who have left the community or who have been dismissed therefrom at the expiration of temporary vows; [37] they who have been dismissed while in temporary vows, since the law declares that the dismissal effects their release from all religious vows; [38] they who have voluntarily left or who have been dismissed from an institute of simple vows if in that institute the vows are pronounced with the following or a similar condition: "as long as I shall live in the Congregation," so that if the person leaves of his own accord or is dismissed by the superior, he is by that very fact free from his vows;[39] finally, they who have received a decree of secularization from the local ordinary or from the Holy See.[40] All the aforementioned persons will have to secure a dispensation from the Holy See from the impediment which prevents the entrance into the novitiate of those who have been bound by a previous religious profession. Their admission without such an indult would be invalid.[41]

(b) Canon 632 includes in its scope transfer to any other religious institute—

The permission of the Apostolic See is necessary when a religious transfers *to another religious institute.* This term of canon 632, namely, *another religious institute,* is quite as universal in its application as the term *religious.* Transfer cannot take place without apostolic authority when made to *any* other institute. It does not

with the vote of his council or chapter, as directed by the constitutions (can. 543)—Hofmeister, 441-442.

[37] Can. 637; Schaefer, p. 928; Chelodi, p. 428, note 2.

[38] Cf. can. 648.

[39] A decision of the Commission for the Interpretation of the Code (March 1, 1921) mentions such communities; the description given of them makes it evident that those who leave them are no longer religious, since the vows are taken with a condition which implies an automatic release from them upon a voluntary departure or upon a dismissal from the community.—*AAS,* XIII (1921), 177.

[40] Cans. 640, § 1, n. 2; 638.

[41] Cf. can. 542, 1°.

matter whether this be an order or a congregation, clerical or lay, of pontifical or of diocesan approval. To obviate any doubt which might arise from the former law, which remained in force at least in theory until the Code,[42] canon 632 declares explicitly that apostolic permission is required for transfer even to a more rigorous institute. By a more rigorous institute is meant one that surpasses others with regard to bodily austerities and mortifications, such as fasting, abstinence, vigils, silence, labor and the enclosure.[43]

What is meant by *another* religious institute? The authors point out that when the same rule and constitutions are followed and when the same superior general holds authority over the persons concerned, then such persons belong to one and the same religious institute.[44] When the rule or constitutions and the superiors general are not the same the institutes are different and distinct.[45]

One might ask whether different branches of the same Order are to be considered as distinct institutes with regard to transfer. As was seen in the historical section of this dissertation,[46] Suarez (1548-1619) inclined to the opinion that a transfer was possible, despite the prohibition of the Council of Trent, between branches of the same Order which did not have the same superior-general. Probably for the reason that the precise definition of a religious institute given by the Code implies quite plainly a society which has the unity of a political body and constitutes a moral person, post-Code authors who have been consulted by this writer are unanimous in rejecting this opinion. As an example, the three branches of the Franciscan family, that is, the Friars Minor, the Conventuals, and the Capuchins, are held to be distinct institutes as far as the law

[42] See above, pp. 22-24, 39-40, 50-51.

[43] See above, pp. 41-44; Augustine, III, 364; Fanfani, *De Iure Religiosorum ad Normam Codicis Iuris Canonici* (2. ed., Taurini-Romae: Marietti, 1925), p. 476 (hereafter to be cited as Fanfani); Oesterle, *Praelectiones Iuris Canonici*, I (Romae: Cuore di Maria, 1931), p. 357 (hereafter to be cited as Oesterle).

[44] Bastien, p. 432, n. 680, 4; Beste, p. 429; Vermeersch-Creusen, *Epitome*, I, p. 586, n. 792 (734); Gerster a Zeil, *Ius Religiosorum in Compendium Redactum pro Iuvenibus Religiosis* (Taurini: Marietti, 1935), p. 133 (hereafter to be cited as Gerster a Zeil).

[45] Bastien, *loc. cit.*

[46] See above, pp. 68-69.

of transfer is concerned, since they have neither the same constitutions nor the same superiors-general.[47] Goyeneche indicates plainly that, in consequence simply of a difference in superiors, two houses of a diocesan institute which separated with the consent of the ordinary are to be reckoned as different institutes. In the case cited, the two houses had not only a common origin but also a common rule.[48]

Because canon 632 states that the permission of the Holy See is required when the transfer is made to *another institute,* it is not required for transfer to another house or province of a centralized religious institute.[49] The reason is that a province is merely a part of a religious institute.[50] For a transfer to another province of the same institute the consent of the superior according to the constitutions suffices.[51]

The transfer from a religious institute to a society of the common life does not receive explicit mention in the Code, but as Goyeneche observes, the norms which regulate it are easily derivable from other prescriptions in the law. The apostolic indult is certainly required whenever anyone wishes to effect this sort of transfer. One who has left his own institute cannot, without an apostolic idult, be received validly into the novitiate of another religious institute or of a society of the common life. The reason is the provision of canon 542, 1°, which impedes his entrance into the novitiate of another religious institute, and canon 677, which provides that the impediments of canon 542 concerning the entrance

[47] Vermeersch-Creusen, *Epitome,* I, p. 586, n. 792 (734); Papi, *Religious in Church Law* (New York, 1924), p. 15; Prikryl, "Übertritt in eine andere Ordensgenossenschaft"—*Theologisch-praktische Quartalschrift* (Lenz, 1848—), XCII (1939), 124; Schaefer, p. 936, n. 525; Claeys-Bouuaert-Simenon, *Manuale Juris Canonici* (3 vols., Vols. I et III, 5. ed., Vol. II, 3. ed., Gandae et Leodii: Apud Auctores, 1939), I, p. 420, n. 685, I, 1 (hereafter to be cited as Claeys-Bouuaert-Simenon). There is a distinction between the concept of the diversity of religious institute as used by can. 632 and as just explained, and that of Order as used by can. 633, § 3, which will be pointed out in the commentary given to can. 633, § 3, in the next chapter, pp. 139-142.

[48] "Consultationes"—*CpR,* VI (1925), 432-434.

[49] Beste, p. 427; Gerster a Zeil, p. 133.

[50] Can. 488, 6°.

[51] Gerster a Zeil, *loc. cit.*

into the novitiate of a religious institute are obstacles likewise to the admission of candidates into societies of the common life.[52]

2. The Transfer of Religious from One Independent Monastery to Another Independent Monastery.

Canon 632 also declares that the apostolic authority is necessary in the case of a transfer from one independent monastery to another. The reason for this provision is to be found in the decentralized character of some of the religious Orders, which makes local units of the Order practically autonomous. Because of this autonomous character, the religious, by a special promise or oath, or implicitly by the act of profession itself, contracts the obligation of persevering in the same house or monastery. This is true especially of the Benedictine Order. It is this autonomy which makes the independent units in a sense similar to distinct religious institutes in the matter of transfer. It is for this reason that canon 632 requires an apostolic permission for the transfer not only to another religious institute but also to another and independent monastery.[53]

(a) *Monasteries of men.* The term *monastery* is nowhere defined in the Code, though this had been done in the preparatory schemata.[54] The authors state that in the Code the word *monastery*

[52] Goyeneche, *art. cit., CpR,* I (1920), 363.

[53] Cf. the historical synopsis, pp. 5 to 8; Coronata, III, p. 848, n. 636; Hippolytus a S. Familia, "Annotationes"—*Analecta Ordinis Carmelitarum Excalceatorum* (Romae, 1926—), I, (1926), 490; Toso, *Ad Codicem Iuris Canonici Benedicti XV Pont. Max. Auctoritate Promulgatum Commentaria Minora* (5 vols., Vol. V, Romae: Ius Pontificium, 1927), V, 224 (hereafter to be cited as Toso); Wernz-Vidal, III, 449-450. The bond between the religious and his monastery is expressed very well in the *Declarations on the Holy Rule and Constitutions of the Swiss-American Congregation, O.S.B.* (translated from the Latin original by order of the general chapter, Oct., 1935, Conception: Altar and Home Press, 1938), n. 95: "By the vow of stability in the Order a person is, in the first place, associated with and united to the monastic family to whose abbot he made his profession. . . . Wherefore a monk, if his act is gravely imputable, sins grievously against his vow . . . if he unlawfully leaves his own monastery in order to go over to another, whether of his own or of a different congregation or order. . . ."

[54] Larraona, "Commentarium Codicis"—*CpR,* II (1921), 202. The word is however frequently used throughout the Code.

refers, first of all, to a religious house of monks or of canons regular.[55] In the case of men religious, therefore, it refers only to the houses of regulars, that is, to houses which belong to institutes in which the members take solemn vows. It does not apply to all houses of regulars, for some of these houses are designated with a term exclusive of the term *monastery.* So, for example, the houses of the Mendicants are called convents.

When is a monastery independent or autonomous, that is to say, *"sui iuris"?* Fanfani states briefly that a monastery is *sui iuris* when it is not dependent on any but local superiors; and that it is not *sui iuris,* when it has other superiors besides local superiors on which it is dependent, such as a provincial or a superior-general.[56] This statement requires amplification. The most complete discussion of the point is to be found in two articles written in 1922, one by Vermeersch in *Periodica,* and the other by Larraona in the *Commentarium.*[57] The term *"sui iuris"* is taken from the Roman Law. There it was used as characteristic of the *paterfamilias,* the father of the family, who was the true juridical head of the family and who alone had full civil capacity and independence. It indicated independence of the control of any private person.[58] As is well known, St. Benedict's concept of the monastic family was a spiritual counterpart of the juridical notion of the Roman family: the monks were the *filiifamilias,* or dependents; the abbot (from "abba," meaning father), the head and family father. The monastic family was *sui iuris* inasmuch as each monastery was independent, as to its internal rule, of higher religious superiors.

In what does this quality of autonomy consist? It consists in the fact that the monastery in question is self-ruling in its internal

[55] Larraona, "Commentarium Codicis"—*CpR,* III (1922), 133; Schaefer, p. 79. Cf. cans. 488, 2° and 8°; 494, § 1; 625; 632; 633, § 3; 635; 647; 896; 1395, § 3; 1579, § 1 and § 2; etc.

[56] Fanfani, p. 28.

[57] Vermeersch "De monasteriis seu domibus sui iuris"—*Periodica,* X (1922), (7)-(9); Larraona, "Commentarium Codicis"—*CpR,* III (1922), 133-138.

[58] Cf. Leage, *Roman Private Law* (2. ed., ed. by C. H. Ziegler, London: Macmillan Book Co., Ltd., 1942), pp. 77, ff.

government.[59] This autonomy as to the internal rule of the monastery is not destroyed by the subjection and obedience which all religious owe to the Holy See, nor by the subjection of non-exempt houses to the local ordinary. It is important to note in this connection that autonomy is not at all the same as exemption. All Orders are exempt by law, and some congregations by privilege. But only certain houses of certain Orders and of certain congregations are independent.[60] This autonomy need not be so great as to constitute the monastery as an independent religious institute which precludes all union with other monasteries subordinated to a common superior. Canon 488, 2° expressly includes the notion of independent monasteries in its definition of a monastic congregation so as to make it perfectly clear that the union of several monasteries into a monastic congregation can leave intact the autonomous government of the individual monastery.[61]

According to the sense of the words used, the term *"sui iuris,"* like the term *autonomous,* is employed for the purpose of designating that which is ruled by its own law, that which is a law to itself. This means, not that an autonomous monastery does not have some laws which are common to other monasteries, but that it rules itself in applying these laws to itself and in complementing them with further interpretations through a superior chosen by the community itself. It must have no other *ordinary* superior who exerts authority over its internal discipline. It is comparable to an adult, who is said to be *"sui iuris"* after he has reached his majority, not because he does not have to observe laws, but because in observing them he is not subject to any other person in private life.[62]

Criteria of autonomy in a monastery are its unity and its completeness. It must be a moral entity which is so compact that it forms one single individual whole and so complete that it is sufficient for itself. A dependent abbacy or monastery which is subordinated

[59] Larraona, *art. cit.*, p. 134; Vermeersch, *art. cit.*, (7).

[60] Cf. O'Neil, *The Dismissal of Religious in Temporary Vows,* p. 80. For the notion of exemption, cf. canons 615 and 618.

[61] *"Congregationis monasticae,* plurium monasteriorum sui iuris inter se coniunctio sub eodem Superiore." Cf. Larraona, *loc. cit.*

[62] Vermeersch, *art. cit.*, p. (7).

to another monastery lacks autonomy precisely because it lacks unity and completeness; it is a part, and not a whole. To be autonomous it must be so complete in itself in that its superior is chosen by the monastery itself, and not by some higher superior. He must rule, not in virtue of authority delegated to him by some higher superior, but in his own name and by authority derived from the community over which he rules. Another element necessary for this completeness is that the community have its own professed religious, incorporated into the monastery, and its own novices; for it must have all those elements which are necessary for its own continuance and preservation.

A dependent monastery, on the other hand, is dependent even as to its internal rule on some superior other than the local one, and subject to another chapter which is not its own. It is therefore not ruled by itself, but by another, and its religious are incorporated in another monastery to which it is subordinated, or in a religious institute of which it is a part.[63] Larraona gives another criterion for judging whether or not a monastery is autonomous. If the superior of the house is a major superior in the sense of canon 488, 8°, the house is autonomous.[64]

Vermeersch gives a list of religious institutes which have autonomous monasteries. The Cistercians, he holds, with the exception of the Italian Congregations of the ancient observance, have truly autonomous houses. In the independent monastic congregation of the Vallombrosians, the local abbots have been subjected to such an extent to the general abbot that true autonomy is no longer to be found in their monasteries. The Premonstratensians have monasteries which are *sui iuris*. In orders which have houses which are autonomous, among the Black Benedictines for example, one will find some houses which are truly independent, such as abbacies and independent priories. The Black Benedictines call them conventual priories. One may also find simple priories, which must be distinguished from conventional priories because they are subject to another and independent monastery.[65]

[63] Cf. Vermeersch, *art. cit.*, p. (8).

[64] *Art. cit.*, p. 135.

[65] *Art. cit.*, p. (8).

With regard to the temporary transfer of monks to another independent monastery, this is often provided for by the constitutions themselves. So a temporary, even a protracted transfer for reason of studies (canon 606), or help, or for removing occasions of sin (canon 661, § 2), or for other just reasons, needs no apostolic idult. The permission of the superiors suffices. The reason is that the religious retains his filiation in the monastery of his profession and is not incorporated in the monastery to which he has been transferred. In such cases the constitutions of each monastic congregation must be observed.[66]

(b) *Monasteries of nuns.* The term *independent,* or *autonomous monastery* can be defined more easily when one speaks of the monasteries of nuns. Nuns are here understood according to the strict sense of the Code, that is, as *moniales,* women religious who take solemn vows or whose vows are solemn at least by institute, though actually simple in certain places because of the prescription of the Holy See.[67] The houses of nuns are always called monasteries. It does not matter to what Order they belong, whether it be a monastic or a Mendicant Order. It applies to both.[68] The word is frequently used in the Code in this sense.[69]

With regard to the autonomy or independence of monasteries of nuns, the former Secretary (later, Prefect) of the Sacred Congregation for Religious. His Eminence Cardinal La Puma (January 22, 1874-November 4, 1943) stated that the monasteries of nuns are always autonomous. He immediately, however, admitted an exception to this general rule, namely, the dependence of a new house on its parent monastery at the time of its foundation.[70] The jurisdiction exercised over a monastery of nuns by the regular superior or

66 Schaefer, pp. 929, 930; Berutti, III, 318; Augustine, III, 365; Goyeneche, *art. cit.—CpR,* I (1920), 362.

67 Can. 488, 7°.

68 Larraona, "Commentarium Codicis"—*CpR,* III (1922), 133.

69 Larraona, *loc. cit.*; Schaefer, p. 79; cf. canons 497, § 1; 504; 501, § 2; 512, § 1, 1° and § 2, 1°; 533, § 1, 1°; 534, § 1; 535, § 1, 1°, 2°; 540, § 3; 547, § 1, § 2 (compared with § 3); 548; 550, § 1; 580, § 3; 600, 1°; 601, § 1; 602; 647, § 1; 1267; 2342, 1°; etc.

70 La Puma, "Statuta a Sororibus Externis Servanda"—*CpR,* XV (1934), 13.

by the local ordinary to whom they are subject does not prevent the monastery from being autonomous, as long as the authority of the abbess is not limited by a higher superior within the Order itself. The superiors of these communities are called by the authors major superiors in the canonical sense in virtue of an analogy of law justified by canon 20.[71] Examples of institutes of nuns with autonomous monasteries are the Carmelites, the Colettines, and the Visitandines. It would certainly include all nuns bound with the papal enclosure. There is some doubt, however, about the autonomy of the monasteries of the Ursulines which belong to the Roman Union.[72]

For a time there was doubt concerning the autonomy of the monasteries of nuns in France and in Belgium who by special order of the Holy See did not take solemn vows. These had been subjected to the local ordinaries. In 1919 the Sacred Congregation of Religious declared that the Code of Canon Law had not changed their dependence upon these ordinaries.[73] This was understood as a confirmation of the pre-Code practice in virtue of which a nun could transfer from one monastery to the other within the same order without an apostolic indult. She needed only the permission of the two bishops of the places where the monasteries were situated.[74]

In 1923, however, the same Sacred Congregation declared not only that the nuns in these monasteries were true nuns of pontifical law in the sense of canon 488, 7°, but also that they were subject to the local ordinaries (because not subject to regular superiors) *in those matters in which the Code gave bishops jurisdiction over monastic nuns.*[75] Since the Code nowhere gave the bishops the power to permit such transfers, it was plain that an apostolic indult was to be required in virtue of canon 632.[76] This was placed beyond all possibility of controversy in 1926 by a response of the Sacred

[71] Schaefer, p. 90; Larraona, "Commentarium Codicis," *CpR,* IV (1923), 41; VII (1926), 376-7; Vermeersch-Creusen, *Epitome,* I, pp. 428-429, n. 594 (546); Vermeersch, *art. cit., Periodica,* X (1922), (9).

[72] Vermeersch, *Periodica, loc. cit.*

[73] S. C. de Religiosis, 22 maii 1919—*AAS,* XI (1919), 240.

[74] Mothon, p. 631, n. 534.

[75] S. C. de Religiosis, decr. 23 iun. 1923—*AAS,* XV (1923), 357-358.

[76] Vermeersch, "Annotationes"—*Periodica,* XV (1926), 230.

Congregation of Religious. In answer to two doubts which had been proposed, it was declared that these nuns of simple vows could not transfer from their own monastery to another autonomous monastery of the same Order solely by the authority of the ordinary or ordinaries; furthermore, the ordinary or ordinaries could not transfer them to another monastery even though it was only for a time, with their consent, and with that of both communities, if the transfer implied that while in the second monastery they would enjoy the rights and be able to fulfill the duties of nuns belonging to that religious family. The permission of the Holy See was required.[77] A temporary transfer, however, if it does not imply a share in the rights and obligations of the new monastery, and if it was effected for reasons of convalescence or study, is not forbidden by this response.[78] Such a transfer, therefore, can be allowed, provided that the necessary permission to leave and to live outside of the enclosure has been obtained.

The need for apostolic authority in the effecting of a transfer extends not only to the professed nuns of the monastery, but also to the extern sisters who are attached to it. The statutes for extern sisters which were approved in 1931 provide that these sisters cannot transfer from one monastery to another even of the same order

[77] "Sacrae Congregationi Religiosorum Sodalium negotiis praepositae sequentia dubia pro opportuna solutione subiecta fuere:

"I. Utrum moniales monasteriorum, in quibus vota dumtaxat simplicia emittuntur iuxta can. 488, n. 7 Codicis iuris canonici et decretum Sacrae Congregationis de Religiosis, sub die iunii 1923, e proprio ad aliud huiusmodi monasterium sui iuris et eiusdem ordinis transire queant sola Ordinarii vel Ordinariorum auctoritate.

"II. Utrum eaedem moniales ab Ordinario vel Ordinariis e proprio ad aliud monasterium, uti supra, de ipsarum et utriusque communitatis consensu, transferri queant saltem ad tempus, ita ut in novo monasterio, dum ibidem commorantur, iuribus gaudere et officiis fungi valeant ut moniales de familia.

"Porro Sacra Congregatio, in Congressu diei 26 iunii 1926, re mature perpensa, respondendum censuit prout respondet:

Ad I. *Negative* et servetur can. 632 Codicis iuris canonici.

"Ad II. *Negative* sine praevia Apostolicae Sedis licentia." Pius XI adprobavit die 9 nov. 1926.—*AAS,* XVIII (1926), 490-491.

[78] Cf. Coronata, I, p. 848, n. 636, note 6.

without the authority of the Apostolic See.[79] Cardinal La Puma, in commenting upon this statute, declared that if by exception a monastery were not autonomous, the transfer from the dependent monastery to the motherhouse, or to another monastery dependent on the same motherhouse, was of course not forbidden. He wrote also that this statute was only a restatement of the general law of canon 632.[80]

(c) *Independent Houses in Institutes of Simple Vows.* Canon 632 requires the permission of the Apostolic See for transfers from one independent monastery to another. The question may be asked whether this requirement should be extended to transfers from one independent religious house to another in institutes of simple vows. Tabera denies that there are such houses. Admitting them hypothetically, however, he says that in the case of institutes of women they are to be considered as nuns.[81]

It can be said with certainty that there are truly independent houses in congregations, at least in congregations of women. Examples are the branches of the Sisters of Mercy and of the Sisters of St. Joseph which have not been amalgamated into the union of houses which took place in comparatively recent times. An examination of their constitutions demonstrates both that their vows are simple and that the houses are truly independent of each other.[82]

At first glance, independent houses in congregations of simple vows would not seem to come under the law of canon 632. The reason is that the term *independent monastery* refers, in its strict sense, only to independent houses of monks, canons regular and nuns. This was explained above. The Holy See, in fact, had indicated in the *Normae* which contain directions for the founding of new institutes of simple vows that the constitutions of these institutes

[79] Cap. IX, art. 113- "Statuta a Sororibus Externis Servanda"—*Apollinaris* (Romae, 1928—), IV (1931), 358. The text of these statutes is not contained in the *AAS.* But mention is made of the approval of these statutes and of the possibility of obtaining a copy of them from the Sacred Congregation of Religious.—*AAS,* XXIII (1931), 380.

[80] La Puma, "Statuta a Sororibus Externis Servanda"—*CpR,* XV (1934), 13; Berutti, III, 318.

[81] Tabera, "De dimissione religiosorum"—*CpR,* XII (1931), 144.

[82] Cf. O'Neill, *The Dismissal of Religious in Temporary Vows,* pp. 84-85.

should not use the term *monastery,* but rather the term *house,* since the former term cannot be applied to congregations.[83]

However, some of these decentralized communities of simple vows used the word *monastery* in their constitutions to designate their own houses, and these constitutions have been approved after the enactment of the Code.[84] Furthermore, the same reason for requiring the apostolic permission for a transfer to another independent house is present as in the case of independent monasteries in the strict sense. For, as has been pointed out in section (a) above, the reason for the law with regard to independent monasteries is founded, not in the fact that they are the houses of regulars, but in that their autonomy likens them to independent and distinct religious institutes. Their members are primarily united, by their profession, with the local community in which they are professed.

If the term *monastery* cannot be applied to them in the strict sense, one must say that in this instance there is a true *lacuna* in the law, in which case canon 632 should be applied to them in virtue of an analogy of law. For the transfer from one independent house to another of the same institute is certainly very similar to the transfer to another independent monastery of the same order, and the reason for a restriction of freedom in the act of the transfer seems to be the same in both.

In such a case one can apply the legal maxims, *"in similibus idem est iudicium,"* and *"ubi eadem est ratio, eadem debet esse iuris dispositio."* [85] Canon 20 provides that if an express prescription of general or particular law is not had concerning a certain matter, then a norm is to be taken, except with regard to the application of penalties, from laws issued for similar matters; from general principles of law applied with canonical equity; from the style and

[83] "22. Excludenda sunt a textu constitutionum: . . . h) termini iuris canonici qui Congregationibus religiosis applicari non possunt; verbi gratia, . . . *Monasterium,* . . . Quorum loco respective dicendum est: . . . *Domus,* . . ."—S. C. de Religiosis, *Normae Secundum Quas Sacra Congregatio de Religiosis in Novis Religiosis Congregationibus Approbandis Procedere Solet—AAS,* XIII (1921), 312 ss.

[84] Cf. for example, *The Rule and Constitutions of the Religious Called Sisters of Mercy* (Dublin, Brown & Nolan, Ltd.), n. 166, and *passim.*

[85] Cf. Beste, p. 84.

practice of the Roman Curia; from the common and constant teaching of learned men.[86] Canon 632 certainly is a *"lex lata in similibus."*

A further consideration which confirms the application of canon 20 to the case of independent houses in religious institutes is the following private response, which is reproduced here through the kindness of the Most Reverend Raymond A. Kearney, Chancellor of the Diocese of Brooklyn. Doubts had arisen with regard to the application of canon 632 and of the response of the Sacred Congregation of Religious in 1926 to a convent of a contemplative community of simple vows, the Sisters Adorers of the Most Precious Blood, with a house in the Diocese of Brooklyn. The following inquiry was sent to Cardinal Lepicier, prefect of the Sacred Congregation of Religious:

Brooklynii, die XXVII Augusti 1931.

Eminentissime Princeps:

". . . Prae oculis habentes praescripta canonis 632 C. I. C. et responsa S. Cong. Religiosorum Sodalium negotiis praepositae sub die IX Novembris 1926 editorum, quaerimus utrum religiosae quae secundum constitutiones vota dumtaxat simplicia undique emittant, praescripto canonis 632 C. I. C. tenantur, si unaquaeque earum domus ab aliis eiusdem religionis domibus independens prorsus sit?

"Tales enim religiosae nullam praeter localem superiorissam agnoscunt, proindeque earum domus quasi sui iuris esse apparent. In constitutionibus autem earum domus monasteria passim appellantur. Ex alia autem parte moniales nullimode dici poterunt, ita ut sub tenore responsorum iam memoratorum comprehendi negueant.

"Cum una non sit peritorum quibus consuluimus sententia, instructiones opportunae in causa utiles valde fore Nobis videntur. . .

Sacram Purpuram reverenter deosculans permaneo

Eminentiae V. Revmae

Addictissimus servus

EPISCOPUS BROOKLYNIENSIS

The following answer was received:

[86] Can. 20.—"Si certa de re desit expressum praescriptum legis sive generalis sive particularis, norma sumenda est, nisi agatur de poenis applicandis, a legibus latis in similibus; a generalibus iuris principiis cum aequitate canonica servatis; a stylo et praxi Curiae Romanae: a communi constantique sententia doctorum."

N. 26/31

Romae, die 19 novembris, 1931.

Secretaria Sacrae Congregationis
de Religiosis

Excm̃e Domine,

Haec S. Congregatio, mature perpenso dubio ab Exc. Tua exposito: utrum religiosae Adoratrices Pretiosissimi Sanguinis quae secundum Constitutiones vota dumtaxat simplicia undique emittant, praescripto can. 632 C.I.C. teneantur, si unaquaque earum domus ab aliis eiusdem religionis domus independens prorsus sit? . . . attentis omnibus ad rem facientibus, rescribendum censuit prout rescribit: "Dispositio can. 632 (633, § 3) servanda est etiam in transitu Religiosarum a Pretiosissimo Sanguine ad aliud monasterium sui Instituti."

Haec a me communicanda erant cum Excellentia Tua, cui fausta omnia adprecor a Domino.

Addm̃us servus

Vinc. La Puma, Secr."

Translated, the response reads as follows:

"This Sacred Congregation, after a mature consideration of the doubt explained by Your Excellency: whether the Sisters Adorers of the Most Precious Blood, who everywhere according to their constitutions take only simple vows, are bound by the prescript of canon 632 of the Code of Canon Law, if each of their houses is entirely independent of other houses of the same institute? . . . has determined, after weighing all relevant circumstances, to answer as follows: 'The disposition of canon 632 (and of canon 633, § 3) is to be observed also in the transfer of Sisters of the Most Precious Blood to another monastery of their institute'."

It is to be noted that this is a private response, and therefore does not have the force of law, and binds only the persons and affects only the matters with regard to which it was given.[87] But it is an indication of the mind of the Holy See, and as an indication of the practice of the Curia adds weight, in virtue of canon 20, to

[87] Can. 17, § 3.

the application of the law of canon 632 to transfers between independent houses of institutes of simple vows.

The houses of the institute in question are so independent of each other that there is no superior general, but only a local superior for each house. The same is true of the independent monasteries of the Sisters of Mercy, for example, and of other de-centralized institutes. Where (as is the case with the Sisters of Mercy of the Union) various independent branches of such institutes have become amalgamated into one centralized institute, the transfer of a religious from one province to the other can be accomplished by the superior general with the advice of the provincial concerned, in accordance with the constitutions.[88] The separate branches have therefore lost their autonomy to such an extent that they no longer come under the law of canon 632.

Could there be congregations which have a superior general but whose houses remain independent or autonomous? It is not possible for this writer to say whether there are any such in fact, but it does not seem to be intrinsically impossible that there should. Several authors speak of this possibility.[89] The present writer holds the opinion that such houses, if they are truly autonomous according to the norms for autonomy given in section (a) above, fall under the norm of canon 632 in virtue of an analogy of law.

One could also raise the question whether or not a temporary transfer between such houses is possible. Such a transfer, without permission of the Holy See, has been forbidden in the case of nuns whose vows are actually simple, if the transfer is to imply that the nuns share in the *rights* and *obligations* of the new monastery.[90] The reason for this prohibition is that such a transfer implies a true and juridicial, even if only temporary, incorporation into the new community. It seems that the same reason is present in the case of a temporary transfer which would imply a share in the

[88] Cf., for example, the *Constitutions of the Institute of the Religious Sisters of Mercy of the Union in the United States of America* (Washington, D. C.: Sisters of Mercy, General Motherhouse, 1941), nos. 98, 243.

[89] Larraona, "Commentarium Codicis"—*CpR,* III (1922), 138; Vermeersch, "De monasteriis seu domibus sui iuris," *Periodica,* X (1922), p. (9); Bastien, p. 432, n. 608, 3.

[90] See above, pp. 98-99.

rights and obligations of the new community for women religious in independent houses of congregations of simple vows. Therefore, in the writer's opinion, such transfers should not be made without the permission of the Holy See. A temporary transfer for reasons of health or for any other just cause, if it does not imply an incorporation in the new community, appears not to be forbidden.

3. Transfer from a Society of the Common Life to Another Such Society Or to a Religious Institute.

Canon 632 requires the authority of the Apostolic See, for the transfer from one religious institute to another and for the transfer from one autonomous monastery to another. Canon 681 extends the rule of canon 632 as also of canons 633, 634 and 635, to the transfer from one society of common life to another, and to the transfer from a society to a religious institute. There is, however, a double limitation stated in canon 681: first, it indicates that not only canons 632 to 635, but also the constitutions of each society are to be observed; second, the canons on transfer are to be applied *"congrua congruis referendo,"* that is, to the extent that their prescriptions will fit the society in question.[91]

How, then, is one to judge when the norm of canon 634 will fit a particular case of transfer from a society of the common life and when it will not? This judgment one must gain through an examination of that juridical element in the status of a religious or of a member of a society of the common life which is primarily affected by a transfer, namely, the juridical bond which incorporates him in a stable way in his community and which makes him a member of that particular ecclesiastical collegiate moral personality.[92]

One must distinguish, first of all, the societies in which the members have no juridical obligation to persevere in the community, as is the case with the Society of St. Sulpice and of the Congregation

[91] Can. 681.—Praeter proprias cuiusque societatis constitutiones, circa transitum ad aliam societatem vel ad aliam religionem aut circa sodalium exitum a societate etiam iuris pontificii, serventur, congrua congruis referendo, praescripta can. 632-635, 645; circa eorum dimissionem, praescripta can. 646-672.

[92] See above, pp. 81-84.

of the Secular Clerics of the Oratory of St. Philip Neri,[93] from those in which there is such a juridical obligation, as is the case with the Pious Society of the Missions (the Pallotine Fathers).[94] If there is no juridical obligation to persevere in the society, it would be incongruous to apply for an apostolic indult to transfer, since on the one hand the member is free to leave the society, and on the other there is no obstacle in the common law which would prevent his reception into another society or into a religious institute.[95] It must be pointed out, however, that the procedure to be used in this case is not that of a transfer in the strict sense, but one of egress from one society followed by ingress into another.[96] Such a procedure is impossible for a religious unless an apostolic indult has been obtained, since canon 542 prevents his reception into another religious institute, and canon 677 bars his reception into a society of the common life. Disregard of either of these canons will invalidate the admission of a candidate.

Goyeneche, however, followed by a number of other authors, makes a further distinction. He differentiates societies of pontifical approval, where a dispensation from the obligation to persevere in the society is reserved to the Holy See, from societies of diocesan approval, where a dispensation from the obligation can be given by the local ordinary. In the first case, he maintains, it is necessary to ask the Holy See for an indult to transfer to another society or to a religious institute. This is certain, he believes, because on the one hand, members of pontifically approved societies are like religious who cannot dissolve the bond which incorporates them in their institute, not even in order to transfer to a more perfect community (canon 632) and on the other, the very nature of the bond is such

[93] Cf. Goyeneche, "De transitu ad aliam religionem"—*CpR,* I (1920), 298; Stanton, p. 161.

[94] Cf. Goyeneche, *loc. cit.*

[95] Goyeneche, *loc. cit.*; "Consultationes," *CpR,* VIII (1927), 114, 115. Wernz-Vidal, III, 500. Schaefer, p. 930, n. 517; Creusen-Garesché-Ellis, p. 249.

[96] See above, pp. 85-86. "Sane transitus proprie talis non habetur, nisi quando is, qui adstringitur obligationibus erga determinatam societatem, cuius est sodalis, illas vult commutare in obligationes alterius societatis vel alicuius instituti religiosi, nec ipse religiosus post egressum a religione dicitur ad aliam religionem transire si in hanc petit ingressum."—Wernz-Vidal, III, 500.

that its dissolution is reserved to the Holy See. Members of societies of diocesan approval, however, are said to be free to transfer to another society or to a religious institute without previously obtaining an apostolic indult. The arguments for this view are: first, the bond which incorporates them can be broken by the local ordinary (canon 638 is here cited); second, their admission into another society or into a religious institute has been nowhere interdicted.[97]

The present writer considers this opinion to be untenable, and thinks that its application should not be allowed in practice. The two arguments as brought forward prove only that the member of a society of diocesan approval who has a juridical obligation to persevere in the society can obtain from the local ordinary an indult which severs his connection with the society. This indult is similar to an indult of secularization in the case of a religious who belonged to a community of diocesan approval. Such a person is subsequently free to enter into another society or into a religious institute. But, as has been pointed out before,[98] such a process is not a transfer in the strict sense, but simply an egress from one community, and ingress into another.

As Vermeersch-Creusen observe, there is no transfer in its strict and proper sense, unless a religious or a member of a society in which public vows are not taken seeks, without having obtained a dissolution of his obligations in the first community, to substitute for them new obligations as assumed in another religious institute or society. For such a transfer the intervention of the Holy See is always required.[99] Vermeersch-Creusen go on to indicate that it is true, however, that if the former obligations have been extinguished in some other way than by an indult of transfer, it is permitted to the former member of a society of common life to enter the novitiate

[97] Goyeneche, "De transitu ad aliam religionem," *CpR*, I (1920), 297, 298; "Consultationes," *CpR*, VIII (1927), 114, 115; Creusen-Garesché-Ellis, p. 249; Coronata, I, p. 848, n. 636; Schaefer, p. 930, n. 517; Stanton, pp. 161, 162; Wernz-Vidal, III, p. 449, note 1.

[98] See above, p. 86.

[99] "Transitus non habetur proprie nisi quando, non soluta priore obligatione, religiosus vel sodalis societatis sine votis, suas obligationes in alias diversae religionis vel societatis convertere vult. Ad huiusmodi transitum semper requiritur interventus S. Sedis"—*Epitome*, I, pp. 616, 617, n. 839 (780).

of another society or of a religious institute, since canon 542 excludes only those who have been bound by the bond of religious profession.[100] This is obviously a case of egress and subsequent ingress. This is distinct from a true transfer, in which case the person is still a member of the first community while undergoing a period of probation in the other. In the case of egress and ingress he has already lost his membership in the releasing community when undergoing probation in the new society or in a religious institute.

Berutti supports this view in that he states simply and without qualification that a member who is actually bound to one society needs special permission of the Sacred Congregation of Religious in order to be able to transfer to another society or to an institute of simple or of solemn vows.[101] Cappello likewise states that the words *"congrua congruis referendo"* of canon 681 are to be understood as follows: If the members are not obliged by any bond to remain in the society, each can freely leave and therefore can transfer [*sic*] without the permission of the Holy See to another society or to some religious institute; if, however, as most often happens, some bond exists, then the permission of the Holy See is necessary.[102] It is plain that Cappello used the word "transfer" in a wide and improper sense.

A conclusive consideration against the opinion that members of a society of diocesan approval do not need an apostolic dispensation to transfer is that the power to sever the affiliation of a member with his community is not necessarily the same as the power to grant a transfer to another community. A perfect parallel in this re-

[100] "Verum, si aliter obligationes exstinctae sint, integrum erit sodali novitiatum vel alius societatis vel religionis ingredi, cum c. 542 eos solos excludat qui vinculo professionis religiosae adstricti fuerint."—*loc. cit.*

[101] "Sodalis qui actu uni Societati adstringitur, speciali licentia indiget S. Congr. de Rel. ut ad aliam Societatem transire valeat, vel ad aliquam Religionem votorum simplicium aut solemnium (can. 632)"—Berutti, III, 372.

[102] "Verba *congrua congruis referendo* (can. 681) ita videntur intelligenda: si nullo vinculo sodales in societate ligentur, unusquisque libere egredi potest ideoque transire valet sine licentia S. Sedis ad aliam societatem vel ad aliquam religionem; si vero, uti plerumque, vinculum aliquod existit, venia S. Sedis necessarium est."—*Cappello, Summa Iuris Canonici* (3 vols., Romae: Vol. I, 1928; Vol. II, 1930; Vol. III, 1936), II, 223.

gard to members of a society of diocesan exists in the case of religious of diocesan approval. Canon 638 empowers the local ordinary to grant such religious an indult of secularization, which severs the bond between the religious and his community so as to permit him to return permanently to the world. But canon 632 prevents the ordinary from granting to these very same religious an indult to transfer to another community. It is important to emphasize that it is canon 632, and not merely canon 542, which makes it impossible for the ordinary to grant the indult to transfer. This means that his power to grant an indult of transfer to a religious of diocesan approval has been destroyed in the root by canon 632, and not merely that its exercise has been impeded in consequence of the extant invalidating impediment against entrance into another community as set up by canon 542. To apply the analogy now to members of societies of diocesan approval: It is canon 632 which is applied by the Code itself (canon 681) to members of religious societies, and not canon 638. Even if the ordinary can permit a member of a society of diocesan approval to leave it and to return to the world, canon 632, applied to these societies by canon 681, has destroyed in the root his power to grant permission to leave the society by way of transfer to another. The fact that the entrance of dispensed members into another society is not impeded by canon 542 proves only that, after the ordinary has permitted egress from the community, a subsequent ingress into another community is not impossible. This is not a transfer.

In practice, then, there are two possibilities. If the Ordinary dispenses from the obligation to persevere in affiliation, the member is free to seek admission into another society. But in that case, canon 681 with canons 632 to 635 will not apply to him, since he is not transferring in the proper sense of the term as it is used in the law; if, however, it seems preferable in a particular case to secure the permission to transfer, and not the definitive and final separation of the member from the society so as to permit subsequent ingress into another society or into a religious institute, then an apostolic indult will be necessary. Which of the two courses will be pursued depends on the particular circumstances of each case and on the desires of the parties involved.

When the ordinary is asked to permit the member's withdrawal from the society, the member will not be obliged to return to it if during the lapse of the probationary period he decides not to enter the new community, or if he is dismissed by the new community. Likewise, the first society will not be obliged to receive him back. If it does receive him, he is to be treated like a new aspirant. The cessation of his rights and obligations in his former community occurs at the moment of his withdrawal, and not at the moment of his affiliation with the new society or institute.

In summary, therefore, the following may be said: (1) If there is no juridical obligation to persevere in a particular society, the indult to transfer should not be requested; it will be better to withdraw from the society and to seek entrance into the new community. (2) If there is a juridical obligation to persevere, a true transfer will always require an apostolic indult; in the case wherein the local ordinary can dispense so as to permit the member to sever his relationship with the society, it will depend on the circumstances whether the person will seek an apostolic indult to transfer, or will seek rather a dispensation from the ordinary to leave the society in order subsequently to seek admission into another society or into a religious institute.

B. Privileges Exempting from the Observance of Canon 632.

In the past, as was seen in the historical synopsis, some communities had privileges to receive members who transferred from other Orders. All such privileges were revoked by Pope St. Pius V in 1569.[103] There were also extant some privileges permitting religious to transfer to other Orders or monasteries. The Jesuits had the right to transfer to the Carthusians,[104] and the superior general of the Jesuits was given power to dismiss subjects and permit them to transfer to any other Order which he prescribed, provided that he had the consent of the superiors of the place to which the transfer

103 See above, pp. 31-33.

104 See above, pp. 35-37; Fanfani (p. 46) says that the Dominicans had a similar privilege.

was to be made.[105] According to Suarez, this privilege did not confer an unlimited power to grant to a professed member of the Society the permission to transfer simply on the ground that he desired another kind of life, or hoped for greater happiness in another Order, and so forth. It conferred on the superiors the power to grant a transfer only to those who had given cause for their dismissal from the Society. Such a cause implied that grave offences had been committed, for lesser reasons did not suffice for the dismissal of a member from the Society.[106]

There is a dispute about this question and similar privileges. Canon 632, which makes the authorization of the Holy See a necessary condition for all transfers, does not contain any clause which derogates privileges to the contrary, and canon 4 declares that privileges granted by the Apostolic See which were still in use and which had not been recalled at the time were not abolished by the Code unless the canons expressly revoked them. In consequence of this, it seems that the Jesuits still have their ancient right. This conclusion has been maintained by several post-Code canonists.[107]

A number of weighty authors, however, deny that the use of such a privilege is still possible. It is conceded that there is no express revocation of such privileges in the Code. But it is argued that canon 632 is the first general law which requires apostolic permission for the transfer to a more rigorous or to an equally rigorous community. Therefore one cannot consider ancient privileges as having been privileges *contra legem,* and they cannot be now maintained.[108]

A stronger argument is drawn from canon 542. It is maintained that while the superior-general may be free, by privilege, to permit a transfer to even a less rigorous community, this does not necessarily give the superior of the receiving community a right to admit the

[105] See above, p. 37.

[106] Suarez, *De Religione,* tract. VIII, lib. III, cap. 12, n. 40—*Opera Omnia,* XVI, pt. 1; cf. Goyeneche, "De transitu ad aliam religionem"—*CpR,* I (1920), 299.

[107] Beste, p. 427; Claeys-Bouuaert-Simenon, I, 419; Vermeersch-Creusen, *Epitome,* I, 585, n. 791 (733); Prümmer, *Manuale Iuris Canonici* (3. ed., 2 vols., Friburgi Brisgoviae, 1922), I, 333 (hereafter cited Prümmer).

[108] Cf. Chelodi, p. 452, note 4.

candidate. For the Code has created an invalidating impediment to the admission into the novitiate of a candidate who is bound by vows. Therefore the use of the privilege is impeded in practice.[109] The argument drawn from canon 542 has not been answered by any of the canonists who hold the opposite opinion. Therefore it seems that a superior-general who has such a privilege should not use it without consulting the Holy See.

Before the Code the Abbot Primate of the Black Benedictines received the power, *durante ipsius oratoris munere,* to grant transfers from one monastic congregation of his Order to another.[110] Since all these congregations were within the same Order, this power involved, as is evident, the ability to grant the permission to transfer as well as the permission to receive the transferring religious. This procedure is, therefore, not open to the objection drawn from canon 542 in the case of a transfer to another religious institute. Consequently one can agree with Hofmeister that this power is to be reckoned as a habitual faculty, and that it is therefor a *privilegium praeter ius,* and that in accordance with the norms of canons 4 and 66 it was not abolished upon the promulgation of the Code.[111] It ceased only with the end of the term of the Prime Abbot who had received the faculty.

These faculties have been given to the Benedictines again since the promulgation of the Code. Beste reports that in 1929 the incumbent Abbot Primate of the Black Benedictines received the faculty *ad quinquennium* to permit the transfer from one monastic congregation of the Benedictine Order to another. This temporarily granted faculty must again have been renewed, since recent editions

[109] Among those who hold this opinion are the following: Chelodi, *loc. cit.*; Coronata, I, 849, note 5; Goyeneche, "De transitu ad aliam religionem"—*CpR,* I (1920), 299, 300; Schaefer, p. 928, n. 515 (note 23); Wernz-Vidal, III, 453, note 15. Goyeneche (*loc. cit.*) gives a further argument against the use of the privilege which was conceded to the Jesuits. Under the discipline of the Decretal and Tridentine legislation one who had been permanently dismissed from a religious institute could enter another institute without any permission, since he was free also to remain in the world (Suarez, *ibid.,* n. 42).

[110] Decr. S. C. Ep. et Reg., 21 dec. 1907—*ASS,* XLI (1908), 44.

[111] Hofmeister, *art. cit., AKKR,* CVIII (1928), 441. Augustine disagrees but gives no reason for his opinion—III, 365.

of the constitutions of some of the Benedictine monastic constitutions make mention of this power.[112] In the case of some monastic congregations the constitutions give the power to permit the transfer from one monastery to another within the congregation to the abbot president. This power is delegated to him by the Holy See.[113] In others, the constitutions simply repeat the prescription of canon 632 with regard to the need of an apostolic dispensation for transfer to another monastery.[114] These constitutions prescind from the fact that the Abbot Primate has the faculty to grant permission to transfer from one monastic congregation to another, and it is not unlikely that they do so in virtue of the fact that the faculties of the Abbot Primate are temporary in nature. Both when the Abbot Primate permits a transfer from one monastic congregation to the

112 *Declarations of the Holy Rule and Constitutions of the Swiss-American Congregation, O.S.B.*, n. 95; *Acta et Decreta Capituli Generalis XIX Congregationis Helveto-Americanae O.S.B. habiti diebus 26, 27, 28, 29 Septembris 1941*, VII, Decl. et Const. 95. The Prime Abbot may subdelegate this faculty to others. Cf. can. 199, § 2, and the competent commentary on this canon to be found in Kearney, *The Principles of Delegation*, The Catholic University of America Canon Law Studies, n. 55 (Washington, D. C.: The Catholic University of America, 1929), pp. 82-85.

113 *Declarations . . . of the Swiss-American Congregation, O.S.B., loc. cit.*; *Constitutiones Congregationis Benedictinae Bavaricae* (Augustae Vindelicorum, 1922), n. 107.

114 The Constitutions of the American Cassinese congregation of the Benedictine Order, for example, provide that an apostolic dispensation is necessary for a permanent transfer to another monastery. This requires a reasonable cause, a year's probation in the new monastery, and the consent of the monk himself, of both superiors and of the chapter of the monastery to which the transfer is to be made. "Potest tamen etiam ob causam rationabilem, obtento prius licentia Sedis Apostolicae, translatio in perpetuum fieri ab uno monasterio ad aliud, si, postquam talis monachus per integrum annum in illo monasterio degerit in quod transferendus est, adest consensus tum monachi tum praelatorum necnon Capituli monasterii, ad quod fit translatio. In hoc casu fiat decretum a D. Praeside illisque Praelatis, quorum intererit, subscribendum et obsignandum; cuius exemplaria cum in Congregationis archivo, tum in utriusque monasterii tabulario reponendus. . . ."—*Declarationes in Regulam S. P. N. Benedicti et Statuta Congregationis Americo-Cassinensis* (approved by the S. Cong. for Religious, Feb. 3, 1935, Atchison, Kansas), n. (78); see also the *Declarationes et Statuta sive Constitutiones Congregationis Ottiliensis O.S.B.*, 1925, n. 197; *Constitutiones Ordinis Cisterciensium Strictioris Observantiae* (Westmalle, 1925), n. 169.

other, and when the Abbot President permits a transfer from one monastery to the other, the following conditions are usually required: (1) that the transferring religious have lived an entire year in the monastery to which he is to be transferred, and (2) that both abbots, as well as the absolute majority of the chapter into whose community he wishes to be received, give their consent.[115] Hofmeister reports that the apostolic permission has also been given *semel pro semper* in the case of the Black Benedictines, for the transfer of a monk who is postulated as abbot by a monastery other than his own, but within his own congregation. From the day on which his election is confirmed such a man becomes permanently affiliated with the new monastery.[116]

C. Neglect in Complying With Canon 532

Validity—An interesting question is the consideration of the purport of the word *"nequit"* in canon 632. Does this word imply that a transfer made without apostolic permission is invalid, or does it contain only a prohibition which makes it illicit?

In the earlier law the neglect to secure the necessary permission was more commonly held to entail the invalidity of the transfer, and this was a reasoned conclusion from a series of legal texts of the Pre-Code period.[117] But it cannot be certainly maintained that canon 632 is an invalidating law. It is true that at first sight a negation of the ability to transfer seems to imply that a contrary act would be null and void. But in the Code of Canon Law the mere

[115] Cf. *Declarations . . . of the Swiss-American Congregation, O.S.B.*, n. 95; Hofmeister, *art. cit.*, *AKKR*, CVIII (1928), 441, 444.

[116] Hofmeister, *ibid.*, p. 441.

[117] Cf. Hofmeister, *art. cit.*, p. 446; C. 2, C, XX, q. 4; c. 2, C. XIX, q. 3; c. 5, X, *de regularibus et transeuntibus ad religionem*, III, 31; c. 1, *de regularibus et transeuntibus ad religionem*, III, 8, in Extravag. com.; Const. *"Super gregem,"* 31 oct. 1547—*Bull Rom. Taur.*, V, 141; Const. *"Sedis Apostolicae,"* 6 oct. 1567 —*Bull. Rom. Taur.*, VII, 617; decr. S. C. C., 24 mart. 1713—Pallottini, s. v. "Regulares," I, n. 41; Const. *"Emanavit,"* 12 iul. 1655—*Bull. Rom. Taur.*, XIV, 34, 35; decr. S. C. C., 17 ian. 1693—Pallottini, s. v. "Regulares," I, n. 48; S. Ep. et Reg., decr. 30 iul. 1683—*Analecta Ecclesiastica*, XI (1903), 179; Const. *"Licet sacra,"* 13 febr. 1726—Ferraris, s. v. "Regulares," n. 61; etc. Many of these texts imply, declare or decree the invalidity of forbidden transfers in particular cases.

negation of ability to act seems equivalent to a mere prohibition, and does not imply invalidity unless this is expressly stated in the law. The reason is that the terms ***nequit*** and ***non potest,*** according to many authors, are ambiguous in the Code. Since the terms are ambiguous, disobedience to a precept or a law in which they are used implies only that the act is illicit. For canon 11 declares that only those laws must be considered as invalidating which expressly or equivalently state that an act is null.[118] In itself, therefore, the use of the term *"nequit"* in canon 632 implies no more than that a transfer made without apostolic permission is illicit.[119]

A transfer made to another religious institute, however, will be certainly invalid if made without the proper permission of the Holy See. The reason is that the novitiate, and consequently also the new profession, would be invalid in consequence of the provisions of canons 542, 1°, and 572, § 1, 3°.[120] A transfer from a religious institute to a society of the common life would also be invalid if made without the apostolic permission, since a valid admission into the society is impeded by the same obstacles as those which canon 542, 1°, sets up against a valid admission into the novitiate of a religious institute.[121] Transfers in which no novitiate is required, however, cannot be said to be certainly invalid. This is true of the transfer from one autonomous monastery to another of the same order.[122] Nor can the apostolic permission be said to be required for the validity of a transfer from a society of the common life to another society or to a religious institute, for the simple rea-

[118] Cf. also canon 15. Beste, p. 68; Vermeersch-Creusen, *Epitome,* I, p. 101, n. 103; Coronata, I, p. 35, note 6; Van Hove, *Commentarium Lovaniense in Codicem Iuris Canonici* (1 Vol. in 5 tomes, Mechliniae-Romae: Dessain, 1928-1939), Tom. II, *De legibus ecclesiasticis* (1930), p. 165, n. 161.

[119] Hofmeister, *art. cit.*, p. 446; Eichmann, *Lehrbuch des Kirchenrechts* (2. ed., Paderborn, 1926), p. 38, note 2. *Contra,* Toso, V, 224

[120] Can. 542, 1°: "Invalide ad novitiatum admittuntur: . . . Qui obstringuntur vel obstricti fuerunt vinculo professionis religosae"; can. 572, § 1, 3°: "Ad validitatem cuiusvis religiosae professionis requiritur ut: . . . Novitiatus validus ad normam can. 555 praecesserit"; can. 555 in turn includes the provisions of can. 542, 1°. Cf. Hofmeister, *ibid.*, p. 447.

[121] Can. 677.

[122] Can. 633, § 3. Hofmeister, *loc. cit.*

son that nowhere in the law does one find a prohibition against the reception of such persons under pain of invalidity.[123]

Penalties—No mention of penalties can be found in the law of today, or in the constitutions of religious orders, even of the Mendicants, for illegitimate transfer as such. The reason for this is probably that such transfers are comparatively rare.[124] It seems, however, that a religious in perpetual vows, whether they be solemn or simple, who leaves his institute and transfers to another without having secured the permission of the Holy See fits the definition of an apostate from his institute as delineated in canon 644, § 1,[125] since he leaves the religious house to which he belongs illegitimately and with the intention of not returning, or if he leaves it legitimately does not return because he has formed the intention to withdraw himself from the obedience which he owes to his legitimate religious superiors. He in consequence incurs the penalties of an apostate from his institute.[126]

If the delict meets the conditions required by canon 2242, §§ 1 and 2, for the incurring of a censure, he is bound by an excommunication reserved to his major superior, or, if his institute is a lay institute or is not exempt, an excommunication reserved to the ordinary of the place in which he is staying. He is also excluded from the legitimate performance of ecclesiastical acts, and is deprived of all the privileges of his institute; if he returns, he will always lack the active and passive vote in his community, and can be punished by his superior with other penalties in proportion to the gravity of his fault, according to the norms of the constitutions.[127]

Before the Code, many Orders received by privilege a special law in virtue of which religious of their Order who transferred to other

123 Cf. Hofmeister, *loc. cit.*

124 Hofmeister, *loc. cit.*

125 "Apostata a religione dicitur professus a votis perpetuis sive sollemnibus sive simplicibus qui e domo religiosa illegitime egreditur cum animo non redeundi, vel qui, etsi legitime egressus, non redit eo animo ut religiosae obedientiae sese subtrahat."

126 Cf. Prümmer, I, 334.

127 Cf. can. 2385.

Orders without due permission incurred the penalties which were incurred by apostasy from a religious community.[128] It seems to the writer that these privileges have now been made unnecessary, since the definition of apostasy as given by the Code itself is wide enough to include those who attempt to transfer without due permission to another institute, at any rate with regard to those who have made profession of perpetual vows.

II. Conditions Required for Seeking Permission to Transfer

A. A Just Cause.

Transfer to another religious community is opposed to that stability which is normally required for progress toward perfection in any vocation, and which cannot but be necessary for progress in the religious state, which is ordained for the struggle toward the ideal of perfection that was taught and lived by Jesus Christ. Therefore, the general rule laid down by St. Paul, "Let every man remain in the calling in which he was called," [129] applies with peculiar force to the religious life. What is required here is not only stability in the religious state but also stability in that particular spiritual family with its own proper purposes, spirit, and works, of which the individual became a member at the time of his entrance into the community.

St. Thomas Aquinas (1225-1274) succinctly stated several reasons which make transfer inexpedient unless it is very useful or necessary: first, that it usually causes scandal to other members of the community; second, that, other things being equal, a religious can progress more easily in virtue in a community to which he has become accustomed than in one which is new to him; third, that it is impossible for a man to excel in all virtues, so that if he strives to do so he will excel in none—that therefore a man should remain in the profession which he had chosen and strive with all his energy to bring to perfection the work which he has there begun—that this is true of religious communities, too, all of which are preeminent in

[128] See above, pp. 34-38; Schaefer, p. 975.

[129] I Cor., 7:20.

different works of virtue.[130] Reiffenstuel (1624-1703) confirmed this with the observation that experience testified that a religious rarely bettered himself by means of a transfer.[131]

Other reasons can be brought forward which make transfer inexpedient unless it is very useful or necessary. So the affiliation of the member with his community, whenever perseverance in the affiliation is obligatory, gives the community an acquired right to his services of which it ought not to be deprived without reason.[132]

Furthermore, a transfer from one religious institute to another or from an institute to a society usually implies a commutation or a dispensation from vows already taken. The commutation is implied by the fact that while the substantial obligations of the religious life are everywhere the same, there is a great variation as to detail. Thus the vow of obedience really implies obedience to the superiors of the community in which profession is made, under the constitutions of that particular community. A change of affiliation, then, certainly implies a commutation of this vow.

The commutation of any vow is the transfer of the obligation of the vow from one matter to another; it is the substitution of one good work for another which was promised under vow. The new work is obligatory in virtue of the original vow. If the work to be exchanged for the original is a better one, no cause is ordinarily required, since it is always licit to do what is objectively and subjectively better, that is, better in relation to all the objective and subjective conditions of the one who makes the vow.[133]

The commutation of any vow to an equally good work requires at *least a slight reason,* for if there is none, the commutation would be open to the charge of inconstancy, and therefore cannot be pleasing to God. Examples of good and sufficient reason given by authors who treat of vows are greater devotion, or a lesser danger of breaking the vow. The commutation of a vow to a less perfect

[130] *Summa Theologica,* II-IIae, q. 189, a. 8.

[131] Lib. III, tit. 31, n. 274.

[132] Schmalzgrueber, Lib. III, tit. 31, n. 237; Pirhing, Lib. III, tit. 31, n. 105.

[133] Cf. Teodori, "Commutatio Voti"—*Apollinaris,* VI (1933), 508.

work amounts to a partial dispensation from the vow, which requires a serious and a sufficient cause.[134]

It is not certain whether a serious reason is required for the validity of the commutation. Both the affirmative and the negative opinion concerning the validity of a commutation without cause are truly probable, according to St. Alphonsus (1696-1787).[135]

Finally, if a complete dispensation of a vow is required, moral theology requires an even more serious reason than in the case of a commutation to a less perfect work. A just cause is necessary for a valid dispensation.[136]

All these considerations indicate that a transfer will only be expedient when it is very useful or necessary. There must be a reason sufficient in each particular case to outweigh the moral obstacles which ordinarily make a transfer to another religious community inadvisable, and which will therefore induce the Holy See to grant the transfer which has been requested.[137]

It would be hard to furnish an exhaustive list of the reasons for which a transfer could be granted. These depend of course on the practice of the Sacred Congregation of Religious (the *stylus curiae)*, which will only be well known to those who have a practical and extensive knowledge of the mind of the Sacred Congregation. But it will not be impossible to draw up a list of some of the traditional reasons for which transfers have been granted in the history of this institute.

St. Thomas mentioned three: if the transfer is made to a more rigorous community in consequence of a great desire for a more holy life; if one's own community has declined from the perfection which it should have; if one suffer from sickness or

[134] Teodori, *loc. cit.*; Arregui, *Summarium Theologiae Moralis* (13. ed., Westminster: The Newman Bookship, 1944), n. 217; Noldin, *Summa Theologiae Moralis* (27. ed., 3 vols., Oeniponte-Lipsiae: Rauch, 1940-1942), II, n. 238.

[135] Teodori, *loc. cit.*

[136] Noldin, *ibid.*, n. 230.

[137] Goyeneche, *art. cit., CpR,* I (1920), 220, 221; Pejška, *Ius Canonicum Religiosorum* (3. ed., Friburgi Brisgoviae: Herder, 1927), p. 182 (hereafter cited Pejška); Prümmer, I, 333; Schaefer, p. 941, n. 534; Sipos, *Enchiridion Iuris Canonici* (2. ed., Pécs: Ex Typographia "Haladás R. T.," 1931), p. 390 (hereafter cited Sipos).

weakness, which will justify a transfer to a less rigorous community when these incapacitate the member from observing the statutes of his own community, but not those of a less rigorous one.[138] Transfers have been permitted when there was need of obtaining a competent superior, as when a community could not find a suitable candidate among its own members, [139] or also for reasons of health, as, for example, when a change to another climate was required.[140] The indigence of parents, when this could not be relieved without a member's transfer to a less rigorous community, has also been considered as a sufficient reason by the Holy See in the past.[141] Cardinal Nervegna, writing at the turn of the century, stated that it had even happened on several occasions that the Sacred Congregation of Bishops and Regulars, then in charge of these matters, granted a transfer when the religious himself had no just cause. It was granted out of pure mercy, to prevent his total return to the world.[142]

Despite the fact that the present law makes all religious institutes and many religious societies equal in that a transfer from any one of them requires the apostolic permission, this does not change the intrinsic differences between communities, which make it inevitable that a transfer to some will be more favored than a transfer to others. Transfer to a more rigorous community has always been favored in the law of the past, and the Code of Canon Law insinuates that it recognizes the special consideration given to this sort of transfer when it forbids a transfer *even* to a stricter community *(etiam ad strictiorem)* without apostolic authorization.[143] It is well known that such transfers are quite frequently granted by the Sacred Congregation even today, provided that it has assurance that the transfer does not connote a rash and ill advised act,

[138] *Summa Theologica,* II-IIae, q. 189, a. 8.

[139] The constitutions of some monastic orders provide for such transfers, and even permit a 2/3 majority vote in such a case to override lack of consent of the abbot of the person postulated.—Cf. Hofmeister, *art. cit., AKKR,* CVIII (1928), 44.

[140] S. C. Ep. et Reg., decr., 21 febr. 1687—*Analecta Ecclesiastica,* X (1902), 135. See above, p. 61.

[141] Cardinal Nervegna, *De Iure Practico Regularium,* p. 214.

[142] *Loc. cit.*

[143] Can. 632.

and that the consent of the superiors of both communities has been secured.[144]

It will therefore not be unreasonable to suppose that it would not be very difficult to secure transfers to the more rigorous and contemplative communities, such as the Carthusians, the Trappists, or the Discalced Carmelites, and, in the case of women religious, the second orders of these institutes. A reasonable cause will have to be present to induce the Sacred Congregation to grant a transfer to communities of merely equal rigor, and very serious reasons for a transfer to communities which are of lesser rigor. It can also be said that a transfer from a community of solemn vows to a community of simple vows will be less favored than a transfer from a religious congregation to a religious Order, for in its very nature the bond induced by solemn vows is more firm and requires a greater

[144] Goyeneche has gone so far as to say that the right to transfer to a more rigorous community is a natural right. His reasons are, first, that in profession there is implicit the condition that what is promised should not be an impediment to greater perfection; second, that the religious gives himself to the superior principally for the sake of God's glory—and for his own perfection, and that therefore this offering of himself cannot preclude the transfer to a more rigorous institute, for in this God will receive greater glory and he will be enabled to lead a life of greater perfection. Goyeneche states that the limitations placed on such transfers in the earlier law and by canon 632 of the Code must not be understood in the sense that they take away the right, since it belongs to the religious in virtue of the natural law. It cannot therefore be taken away by any human power. The limitations are therefore to be understood as precautions which circumscribe the exercise of the right, so that it will not become subject to the whims and to the fallible judgment of private persons. These precautions also forestall anxiety on the part of scrupulous religious, who might be disturbed and induced to depart rashly from the vocation to which they had been called by God. (This doctrine is that of Passerini, *De Hominum Statibus et Officiis,* III, q. 189, a. 8, pp. 333-334.)—Goyeneche, *art. cit., CpR,* I (1920), 225, 226. This view was countered by Chelodi (1880-1922), who argued as follows: first, that no one is forbidden, if he wishes, to tend to the highest degree of perfection in his own institute; second, how can the right to transfer to another institute be a natural right if religious institutes are ecclesiastical institutions which at any moment can be suppressed by the Holy See? He points out also that the juridic evolution of transfer was in the direction of greater opposition to transfer.—*Ius Canonicum de Personis,* p. 452, note 4.

reason for an eventual commutation or dispensation.[145] Similarly, a transfer from a society of the common life to a religious institute will surely find more favor and require lesser reason than a transfer from an insitute to a society, while a transfer from a society in which the bond of affiliation and the obligations are stronger and greater will find less favor than a transfer from a society wherein the bond of affiliation is weaker and the obligations are not so extensive.

The cause for a transfer, then, will be a just one if, in consideration of all the subjective and objective circumstances which affect the individual for whom it is sought, the grant of the transfer rather than its denial proves better suited for his spiritual welfare and for the general good. But if the life of religious institutes and societies in the Church is to remain flourishing and fruitful, then the transfer from one community to another must likewise remain a factor which appears only as an exception, and not as the rule. The whole history of this institute is marked by the Church's growing realization of this truth, and by her effort to keep the proper balance by indeed permitting a transfer when there was a sufficient reason, but by simultaneously safeguarding the person's freedom to transfer only under such restrictive conditions which would ensure the due maintenance of religious stability, so necessary for the good of the individual religious, as well as for the good of the religious state in general and of the Church. "Let every man remain in the calling in which he was called" is still a salutary counsel which in its acceptance ordinarily offers the best guarantee for attaining perfection in the work, the state and the community with which an individual has definitively linked his life's efforts.

B. The Consent of the Superiors.

According to the testimony of post-Code canonists, it is the practice of the Sacred Congregation for Religious to require the consent of the superior-general of the community from which the transfer is to be made. It also requires evidence that the com-

145 Cf. Fanfani (p. 476), who says an Order is counted as stricter than a congregation.

munity with which the person seeks affiliation through the transfer has promised to receive the person in question. It is useless to remark that a religious should always inform his own superior of the intention to transfer before requesting the indult, since the community with which he is affiliated has an acquired right to his continued services, which right ought not to be violated.[145a]

The prudent thing will be always to add to the petition for the apostolic indult a certification of the consent both of the superior of one's own community and of the superior who is competent to admit one to the community with which affiliation is sought through the act of transfer.[146] The promise to admit the transferring religious into the novitiate can be made on the basis of the testimonial letter required by canon 544, § 5, which is discussed below.

C. Testimonial Letters.

Can. 544, § 5. Religioso professo, ad aliam religionem ex apostolico indulto transeunti, satis est testimonium Superioris maioris prioris religionis.

Canon 544, § 5, declares that when a professed religious transfers to another religious institute by means of an apostolic idult he needs only the testimonial of the major superior of the former religious institute.[147] The superior competent to admit aspirants to the community to which the transfer is to be made may well use this letter, as well as the petition of the religious, as a basis for refusing or agreeing to signify his willingness to receive the religious as an aspirant for his community.[148]

Testimonial letters as a requirement for transfer to a new religious institute date from about the middle of the last century.[149]

[145a] Cf. New Code above, p. 121, note 144.

[146] Cf. Bastien, p. 431, n. 608. Beste, pp. 427, 428; Gerster a Zeil, p. 133; Lanslots, *Handbook of Canon Law for Women Religious* (10. ed., New York, 1922), p. 91; Pejška, p. 182; Fanfani, pp. 476, 477; Hofmeister, *art. cit.*, *AKKR*, CVIII (1928), 443.

[147] Cf. Gerster a Zeil, p. 133; Goyeneche, *art. cit.*, *CpR*, I (1920), 313.

[148] Hofmeister, *loc. cit.*

[149] See above, p. 63.

The present law is substantially the same as the former law. The one exception is in the wording. Whereas the former law established detailed requirements with regard to the person of the superior who was to give the testimonials, the present law states simply and concisely that it is to be the major superior of the former religious institute. In the former law it had been provided that it was to be the superior-general or the provincial, or, in the case that there were no provincials in an institute, the local superior.[150]

It is evident from the wording of canon 544, § 5, that testimonials are not required by law when the transfer is from one house to another within the same institute, or from one province to another of the same institute. The paragraph of the canon quoted refers only to professed religious; postulants and novices are considered in paragraphs 1 to 4 which precede it.[151]

The canon applies expressly to religious who transfer by virtue of an apostolic indult. This is the only way by which a transfer which is recognized in the common law can be made to another religious community. Because of the purpose of the law, however, the testimonial letters would be required even if the transfer, by reason of a special privilege, were made without an indult from the Holy See.

The superior to give the testimonials if the religious has been a member of several religious institutes, or of several provinces within the same institute, or of several houses governed by a local superior, is the superior of the last institute, province or house of which he was a member.[152] It is the major superior who must give the testimonials. According to canon 488, 8°, this term includes the abbot primate (e. g., the Abbot of the Monastery of St. Anselm in the city of Rome, who is the representative of the Confederation of the various Congregations of the Black Benedictines with the Holy See), the abbot president of a monastic Congregation, the abbot of an autonomous monastery, even though it belongs to a monastic Congregation, the supreme moderator of a religious institute, the provin-

150 Cf. *supra*, p. 63.

151 Larraona, "Commentarium Codicis,"—*CpR*, IV (1923), 39.

152 This was true in the former law (cf. *supra*, p. 63), and is certainly true in the present law also.

cial superior, the vicars of any one of the above mentioned superiors, and other persons who have authority similar to that of provincial superiors.

There is question whether under the expression *abbot of an autonomous monastery* one can include superiors who are not strictly abbots, either because that title is not found in their institute (e. g., among the Camaldolese and the Carthusians), or because the monastery, though independent, is not an abbey, but a conventual priory. This question seems to have been definitively settled in the affirmative. Larraona states that he knows of two unpublished responses of the Commission for the Interpretation of the Code, one of which includes among major superiors the conventual priors of monastic Congregations, the other, the superiors of independent houses of centralized monastic institutes.[153] Other authors concur in the view that such superiors are major superiors.[154]

There is question also whether abbesses and superioresses of independent houses of nuns are to be classified as major superioresses. A few authors deny that they are major superioresses,[155] but by far the greater number believes that the superioresses of houses which are independent are major superioresses in the sense in which this term is used in the Code. The argument is again drawn from the juridic force which canon 20 acknowledges as inherent in the analogy of law. The monasteries of nuns are truly *sui iuris,* or autonomous. If their superioresses were not major superioresses, there would be many *lacunae* in the law of the Code. Canons 504 and 506 quite clearly insinuate that the superioress of a monastery of nuns is a major superioress. Larraona states that there is a similar insinuation in a circular letter of the Sacred Congregation for Religious

153 Larraona, "Commentarium Codicis," *CpR,* IV (1923), 40, 41.

154 Schaefer, p. 90; Beste, p. 312; Vermeersch-Creusen, *Epitome,* I, pp. 428-429, n. 594 (546); Coronata, I, 617. The argument derives its force from an analogy in law, as justified by an appeal to the principle enunciated in canon 20.

155 Leitner, *Handbuch des Katholischen Kirchenrechts, Das Ordensrecht* (2. ed., 2 vols., Regensburg: Verlag Josef Kösel und Friedrich Pusted, 1921-1927), I, 278-279 (hereafter cited *Das Ordensrecht*); Martinez, Manual de Preladas para la admision de aspirantes a la Religion (Valencia: Falleres de Tipographia la Gutemberg, 1915), pp. 20-21. These authors are cited by Larraona, *art. cit., CpR,* IV (1923), 40.

of the 9th of March, 1920.[156] Examples of such superioresses are had in the case of communities of Benedictine and Cistercian nuns, of the Canonesses of St. Augustine, of Carmelite nuns, of the Poor Clares, etc.[157] The superioress of an independent branch of a non-centralized congregation such as the Sisters of Mercy is also a major superior at least by analogy of law, and can give the testimonial letter required for a transferring religious.

Canon 488, 8°, includes under the expression *major superiors*, the vicars of the above mentioned superiors. However, it includes only those who have ordinary power, even though it be vicarious.[158] It does not include the offices of definitor and assistant general.[159] Whether any given vicar actually exercises vicarious ordinary power must be determined from the constitutions of the religious institute.[160] The vicar who holds power after the decease or incapacity of the superior general until the time when a new superior comes into office certainly is a major superior.[161]

One must note, too, that the term *vicar* is sometimes employed instead of *provincial* in certain institutes. This is done the better to indicate the dependence of the vicar upon the superior-general, and the more clearly to reveal the unity of government in the institute (e. g., the Religious of the Sacred Heart, the Helpers of the Holy Souls). These vicars are major superiors.[162]

Among those who hold power after the manner of provincials the authors include the superiors of divisions of religious institutes

[156] The circular letter is found in *AAS*, XII (1920), 365. Among authors who hold these women are major superioresses are Larraona, *art. cit.*—*CpR*, IV (1923), 41-43; *CpR*, VII (1926), 376; Schaefer, *loc. cit.*; Coronata, *loc. cit.*; Vermeersch-Creusen, *Epitome*, I, *loc cit.*; Beste, *loc. cit.*; Maroto, "Consultationes"—*CpR*, II (1921), 6-7. Cf. Larraona, *art. cit.*, *CpR*, IV (1923), 41-43, for other authors who can be cited as favoring this opinion.

[157] Bastien, p. 28; Creusen-Garesché-Ellis, *Religious Men and Women in the Code* (5. ed., Milwaukee: Bruce, 1940), p. 16 (hereafter cited Creusen-Garesché-Ellis).

[158] Coronata, I, 617; Larraona, *art. cit.*, *CpR*, IV (1923), pp. 45, 46, notes 305, 316.

[159] *"Definitor," "assistens generalis."*—Schaefer, p. 90.

[160] Coronata, I, 627. Cf. also Schaefer, pp. 333, 334 (n. 159).

[161] Bastien, p. 28.

[162] Creusen-Garesché-Ellis, p. 17; Bastien, p. 28.

which are similar to provinces, though they are called by other names, e. g., regions, vice-provinces, quasi-provinces, missionary vicariates, etc.[163] These superiors sometimes have other names, such as *visitator, inspector,* etc.[164] Whether the visitators of men religious are to be counted among the major superiors depends on the power given them by the constitutions of the institute.[165]

No other testimonials than such as are furnished by a major superior are required by the Code. The reason for this is that it is presumed that the other documents which are usually required for entrance into a religious institute have been secured before the aspirant's first entrance into religion.[166] Superiors, however, who are empowered to admit aspirants to religion have a right to demand other testimonials which they may consider to be necessary or opportune.[167]

This general provision allows superiors to call for the attestations of a physician as to the health of the aspirant, a dentist's certificate, and so forth. If a transferring religious of the male sex should have remained in the world for a considerable length of time after leaving the community with which he had been affiliated, then it seems that the testimony of the local ordinary would also be required if the stay was morally continuous for a duration beyond a year.[168]

In the opinion of the present writer, testimonial letters for exclaustrated religious who have dwelt in any one place for more than one year after leaving their institute must be secured from the local Ordinary. The reason is that religious who have secured an indult of exclaustration from the Apostolic See are subject to the local Ordinary of the territory where they have their residence,

[163] Larraona, *art. cit., CpR,* IV (1923), 45-46.

[164] Cf. Schaefer, p. 216, n. 103.

[165] Bastien, p. 28, note 1. Cf., however, Creusen-Garesché-Ellis, p. 16.

[166] Bastien, p. 296; Coronata, I, 722. Thus the documents required in virtue of §§ 2, 3 and 4 of canon 544 are not necessary for religious who by apostolic indult transfer to another institute.

[167] Can. 544, § 6. Goyeneche, *art. cit., CpR,* I (1920), 363.

[168] Cf. can. 544, § 3; Coronata, I, 722; Prümmer, I, 277; Schaefer, p. 495. These authors state merely that testimonials concerning this period are required, without indicating who is to give the testimonials.

even in virtue of the vow of obedience, in place of the superiors of their own community.[169] They are therefore plainly removed from the surveillance and control of their own superiors. In addition to the testimonial from the ordinary, the testimonial of his major superior will also be required in virtue of canon 544, § 5. Similarly, in the case of women who had spent some time in the world after leaving their former institute, it seems that the superioress who is empowered to receive them would be justified in making an investigation of their morals and conduct during that period.[170]

With regard to the attributes required in this testimonial letter, it must be signed and sealed and given, not to the aspirant, but to the religious superior. It must be issued without charge within three months after legitimate request.[171] The oath which is required in confirmation of a testimonial concerning those who have been in a seminary, in a college, in the postulancy or in the novitiate of another religious institute, is not required by the Code for this testimonial.[172] It is, however, recommended in order to assure the truth of the information given in the testimonial.

With regard to the contents of the testimonial, the Code requires that the superior must give information (the accuracy of which he is under a grave obligation in conscience to assure) regarding the natal status, conduct, character, life, reputation, circumstances and knowledge of the aspirant, and also regarding the fact whether he be under any legal inquiry (canon 1939) or under any censure, irregularity, or canonical impediment. The superior must have made a diligent investigation, if necessary by secret inquiry, to secure this information.[173]

Does the provision which requires simply the testimony of a major superior for the religious who transfers to another religious institute apply to the member of a society of the common life (as defined in canon 673) when the latter transfers to a religious in-

169 See can. 639.

170 Cf. can. 544, § 7.

171 Can. 545, § 1.

172 Goyeneche, *art. cit.*, *CpR*, I (1920), 363.

173 Can. 545, § 4.

stitute? At first sight the answer to this question would seem to be in the negative. Since the Code is silent, it would seem that he would be bound to submit the documents required by canon 544 for aspirants coming to the religious institute from the world. It is to be remarked, however, that though the Code does not oblige these societies to require the fulfillment of canon 544 in the admission of aspirants,[174] almost all these communities are accustomed to require their aspirants to fulfill them.[175]

The opinion has been advanced that in this case the testimony of the major superior of the religious society will suffice in connection with the authorized transfer. The arguments advanced are the following: When the documents of canon 544 have been required by a society, it is on a par with religious institutes in this matter; therefore the same law, canon 544, § 5, that applies to religious should apply also in virtue of canon 20 to the members. If these documents were required a second time, then that which had already been accomplished would have to be repeated, and to no good purpose. The Code does apply the discipline regarding transfer to the transfer from religious societies to religious institutes; why should this application not obtain with reference to canon 544, § 5, also?

But the case is different if these documents are not required in a particular society for the admission of aspirants, for then there is no parity between the society and a religious institute in this matter, and the purpose of the law would be frustrated. It would in such circumstances be misdirected to extend the ruling of canon 544, § 5, as applicable to such a society.[176]

D. Freedom From Canonical Impediments

Most of the authors do not discuss the effect of the existence of any of the canonical impediments to valid or licit entrance into the novitiate on the act of transfer to another religious institute. The reason is, most probably, that it would be most unlikely that

[174] Cf. can. 677.

[175] Goyeneche, *loc cit.*

[176] Goyeneche, *ibid.*, pp. 363, 364. Cf. also Stanton, p. 162.

such an impediment would be present in the case of a person who was already a professed member of some other community. It is not, however, absolutely impossible, at least in the case of some of the impediments listed in canon 542, 1° and 2°.

If any of these impediments existed before the entrance of the religious into the novitiate of the original community, and if there was a dispensation from them at that time, then no new dispensation is necessary, even if the conditions which gave rise to the impediment are still present.[177] In transferring to another religious institute the religious does not change his state, but only his juridical relationship with a religious community. One may presume that once the Holy See has dispensed him from the impediment so as to permit him to enter upon the religious state, it will not require a second dispensation in the case of a mere change of community within that state. If, in the case of an impediment which made entrance into the first community illegal, no dispensation had been sought, then the obtaining of a dispensation appears necessary in the case of a transfer.

If, however, any one of these impediments had arisen after the first religious profession, a dispensation would have to be sought from the Holy See together with the indult for the transfer. There is no reason for excluding a transferring religious from subjection to the law as expressed in the general wording of canon 542.

E. The Form Used for Seeking Permission to Transfer

Canon 632 declares that a transfer to another religious community or from one autonomous monastery to another cannot take place without the authority of the Apostolic See. In the Code the term *Apostolic See* includes not only the Holy Father but also the Congregations, Tribunals and Offices through whose instrumentality he carries on the business of the universal Church.[178] Matters relating to religious institutes or to societies of the common life fall

[177] Schaefer, p. 471, puts it in a slightly different way—"Impedimenta quae ingressui in priorem Religionem obstabant et de quibus dispensatio pro valido ingressu concessa fuit, non reviviscunt."

[178] Can. 7.

within the province of the Sacred Congregation of Religious, to which a petition for the transfer must therefore be sent.[179] A copy of an actual petition sent to the Holy See for transfer reads as follows:

Address
Date

HOLY FATHER:
Prostrate at the feet of Your Holiness, Sister M. ....
of the Sisters ...., Province of ....,
humbly presents the following:

That she made profession of simple perpetual vows (date). She humbly begs to transfer to the (*monastery*) of (*place*). The Mother Prioress and her Council have signified their willingness to receive her for trial of her vocation to the contemplative life.

Her reasons for making this petition are:

A strong desire for the canonical cloistered life, with a fair understanding of what it means. This desire began over .... years ago. For the past .... years it has been most active and has been encouraged by her confessor and spiritual director.

Kissing the feet of Your Holiness, I am with all due respect and reverence
Your Holiness' humble and obedient handmaid in J. C.,

....
Secular Name

....
Religious Name

Approved by the General Council of the
Sisters ....
....

....
Mother General.

[179] Can. 251.

A copy of the printed formularies used by the Sacred Congregation of Religious in granting transfers follows:

N. .... Form. 19-A

Beatissime Pater,

Soror (Nomen) ....

in Inst. ....

humillime ad pedes S. V. provuluta petit facultatem transeundi ad ....

Et Deus, etc.

Vigore facultatum a Sm̃o Domino Nostro concessarum, Sacra Congregatio Negotiis Religiosorum Sodalium praeposita, attento consensu (*Instituti a quo et praehabito consensu Monasterii ad quod*) ....

benigne commisit *(Em. mo Card. Protectori)* ....

ut petitum transitum, pro suo arbitrio et conscientia concedat, ad normam Iuris Canonici.

Contrariis quibuscumque non obstantibus.

Datum Romae, die ...., 19.......

CHAPTER IV

THE NEW NOVITIATE AND PROFESSION

Article 1. The Necessity of the Novitiate and of Profession

I. Transfer to a Religious Institute or to a Society of the Common Life.

Can. 633, § 1. Transiens ad aliam religionem novitiatum peragere debet; quo durante, manentibus votis, iura et obligationes particulares, quas in religione derelicta habuit, suspensa manent, et ipse obligatione tenetur Superioribus novae religionis et ipsi noviorum Magistro parendi etiam ratione voti obedientiae.

§ 2. Si in religione ad quam transiit, professionem non edat, ad pristinam religionem redire debet, nisi interim votorum tempus expiraverit.

From ancient times, the novitiate had been required of a religious who transferred to another religious institute, in virtue namely of the fact that it was required of all new members of a community. This practice was confirmed by the Sacred Congregation of the Council in 1633, and has been an explicit requirement of the law ever since.[1]

The law of the Code reaffirms the earlier law, and requires that the religious who transfers to another institute must make a new novitiate and another profession.[2] The novitiate is necessary for a valid transfer.[3] The reasons are: (1) that a valid novitiate is necessary for a valid profession; [4] and (2) that a valid profession

[1] See above, pp. 63-65.

[2] Can. 633, § 1, § 2.

[3] Sipos, p. 340.

[4] Can. 572, § 1, 3°; cf. Hofmeister, *art. cit.*, *AKKR*, CVIII (1928), 451.

is necessary in order to incorporate the transferring religious into the new institute while separating him from the old.

The obligation to make a new profession is quite clear from canon 633, § 2, though the positive precept is phrased in a negative manner: if the transferring religious does not make profession in the institute to which he has transferred, he must return to the releasing institute. This provision of the law of the Code is in accord with the practice before the Code.[5] It is founded on the nature of the religious state, which cannot exist without the profession of public vows in a religious institute, as is evident from canon 488, 1°. Profession is furthermore a solemn contract, which besides the taking of vows includes the aggregation of the novice who makes profession into a determined religious institute, and gives rise to mutual obligations between the institute, and the religious. In short, profession is the only canonical way in which anyone can be adopted into or incorporated by any religious institute.[6]

This is clear also from a consideration of canons 633, § 1, and 635, 1°. According to the first of these canons the vows of the religious who transfers to another institute remain intact, and the rights and particular obligations which were his in the releasing institute are only *suspended.* According to the second, it is the new profession which severs the bond with the releasing institute by causing the religious to *lose* all the rights and obligations which were his before the transfer, and to *assume* the rights and duties of the receiving community. Without a valid novitiate, therefore, a transferring religious cannot make valid profession; but without a valid profession, there can be no valid transfer.

Profession is therefore absolutely necessary for the validity of the transfer to another religious institute. If the community to which the transfer is being made has another rule and constitutions, or another name, it is another religious institute. Thus the Friars Minor, the Capuchins and the Conventuals are three different insti-

[5] See above, pp. 65-66.

[6] Goyeneche, "De transitu ad aliam religionem"—*CpR*, II (1921), 173; cf. also Bastien, p. 433.

tutes within the Franciscan family.[7] The several monastic congregations of the Black Benedictines, however, are all counted as parts of the same Order, as the term Order is understood in canon 633, § 3. A new profession is therefore not required in connection with the transfer from one monastic congregation of the Benedictines to another.[8]

No novitiate or other period of probation is prescribed by the Code before admission into a society of the common life. Such a period will, however, be most generally prescribed before entrance by the constitutions of each society. If such a novitiate or period of probation is prescribed in the constitutions, one who transfers to the society from another society of common life in virtue of an apostolic indult will be obliged to undergo this period in virtue of canons 681 and 633, § 1.

The Code says nothing concerning profession in these societies.[9] Some of these societies have not a word in their constitutions concerning profession, but speak of *aggregation* or *incorporation*. Some provide for incorporation through a profession of private vows, some through the taking of an oath, or of a promise, or by means of a conventional act of consecration.[10] Whatever the ceremony or the formality that is required for incorporation, this will be necessary in order to complete a transfer made from another community into the society.

The postulancy is not required for religious when transferring to another institute.[11] The arguments advanced for the omission of the apostulancy are as follows: first, the silence of the Code.

[7] See above, pp. 91-92, 141. They have not only another name and different constitutions, but also different superiors general.

[8] See below, pp. 140-141.

[9] Schaefer, p. 1032, n. 602.

[10] Cf. Stanton, pp. 136, 137, 138.

[11] Coronata, I, p. 839, note 8; Wernz-Vidal, III, 453; Beste, p. 428; Vermeersch-Creusen, *Epitome,* I, 585, n. 792 (734); Schaefer, p. 932, n. 578, 1; Berutti, III, 319; Goyeneche, *art. cit., CpR,* II (1921), 147; Hofmeister, *art. cit., AKKR,* CIX (1929), 452-453; Pejška, p. 182. Cf. can. 539, § 1; Prikryl, "Übertritt in eine andere Ordensgenossenschaft"—*Theologisch-praktische Quartalschrift,* XCII (1939), 125.

Though the canons on transfer specifically mention the novitiate, the postulancy is not mentioned.[12]

A second argument may be drawn from the purpose of the law. The postulancy was introduced in order to prepare certain aspirants to the religious life for the novitiate. It was meant to guard against a failure of the novitiate to achieve its purpose by reason of the possible ignorance of these aspirants of the nature of the religious life.[13] Such ignorance cannot be presumed to exist in the case of religious when transferring from another community.[14] A third consideration in favor of this opinion is the unanimity of the authors. None, to this writer's knowledge, has held that the postulancy is required for a religious when transferring to another religious institute, despite the general wording of canon 539, §1.

Berutti goes so far as to say that no professed religious can be obliged to make a postulancy before the novitiate in the receiving community; the superiors do not have the power to prescribe or even to permit it.[15] Hofmeister, on the other hand, admitting that the postulancy is not prescribed for a transferring religious, believes that one can deduce from canon 543 that the religious *could* be subjected to an undetermined time of probation before his admission to the novitiate.[16] Canon 543 provides that the right to admit candidates to the novitiate belongs to the major superior who acts in connection with the vote of the council or of the chapter, according to the particular constitutions of each institute.

It is difficult to see how Hofmeister has read an implication of the possibility for a postulancy into canon 543. This canon does not mention the postulancy. Its intent seems to be merely to prescribe who has the right to admit a candidate to the novitiate and to profession. The canon declares that this right belongs to the major

[12] Schaefer, *loc. cit.*; Goyeneche, *loc. cit.* Cf. cans. 632-636.

[13] This is why can. 539, § 1 prescribes a postulancy of six months duration for all women aspirants and for those who wish to become lay brothers if they are preparing to enter an institute in which perpetual vows are taken. In institutes where only temporary vows are the rule this canon permits the constitutions to determine the need and duration of the postulancy.

[14] Goyeneche, *loc. cit.*

[15] *Institutiones Iuris Canonici,* III, 319.

[16] *Art cit., AKKR,* CVIII (1928), 452-453.

superior who acts in connection with the vote of the council or of the chapter, according to the particular constitutions of each institute. The major superior does not need to submit a candidate to a period of probation in order to admit him to the novitiate. An interview with the candidate and the information secured from the testimonial letter required in virtue of canon 544, §§ 5 and 6, should be sufficient to enable him to decide on the admission.[17]

Berutti, on the other hand, gives no reason for his statement that the superiors do not have the power to prescribe or even to permit of postulancy for transferring religious. The writer, however, agrees with him insofar as to say that the framers of the Code did not intend that there should be such a period in the case of a religious transferring to another religious institute. If they had, they would have had to make provisions determining the rights and particular obligations of the religious for such a period. Such a provision was made for transferring religious while in the novitiate of the receiving community by canon 633, § 1. This canon makes it clear that transferring religious, until admission to the novitiate, will be no more than guests in the receiving community. It provides that the rights and particular obligations of the transferring religious in the releasing institute are suspended for the duration of the novitiate. This means, of course, that they are not suspended until the formal admission of the candidate to the novitiate.

Since there is no similar provision concerning the postulancy in the law for transferring religious, their rights and particular obligations in the releasing institute would remain in full force. They would still retain their obligation to obey their superiors in the releasing institute in virtue of the vow of obedience. Their position under such conditions in the postulancy before their entrance into the novitiate of another community would be a juridical anomaly and contrary to the procedure intended by the framers of the Code.

What has been said, however, should not be understood in such a way as to imply that the beginning of the novitiate must coincide precisely with the arrival of the transferring religious in the receiving community. This would often be impossible or at any

17 See the commentary above, pp. 123-129, on canon 544, §§ 5 and 6.

rate very inconvenient. It would certainly not be contrary to the Code to have the transferring religious stay with the new community for a short time as a guest preparatory to the time appointed for his reception into the novitiate. This period, nevertheless, should not be unduly prolonged. It cannot be prolonged for more than six months without an apostolic indult to remain outside of the cloister, in virtue of canon 606, § 2.

It is disputed whether the entrance into the novitiate must be preceded by a retreat of eight days in cases where the postulancy is not required. Beste believes that the word *postulantes* as used in canon 541, which requires postulants to make a retreat before their admission into the novitiate, refers not only to postulants in the strict and technical meaning of the word, but also to all aspirants before their admission to the novitiate.[18] Other authors, however, maintain that the word *postulantes* probably must be understood in its strict sense, and that consequently aspirants who are not postulants need not make the retreat.[19] Very often the constitutions of institutes which do not demand the postulancy nevertheless require the aspirants to make a retreat before their entrance into the novitiate.

The discussion may now be applied to the case of a transferring religious. Since a transferring religious is not obliged to make a postulancy, it cannot be said that he is certainly obliged by the common law to make a retreat of eight days before his reception into the novitiate. But if the constitutions prescribe a retreat for all aspirants, then the transferring religious is bound just as much as the other aspirants.

Canon 552 requires the superiors of women religious to notify the ordinary of the place of the coming admissions of postulants to the novitiate two months in advance, and obliges the ordinary to conduct a canonical examination of the aspirants to determine their

[18] "Vox 'postulantes' heic complectitur omnes, qui admissionem ad novitiatum expetunt, tametsi ad peragendum formalem postulatum, de quo in canonibus antecedentibus, non ligentur."—Beste, p. 359.

[19] Schaefer, pp. 460-461; Coronata, I, 708; Vermeersch-Creusen, *Epitome*, I, 481, n. 669 (620).

intentions, their knowledge of the religious life and their freedom.[20] In the event of a transfer, the postulancy is not required, and consequently the regulation of canon 522 does not apply to transferring religious. It will not be necessary for the superiors to notify the bishops of the admission of the transferring religious nor will it be necessary for the bishop to conduct a canonical examination such as is required of women postulants.

II. Transfer to Another Monastery of the Same Order

Can. 633, § 3. Transiens ad aliud monasterium eiusdem Ordinis nec novitiatum peragit nec novam emittit professionem.

The Code declares that a new novitiate and profession are not required if one transfers to another monastery of the same Order. The reason for this law is that there are only accidental differences between various monasteries of the same Order with regard to the obligations of the religious and the observances of the religious life which are there in use. The rights and obligations in both monasteries will be substantially the same inasmuch as both belong to the same religious institute.[21]

The term monastery refers to a religious house belonging to regulars who are monks, canons regular, or nuns. In the Code the term does not refer to any other kind of religious house.[22] According to many canonists, monasteries are said to belong to the same Order, when they have the same rule and constitutions and the same superior general.[23] In the opinion of the present writer, a slightly better description of the notion of what is meant when the Code uses this term, is to be found in Berutti. He states that several

[20] Berutti, III, 319.

[21] Berutti, III, 323; Blat, *Commentarium Textus Codicis Iuris Canonici* (6 vols., Romae, 1921-1927, Vol. II, *De Personis,* 1921), p. 620 (hereafter cited Blat); Fanfani, p. 477.

[22] See above, pp. 93-94, 97; Schaefer, p. 79, n. 44.

[23] Beste, pp. 428, 429; Claeys-Bouuaert-Simenon, I, 420; Coronata, I, p. 849, note 1; Vermeersch-Creusen, *Epitome,* I, p. 586, n. 792 (734); Gerster a Zeil, p. 134; Prümmer, I, 334; Schaefer, p. 936, n. 525; Wernz-Vidal, III, 456.

monasteries are said to belong to the same Order if they follow the same rule or the same constitutions and are, therefore, called also by the same name: for example, the Benedictine monks (although they belong to different monastic congregations) or the nuns of the Order of Preachers, the nuns of the Visitation of the Blessed Virgin Mary, and so forth.[24]

This is a better definition, for first of all, it excludes all consideration of the centralized Orders, whose houses are not comprehended under the term *monastery.* Secondly it omits mention of the subjection of the monasteries to one and the same superior general, for these Orders do not necessarily have a superior general and, if there be some kind of general superior, his powers are strictly limited. Thirdly, this definition comprehends very readily also such monasteries as may pertain to different monastic congregations which, though they follow the same rule and have the same name, yet have different constitutions, for "monasteries are said to belong to the same Order if they follow the same rule or the same constitutions."

This is a rather wide meaning of the term *Order,* which the Code sometimes uses in a wide and collective sense, and not in the strict sense of the terms *Order* and *religious institute* as these are defined by canon 488, 1° and 2°.[25] The authors therefore generally say that a new novitiate and profession will not be required if a religious transfers from one monastic congregation to another, provided that they belong to the same Order.[26] They agree, for example, that a religious who transfers from a monastery of one monastic congrega-

[24] "Plura monasteria *eiusdem Ordinis* esse dicuntur si eandem regulam seu easdem constitutiones servandas habent, et idcirco etiam eodem nomine appellantur: ut puta, monachi Benedictini (quambis forte ad diversas Congregationes monasticas pertineant), vel moniales Ordinis Praedicatorum, moniales a Visitatione B.M.V., et huiusmodi."—Berutti, III, 323.

[25] Schaefer, p. 71, n. 41; Larraona, "Commentarium Codicis"—*CpR,* II (1921), p. 276, footnote 86. An even wider use of this term, for a case in which one must postulate more than one superior general, is found in canon 613, § 2.

[26] Augustine, III, 366; Blat, II, 620; Coronata, I, p. 849, note 2; Pejška, p. 183.

tion of the Black Benedictines to a monastery of another monastic congregation in the same Order need not repeat his novitiate.[27]

The authors generally state also that the branches of the Order of St. Francis are not to be regarded as branches of the same Order in the sense of canon 633, § 3, on the ground that each branch, the Friars Minor, the Conventuals, and the Capuchins, has a different superior general.[28] In the opinion of the present writer, these authors have come to the right conclusion for the wrong reason. For the Franciscans are truly one Order, if the term Order is taken in its wide and collective sense, and the mere fact that the different branches do not have the same superior general does not nullify this conclusion. The male branches of the Franciscans, however, do not come under the rule of canon 633, § 3, since the term monastery does not refer to a house of men Mendicants, but to a house of monks, of canons regular, or of nuns. Canon 633, § 3, refers primarily to decentralized communities, while the male branches of the Franciscans are centralized religious institutes. However, the matter does not seem to be entirely clear. For while the different branches do not have the same constitutions, they do have the same rule. Furthermore, it is not certain that the rule of canon 633, § 3, should not be applied in virtue of canon 20 to a transfer from one branch to another within the Franciscan group in consideration of the extant analogy. Therefore one may well recommend Prümmer's suggestion, namely, that the Holy See should be asked for a solu-

[27] Claeys-Bouuaert-Simenon, I, 420; Coronata, I, p. 849, note 1; Vermeersch-Creusen, *Epitome,* I, p. 586, n. 792 (734); Schaefer, p. 936, n. 525; Wernz-Vidal, III, 456. It will be noticed that in this case the definition of the expression *the same Order,* as given by these very authors, has been stretched very far indeed; the *abbas primas* of the Benedictines is not a true superior general, since each congregation is a religious institute in its own right, so that all of them together form, not one institute, but a confederation. Furthermore, while all monastic congregations of this Order have the same rule, that of St. Benedict, they do not have the same constitutions. Each congregation has its own.

[28] Claeys-Bouuaert-Simenon, I, 420; Coronata, I, p. 849, note 1; Vermeersch-Creusen, *Epitome,* I, 586, n. 792 (734); Schaefer, p. 936, n. 525; Wernz-Vidal, III, 456. Only one author disagrees. He states that if the particular law does not settle the point, then a solution should be sought from the Holy See.—Prümmer, I, 334.

tion, unless the particular law offers prescriptions which cover this question.[29]

It seems that in virtue of the analogy in the law a transfer from one independent house to another if both belong to a religious congregation of simple vows should not require a repetition of the novitiate. This opinion was advanced by Bastien (1866-1940).[30] It is confirmed in a private response to the Most Reverend Bishop of Brooklyn by the Sacred Congregation of Religious. In this response it was decided that the Sisters Adorers of the Precious Blood, an institute of simple vows in which each house is entirely independent of other houses, and in which there are no superiors except the local superiors, come within the scope of canon 633, §3.[31]

The same situation is had in the case of other communities, for example, the Sisters of Mercy who did not become merged with the "Union." There seems to be no reason why a religious who belongs to a house of the Sisters of Mercy which is not merged with the "Union," should have to repeat her novitiate if she transfers to another house which likewise is not merged with the "Union." There will be certain accidental differences, to be sure, in the religious life, but the sister will be living under the same constitutions as in the first community. There is no substantial difference in the life of the two communities. *Favorabilia sunt amplificanda, odiosa restringenda.*

A problem, however, is presented by the fact that no novitiate is required if the transfer is made to another monastery of the same Order. The purpose of the novitiate is not only to instruct the novice in the life of the community, but also to give the novice an opportunity to acquaint himself with the institute, and the institute an opportunity to acquaint itself with the qualities, temperament and character of the aspirant. If there should be no period during which these purposes could be achieved, it is easy to predict that in some cases there will arise difficulties which could have been prevented if the aspirant had been subjected to a period of probation.

[29] Prümmer, I, 334.

[30] *Directoire Canonique*, pp. 433, 444.

[31] For the text of this decree see above, p. 103.

Some orders have provided for this in their constitutions, which quite commonly demand some probationary period for the religious who has transferred from another monastery of the same Order before he will be admitted as a permanent member of the community. Constitutions at one time distinguished between religious transferring from the same, and religious transferring from another, monastic congregation. In the first case it was usual to require a stay of one-half year or even of a year among the professed of the new monastery.[32] In the latter case the constitutions, even if they did not demand a new novitiate, demanded a year's stay in the novitiate.[33] Since the confederation of the Black Benedictines at the request of Pope Leo XIII there has been a relaxation, so that even when the transfer is made from another congregation of the Order the religious may stay among the professed, and no longer must stay in the novitiate during this prescribed period of probation.[34] These statutes must be observed.[35]

Even when the constitutions have no such provisions, it is the opinion of Bastien that the superior of the monastery to which the transfer is being made is not bound to receive the religious immediately in a definitive manner, until he has received all the necessary information concerning the new aspirant. Furthermore, he believes that he could subject him to a period of probation, preferably to be arranged for with the consent of the superior of the community which the religious is quitting. If in the interval the religious should not persevere, or if he came to be regarded by

[32] *Statuta Congregationis Benedictinae Bavaricae,* n. 107—"ad sex menses"; *Constitutiones Ordinis Cisterciensium Strictioris Observantiae,* n. 169; *Constitutiones Congreg. Belgicae O.S.B.,* P. III, c. II, n. 8. These are cited by Hofmeister in his article in *AKKR,* CVIII (1928), 454-455, note 1.

[33] *Constitutiones Congregationis Beuronensis O.S.B.,* Declaratio in c. 61 S. Regulae. Cf. Hofmeister, *ibid.,* note 2.

[34] *Constitutiones Congregationis Helveto-Americanae,* n. 95; *Statuta Congregationis Americo-Cassinensis O.S.B.* (1925), n. 81; *Constitutiones Congregationis Belgicae,* P. II, c. V, n. 19; *Constitutiones Congregationis Ottiliensis,* n. 197; *Constitutiones Congregationis Brasiliensis* (1911), n. 85, 1919, n. 85; the constitutions of the Cassinese Congregation of the year 1925 demand a trial of at least three years. All these are cited by Hofmeister, *ibid.,* note 3.

[35] Beste, p. 429.

the superior as a subject who is not suited for membership in the community, he would be obliged to return to his former monastery. This would have been impossible if he had not been subjected to any such period of probation, but had been definitely incorporated in the community on the day of his arrival.[36] It is to be noted, however, that under the law of the cloister as found in the Code, the superiors could not extend permission to remain outside of the monastery for a period of more than six months.[37] This will limit a possible probationary period to six months.

One may raise the objection that this probationary period is inadmissible, since, as several authors declare, the incorporation of the individual into the new monastery is effected on the very day of the transfer.[38] The Code itself states that the definitive and final effects of transfer, which are produced by the new profession in the case of those who transfer to another institute, are produced from the day of the transfer (*a die transitus*) in the case of those who transfer to another monastery of the same institute.[39]

Hofmeister suggests the following solution for men religious who transfer to a monastery where the constitutions provide for a probationary period: that the request for the indult be sent toward the end of the probationary period, provided that the religious and the community are satisfied with each other.[40]

[36] Cf. Bastien, p. 434, n. 611.

[37] Can. 606, § 2.

[38] "Unde ut transitus, non quidem ad certum incertumve tempus sed stabili modo et per formalem aggregationem, legitime fiat, requiritur *indultum apostolicum* (can. 632), at nec novitiatus est peragendus nec nova professio emittenda (can. 633, § 3), nam iam primo die perfectus est"—Chelodi, p. 453, n. 285; "Transitus iam primo die statim vim suam obtinet"—Schaefer, p. 936, n. 525.

[39] Can. 635.

[40] Where the Holy See has given the faculty to grant permission for the transfer to another monastery it has done so on the provision that not only the two superiors, but also the chapter of the community to which the transfer is being made, give consent to the transfer—see above, p. 114; see also Hofmeister, *art. cit.*, *AKKR*, CVIII (1928), 444, who notes that in some monastic congregations the lack of consent on the part of the superior of the monastery from which the transfer is being made can be overcome by a two-thirds majority vote by those who have a right to vote in the general chapter. This is provided

The problem cannot be met in this way, however, if the transfer is to be made from an autonomous monastery belonging to nuns. If they are nuns with solemn vows, they cannot, without an indult of the Holy See, leave the monastery even for a short time, or for any reason except in the case of imminent danger of death, or of some other very serious evil. The instruction of 1924 on the enclosure of nuns with solemn vows explicitly states that they cannot transfer from one monastery to the other without the permission of the Holy See. Temporary transfers are included in this prohibition. The permission of the Holy See is required for all transfers. However, the instruction also states that these permissions are usually granted by the Sacred Congregation for a just cause and under reasonably prescribed conditions.[41]

As is evident, the permission for the transfer must therefore be obtained *before* the transfer is made. How then shall one be able to make provision for a period of probation before the definitive affiliation? Hofmeister suggests that the Apostolic Delegate (or Nuncio or Internuncio) be requested for permission to leave the cloister. His faculties permit him to grant nuns an indult of exclaustration in case of infirmity, or for any other just and grave reasons.[42] Hofmeister argues that the greater power always includes a lesser,[43] and that therefore the Apostolic Delegate could give permission to leave the cloister so as to provide for a temporary transfer. After the period of probation, the petition for a permanent transfer together with other information which is required by the practice of the Holy See could be sent to Rome. If, however, the new monastery had decided against admitting the religious, or if she herself desired to return to her original community, she would then be able to do so without having to seek a new indult of transfer.[44]

In the case of nuns who by special prescription of the Holy See

for by the *Constitutiones Congregationis Ottiliensis O.S.B., 1925*, n. 429; *Constitutiones Congregationis Belgicae O.S.B., 1925*, P. III, E. II, n. 8.

[41] Can. 601, § 1; S. C. de Religiosis, instr. 6 febr. 1924, III, 1°, (a) and (b)—*AAS*, XVI 1924), 97-98.

[42] Faculty n. 49.

[43] Reg. 35, R. J., in VI°.

[44] Hofmeister, *art. cit.*, *AKKR*, CVIII (1928), 444, 445.

take only simple vows, permission to leave the cloister can be given by the superiors themselves, but the permission cannot be extended to an absence of more than six months according to the common law.[45]

These solutions have been proposed on the supposition that Hofmeister is correct in his assumption that it is the apostolic indult itself which produces the change in affiliation and effects the definitive incorporation in the new community.[46] This assumption seems to be suggested by the wording of canon 635.[47] Berutti and Bastien, however, indicate that the juridic *completion* of the transfer is accomplished through the admission of the religious by the competent superior of the monastery to which the transfer is being made.[48] This view appeals to the present writer, in that it seems to afford a closer parallel to the admission to profession in the new community on the part of a religious who transfers to another religious institute. This is necessary for the completion of the transfer. If this view should be the correct one, then the apostolic indult may be secured before the probationary period begins, since the permanent incorporation of the religious will not be completed until his admission to the new community on a permanent basis by the competent superior.

Another difficulty, however, presents itself, which will cast doubt upon some of the solutions which have just been explained. It is this: just as the Code has made no provision which explicitly governs the rights and obligations of a religious who transfers to another institute during the postulancy,[49] so it contains no provi-

[45] Can. 606, § 2. An authentic interpretation of the Pontifical Commission for the Interpretation of the Code decided that these nuns were not bound by the law of papal enclosure under cans. 597-600.—1 mart., 1921, III, ad 2um,—*AAS*, XIII (1921), 177.

[46] *Loc. cit.*

[47] "Transeuntes ad aliud monasterium eiusdem religionis a die transitus, ad aliam vero religionem ab edita nova professione. . . ."

[48] "Huiusmodi transitus iuridice perficitur quum primum Superior competens monasterii *ad quod* religiosum legitime admittit, et ex tunc eidem religioso transeunti omnia iura et privilegia *communia* Ordinis in novo monasterio acquiruntur. . . ."—Berutti, III, 323; Bastien, p. 434, n. 611.

[49] See above, p. 137.

sion governing such rights and obligations of a religious transferring to another monastery of the same order during this period of probation which may occasionally seem to be useful and desirable. Unless the constitutions permit a temporary transfer and regulate the rights and obligations of the religious during this period, he would be in the same anomalous position as a transferring religious placed in the postulancy before his entrance into the novitiate of another institute—that is, he would retain all the rights and particular obligations which he had in the releasing monastery, and would remain subject to the superiors of that monastery in virtue of his vow of obedience. Furthermore, the superiors of the new monastery would have no claim to exercise any control over the religious during the period of his probation.

It is therefore the view of the present writer that whenever there is no provision for a probationary period or even for a temporary transfer in the constitutions, the best solution will be the following: Whenever the superiors feel that it would be prudent to submit a religious who wishes to transfer to another monastery to a period of probation before he is definitively and permanently incorporated into that community, they should request the Holy See to grant not only permission for the transfer but also permission to submit the transferring religious to a period of probation before his admission on a permanent basis. It would be well to ask the Holy See also to indicate norms governing the rights and obligations of the religious as well as his subjection to the superiors of the receiving monastery in the course of this period.

Article 2. Admission to the Novitate

Canon 543 states that the right to admit candidates to the novitiate belongs to the major religious superiors, as designated by the constitutions. Major superiors must, moreover, have the consent of the council or chapter, or at least consult the same, as the constitutions require. This canon applies not only to aspirants to the religious life in general, but also to religious who have transferred from other institutes.[50] It seems advisable to consult or

[50] Berutti, III, 319.

to obtain the consent of the council or the chapter, as the constitutions require, before the petition for a transfer is sent to the Sacred Congregation of Religious. Then certification of the consent or consultation of the council or the chapter as well as of the readiness of the superior who has a right to admit the transferring religious if the transfer should be granted, can be included in the petition.

If the superior should neglect to secure the consent of the chapter or of the council when this is required by the constitutions, the admission would be invalid.[51] If the constitutions require only the consultation of the council or of the chapter, then the validity of the superior's act of admitting someone to the novitiate apart from such a previous consultation is in dispute. Some authors hold that the admission would be invalid. Others believe that it would be valid. Practically, until the Holy See has settled the matter, the act is to be regarded as valid, in view of the doubt concerning the demand or requirement of the law.[52] Hence, if the superior should have neglected to consult the chapter or the council, when only consultation is required, no convalidation of the act of admission need be secured from the Holy See.[53]

If the transfer is made to a society of the common life, the formalities required by the constitutions for admission to the novitiate or other probationary period must be observed for the admission of the one who has transferred from some other community to the community in which the novitiate or some other probation is to follow.

ARTICLE 3. THE OBLIGATIONS AND RIGHTS OF THE NOVITIATE.

I. Obligations Arising from the Vows

According to canon 633, § 1, the vows remain in force during the novitiate.[54] This phrase is contrasted with another, which

[51] Can. 105, 1°. The novitiate and the subsequent profession would, like the admission, be invalid also—see above, pp. 123, 124.

[52] Cf. Goyeneche, "Consultationes," *CpR,* III (1922), 265; IV (1923), 120; Schaefer, p. 326, n. 155; pp. 486, 487, n. 223.

[53] Schaefer, p. 487, n. 223.

[54] "Manentibus votis."

declares that the rights and particular obligations which the religious had in the releasing institute are suspended.[55] From this one can rightly infer that the religious retains in full the obligations which are the object of the vows of poverty, chastity and obedience.[56] However, the rights and particular obligations which the religious had in the releasing institute, though they basically remain in existence, are suspended in the sense that the rights cannot be used and that the obligations need no longer be observed for the duration of the novitiate.[57] One must therefore determine precisely in what way the vows affect the life of the transferring religious in the novitiate, and how the obligations arising from his vows can be reconciled with other obligations arising from his status as a novice in a different community than the one in which he made his profession.

A. The Vow of Chastity.

There is no difficulty in the determination of the obligations which arise from the vow of chastity. The matter of this vow has the same extension in all institutes, though the juridical consequences following from a violation of the vow differ according as it is solemn or simple, perpetual or temporary.[58] A person, therefore, who has been simply professed is bound under pain of the illegality of any contrary acts; a solemnly professed religious, however, is bound under pain of the invalidity of any contrary acts if these are such that they can be invalidated.[59] Hence, under pain of invalidity of the attempted act, a religious with solemn vows who is in the novitiate of another religious institute cannot marry. The same is true of a religious with simple vows if by special provision of the Holy See these vows have became accredited with the power of invalidating

55 "Iura et obligationes particulares, quas in religione derelicta habuit, suspensa manent."

56 Blat uses an apt phrase, saying that the vows remain "quoad vim actu obligandi."—*Commentarium,* II, 620.

57 Blat, again summing it up aptly, says that they are suspended "quoad iuris usum et obligationis observantiam."—*Commentarium,* II, 620.

58 Goyeneche, "De transitu ad aliam religionem"—*CpR,* II (1929), 117.

59 Can. 579.

any attempt at the contracting of marriage.[60] Other religious with simple vows are simply impeded from entering into marriage, but the marriage, if contracted, would not be invalid.[61] A perpetual vow of chastity does not cease during the novitiate. A temporary vow expires if the time for which it was taken expires while the religious is in the novitate.[62]

There is, then, the while the religious is in the novitiate of a new community, absolutely no change in the obligations of this vow.

B. The Vow of Obedience.

A slightly more difficult question is the precise extension of the obligations arising from the vow of obedience. Canon 633, § 1, states that the transferring religious is obliged to obey the superiors of the new institute and the master of novices even by reason of the vow of obedience. This indicates that the superiors or the master of novices can impose on him a formal precept which is binding in virtue of the vow.[63]

The obligation of the transferring religious to obey the novice master and the superiors of the institute is, therefore, much more serious than that which binds the other novices. Canon 561, § 2, states that a novice is subject to the power of the master of novices and of the superiors of the institute and accordingly is obliged to obey them. Also noteworthy is the fact that, while this vow remains in its essence just what it was when profession was made in the releasing community, the external reference of the vow has been changed for the duration of the novitiate.

Like the vow of chastity, however, it remains essentially what it was before: solemn or simple, perpetual or temporary. The

[60] Cf. can. 1073.

[61] Cf. can. 1058.

[62] Cf. can. 633, § 2; can. 634.

[63] Berutti, III, 319. Cf. also Vermeersch-Creusen, *Epitome*, I, 585, n. 792 (734).

juridical consequences of its violation as determined by these characteristics remain unchanged.

There may be a decided change, however, in the extension of *the matter* of the vow of obedience. The remote matter of the vow of obedience is whatever is directly or explicitly contained in the rule or the constitutions as well as what is necessary or at least very useful to secure the observance of the rule or the constitutions, and which therefore reducibly, implicitly or indirectly pertains to them.[64] The proximate matter of the vow comprehends precepts in the strict sense of the term, when they have been imposed by the religious superior in virtue of his dominative power or of his power of jurisdiction. Precepts in the strict sense of the term are those by which the superior intends to bind the conscience of the religious. Very often there is required the use of a special formula in the act of imposing them.[65]

In the case of a transferring religious, it is evident that the master of novices or the superiors cannot command anything beyond that which is explicitly or implicitly in the constitutions of the releasing community.[66] To do so would be to demand in virtue of the vow what had not been promised under the vow. This would mean a real change in the vow.[67]

Furthermore, the religious cannot be bound by vow to do anything which is beyond the scope of the rule and the constitutions of the receiving community.[68] In this case the limitation is not occasioned by the original vow taken by the religious. It is rather a limitation which affects the superior, whose power is derived from the rules and the constitutions of his institute, and cannot go beyond their limits. Furthermore, such precepts would be useless: the purpose of the novitiate is to train the aspirant for the community, and it would be futile to compel him to do what is foreign to the nature and purpose of the institute.[69]

[64] Schaefer, p. 672, n. 317.
[65] Schaefer, p. 673, n. 317.
[66] Goyeneche, *art. cit., CpR,* II (1921), 117; Schaefer, p. 932, n. 518.
[67] Goyeneche, *loc. cit.*
[68] Goyeneche, *loc. cit.*, Schaefer, *loc. cit.*
[69] Goyeneche, *loc. cit.*

C. The Vow of Poverty.

Like the vows of chastity and of obedience, the vow of poverty retains its intrinsic nature during the novitiate made in a new community. It remains what it was, solemn or simple, perpetual or temporal. A religious who in solemn vows transfers from an Order to a congregation, accordingly remains incapable, throughout his novitiate, of any act of ownership; conversely, one who transfers, from a congregation to an Order remains capable, throughout the novitiate, of acts of ownership permissible according to his vow.

The vow remains, and thus it retains its actual power to hold the religious to his earlier assumed obligation. So, for example, the religious cannot, under penalty of committing a sin against the vow of poverty, use things without the permission of the master of novices or of the superior.[70]

Goyeneche, whose doctrine is held also by Schaefer, states that the religious cannot be obliged to do more, in virtue of the vow, than was originally promised under the vow. Just as in the case with the vow of obedience, the extent of the obligations of the vow is limited by the rule and the constitutions of the releasing institute. Both authors furthermore maintain that the religious is forbidden to do anything against his vow, even though it would be permitted under the rule and the constitutions of the new institute.[71]

The present writer wishes respectfully to point out that the two illustrious authors just cited are not quite consistent in their treatment of the vows of obedience and of poverty when they indicate that the two cases are similar or parallel. When their statements are examined, it will be found that they do not regard them as

[70] Papi, *Religious in Church Law*, p. 16.

[71] Goyeneche, *art. cit.*, *CpR*, I (1921), 118; Schaefer, p. 932, n. 518. The opinion is summarized by Schaefer as follows: "Cum in citato canone dicatur: *Vota manent*, Superiores secundae Religionis praecipere non possunt, quae terminos voti in prima Religione emissi excedant, sed neque ea, quae ambitum Constitutionum in nova Religione egrediantur, iubere eis licet.

"Pari ratione, transiens nihil facere potest contra terminos voti paupertatis in priore Religione nuncupati, sed neque vi voti ad actus ultra huius ambitum obligatur."

parallel in fact. A limitation is placed on the extension of the vow of obedience which is not placed on the extension of the vow of poverty. It is maintained that the religious cannot be obliged, in virtue of the vow of obedience, to do anything which is beyond the limits of the rule and the constitutions of the new institute, even though it may have been within the limits of the vow in the releasing community. On the other hand, the religious, so they hold, is bound to observe the vow of poverty to the full extent to which it obliged him in the releasing community.[72]

The reason for this difference may perhaps be found in one of the arguments advanced for the limitation of the obligations arising from the vow of obedience. As was seen above, the reason given for the limitation on the extension of this vow is that the superior of the new community did not have the power to bind anyone beyond the limits prescribed in his own rule and constitutions. The limitation was, therefore, not so much a limitation on the extension of the vow, but rather on the power of the superiors of the new community. A second and more general reason was, however, given for the limitation. Precepts which went beyond the rule or the constitutions of the new institute were declared to be useless: the purpose of the novitiate is to train the aspirant for the new community, and it would be futile to compel him to do what is foreign to the nature and purpose of the community.

This argument can also be applied to the vow of poverty. The transferring religious, during his novitiate, is making an experiment of the life of the new institute. It seems quite fitting that the manner in which the vow of poverty is observed in that institute should constitute the norm for the observance of the vow of poverty by the religious who is making an experiment of the life of that community. As will be seen somewhat further on, the authors unanimously declare that the vows which are proper only to the releasing community are suspended in their binding force for the duration of the novitiate. The reason given is that these are particular obligations connected with membership in the releasing insti-

[72] Goyeneche, *loc. cit.;* Schaefer, *loc. cit.*

tute, and as such become suspended and inoperative according to the law as enacted in canon 633, § 1.[73]

It seems to be entirely in accord with the spirit of the law, with the end the legislator had in view in establishing the novitiate for a transferring religious, and also with the demand of canonical equity, that the obligations which arose from the vow of poverty in the releasing community, but which do not at the same time exist for members in the receiving community, are particular obligations which, in virtue of canon 633, § 1, became inoperative for the duration of the novitiate.

It is therefore maintained: (1) that the transferring religious during his novitiate in the new community is excused from observing in virtue of the vow of poverty whatever is not obligatory in the releasing community, and (2) that he is not obliged in virtue of the vow of poverty to observe what goes beyond the limits of the rule and the constitutions of the new community. It must always be borne in mind that his vow retains in full force the juridical limitations imposed by its nature, i. e., by the fact that is solemn or simple, perpetual or temporary.

Those who transfer from one society of the common life to another similar society or to a religious institute do not have public vows. If the transferring member should be bound by private vows of poverty, chastity and obedience, as proper to his society, then it seems that in virtue of canon 681 and canon 633, § 1, he is still obliged by these vows during the novitiate. There would have to be special instructions from the Holy See in the unusual event of a transfer from a society in which these vows obtain to one in which there are no such vows, or in the event of a transfer from a religious institute to a society of the common life. The canonists have not considered these questions. One may rightfully suppose that the vows will continue to oblige the person during the novitiate, but that at the same time there will be granted some modification in the extension of the vows of obedience and of poverty in relation to the constitutions and the nature of the new community. One may

[73] Augustine, III, 366; Berutti, III, 319; Cappello, *Summa Juris Canonici,* I, 202; Goyeneche, *art. cit.—CpR,* I (1920), 365; Coronata, III, p. 850, note 5.

similarly suppose that an oath or a promise of poverty, of chastity, and of obedience, if the time for which it was taken has not expired, will still continue to bind the transferring member during the novitiate, and that he will be bound to obey the superiors of the new community in virtue of his oath or promise of obedience.

II. Other Obligations

Canon 633, § 1, besides declaring that the vows of the transferring religious remain intact during his novitiate in the receiving institute, prescribes that during this period the particular obligations by which he was bound in the releasing institute remain suspended. At the same time it is evident that, in virtue of his status as a novice, he assumes the obligations which are imposed on other novices in the receiving community.

The Code does not define what is meant by the particular obligations referred to in canon 633, § 1. "Particular" is used in the Code as the contrary of "general,"[74] and refers here to obligations which derive, not from the general law, but from the rules, constitutions or special laws enacted for releasing the institute.[75] It seems reasonable to assume also that they include obligations which the religious has assumed toward the community in which he was professed (and toward no other) in virtue of his profession. Certain of these obligations will now be considered in detail.

Special Vows—Vows which are obligatory in the religious institute but which are other than the three substantial vows of the religious life, for example, special vows of abstinence, taken by the Minims of St. Francis of Paula, vows of hospitality, the vow to redeem captives, etc., remain suspended for the duration of the novitiate.[76]

[74] See, for example, the usage of the words particular and general in canons 12 to 14, which speak of the particular as contrasted with the general law.

[75] See, for example, the terms used by Schaefer: to explain this phrase: "Ex. gr. ieiunia particularia, vota specialia (propria illius religionis). . . ."—p. 933, note 45.

[76] Augustine, III, 366; Berutti, III, 319; Cappello I, 202; Goyeneche, *art. cit.—CpR,* I (1920), 365; Coronata, I, p. 850, note 5; Wernz-Vidal, III, *De Religiosis,* p. 454.

Wernz-Vidal state quite clearly that any particular obligations, even if they are derived from vows, cease to oblige during the novitiate of the transferring religious in the receiving community.[77] Though these particular vows are suspended during the novitiate, they remain in existence *radicaliter*.[78] They cease entirely only after profession in the new community.[79] If the religious does not complete the transfer by profession but returns to his former institute they will immediately revive.[80]

The Religious Habit of the Novices—The novitiate begins with the reception of the religious habit, unless some other manner is determined by the constitutions.[81] Furthermore, the habit which is prescribed for novices by the constitutions must be worn throughout the entire period of the novitiate, unless particular local circumstances call for some other arrangement.[82] In answer to a doubt submitted to the Sacred Congregation for Religious, there was issued a decree which stated that a religious who transferred to another institute in virtue of an apostolic indult was obliged to receive the habit of the novices of the receiving institute and to wear it throughout his novitiate in that community.[83]

77 ". . . alia iura et obligationes, quas in religione derelicta habuit, tametsi ex votis derivatas, manent suspensae."—*Loc. cit.*

78 "Vota particularia radicaliter quidem manent, sed suspenduntur tempore novitatus, e contrario vota communia manent ut antea"—Schaefer, p. 933.

79 See below, p. 183.

80 See below, p. 168.

81 Can. 553.

82 Can. 557.

83 "S. Congr. de Religiosis propositum fuit sequens dubium pro opportuna solutione:

"Religiosus, qui in quadam religione professus, obtento indulto Apostolico, ad aliam religionem transit, teneturne ad habitum novitiorum religionis *ad quam* suscipiendum et gestandum perdurante novitiatu in nova religione?"

Sacra autem Congregatio, re mature perpensa, respondendum censuit, prout respondet: *Affirmative*.

Datum Romae, ex Secretaria S. Congregationis de Religiosis, die 14 maii 1923.

The background of this decree is given by Vermeersch in *Periodica.* A sister in perpetual vows had obtained an indult to transfer to a diocesan institute in which, according to the constitutions and canon 553, the novitiate began with the reception of the habit. The local bishop had, however, forbidden her to wear the habit of the novices, on the ground that she belonged to the releasing community until the time of her new profession, and accordingly indicated that she was obliged to wear the habit of that community.

This was clearly an error. Cannon 633, § 1, in suspending all the particular obligations of the religious while in the novitiate, suspends also the obligation to wear the habit of the releasing institute. Furthermore, the bishop could not dispense from the obligation of canon 553. Therefore, since he forbade the sister to assume the habit of the novices, he effectually impeded her entrance into the novitiate. Finally, when the Holy See gives permission for a transfer, it virtually gives also every faculty which is needed to begin the novitiate and to continue it in the usual way.[84]

The Law of the Enclosure—The law of the enclosure is a general one, since it binds all religious communities in virtue of canons 597 to 607 in the Code, and is extended even to societies of the common life, unless the constitutions have a contrary provision, canon 679, § 1. It is not an obligation derived directly from the vows, but from the law of the Church. The effect which a transfer will have on the obligation to observe the enclosure is not discussed by the authors who have been consulted by the writer.

Though the law is general, the law distinguishes between the enclosure in communities of men and those of women, between the enclosure of those in institutes of solemn and those of simple vows. Furthermore, there is room for differences in the regulations concerning the enclosure as found in the rule and constitutions of different communities.

It is the view of the present writer that insofar as the obligations of the enclosure found in the releasing institute are derived from the rule and constitutions they are particular obligations which are

C. Card Laurenti, *Praefectus*—Maurus M. Serafini Ab. O.S.B., *Secretarius. AAS,* XV (1923), 289; *Periodica,* XII (1923), (16), (17).

[84] *Periodica,* XII (1923), (67).

suspended by admission to the novitiate of the receiving community by the operation of canon 633, § 1.

If a nun transfers from a monastery in which the papal cloister must be observed to a congregation which is subject only to the episcopal cloister, what is her obligation to observe the cloister? Is she subject as a *Monialis* to the papal cloister, or as a *novice* to the episcopal cloister after the manner of the other novices. It seems that since she has already left the papal cloister in virtue of the indult to transfer, and since the enclosure in which she is living is episcopal only, she is bound by no stronger obligations than those of the episcopal cloister. As Vermeersch has remarked in another connection.[85] when the Holy See gives permission for a transfer, it virtually gives also every faculty which is needed to continue the novitiate in the usual way.

If a nun transfers from one monastery subject to the papal enclosure to another, she would be bound by the papal enclosure in the receiving community, since novices in monasteries of nuns with solemn vows are subject to the papal enclosure.[86] She would not, however, be subject to the penalty of an excommunication simply reserved to the Holy See prescribed by canon 2342, 3°, if she illegitimately leaves the cloister. She has left the enclosure of her own community legitimately, and is bound only as a novice to the enclosure in the receiving community. Novices in communities which have the papal enclosure do not incur the penalty enacted in canon 2342, 3°, if they illegitimately leave the enclosure.[87] Because canon 2342, 3°, enacts a penalty, it must be strictly interpreted.[88] It is therefore the opinon of this writer that the excommunication is certainly not incurred by the nun who violates the papal enclosure by illegitimately leaving the novitiate of the receiving community.

Miscellaneous Obligations—In the act of transferring to another religious institute a religious remains bound by the general obligations expressed in canon 592, which applies to religious the general

[85] See above, p. 157.

[86] See Instruction on the Enclosure of Nuns with solemn vows—*AAS*, XVI (1924), 96, n. III, 1 (e).

[87] Schaefer, p. 725.

[88] Can. 19.

obligations of clerics expressed in canons 124 to 142, unless they evidently are inapplicable because of the context or from the nature of the obligations. He remains bound also by the obligation to tend to perfection as expressed in canon 593. These obligations are of a general, not of a particular character. They are obligations not only of the individual subject of this or of that religious community, but of any member whatsoever in the religious state.

The obligation, however, to obey the rules and the constitutions of the releasing institute is suspended by canon 633, § 1. This obligation is truly a particular one, insofar as these rules and constitutions determine obligations which are not the common to all in the religious state. The novice religious is obliged to conform himself to the rules and constitutions of the receiving institute, insofar as these apply to the novices of the community.

A transfer to a society of the common life from another community will be subject to the same rules. During the novitiate the particular obligations (i.e., all the obligations which derived from a source other than that of the religious vows in general and which at the same time do not have any binding force in the new community) will be suspended for the duration of the novitiate.

III. Rights

Canon 633, § 1, declares that the rights which the religious had in the releasing community remain suspended relative to their use during his novitiate in the new community. This means that the rights cannot be used, though basically they continue to exist, for they again became operative in case the religious returns to his own community without having made a new profession.[89]

Canon 633, § 1, states that the rights and particular obligations of the religious are suspended relative to their use in the novitiate. In the authorized English translation of this canon the word *particular* modifies only the word *obligations,* and not also the word *rights.* It seems, therefore, that the religious loses the use of *all* the rights which were his as a member of the releasing community. In return, in virtue of canon 567, § 1, which applies to all novices

[89] Cf. Blat, II, 620.

in general, he enjoys all the privileges and spiritual favors granted to the institute to which he is transferring. Should he die during the course of the novitiate, he is entitled to the same suffrages as the professed.[90]

Examples of suspended rights are spiritual privileges proper to the releasing community, such as the privilege of exemption, the right to take part in elections and in chapters, the right to send letters, and so on.[91]

The religious cannot take part in elections in the releasing community even if he has the permission of the superior of his new community. He need not, therefore, be summoned to them.[92] If he did take part in an election, there is question of the validity of the election. Canon 167, § 1, 5°, declares that those who lack an active voice whether because of the legitimate sentence of a judge or by reason of the common or particular law cannot cast a vote.[93] The second paragraph of the same canon states that if any of the preceding should be admitted, his vote is null, but the election is valid, unless it is certain that without his ballot the person elected would not have had a requisite number of votes. . . .[94] Hofmeister declares that he does not dare to settle the question of the validity of the vote of a transferring religious or of the election in which the latter takes part. The answer hinges on the force of the words, *suspensa manent*.[95] It is certain, at least, that these words do not contain as express a declaration of the absence of the right to cast a ballot as is found, for example, in canon 639, with regard to a religious who has received an indult of exclaustration: ". . . during the time of the

[90] Berutti, III, 319.

[91] Cf. Hofmeister, *art. cit., AKKR,* CVIII (1928), 453; Oesterle, I, 359; Vermeersch-Creusen, *Epitome,* I, p. 585, n. 592 (734); Coronata, I, p. 850, footnote 2.

[92] Hofmeister, *loc. cit.*

[93] Can. 167, § 1. "Nequeunt suffragium ferre: . . . 5°. Carentes voce activa sive ob legitimam iudicis sententiam sive ex iure communi aut particulari."

[94] "Can. 167, § 2. Si quis ex praedictis admittatur, eius suffragium est nullum, sed electio valet, nisi constet, eo dempto, electum non retulisse requisitum suffragiorum numerum. . . ."

[95] Hofmeister, *loc. cit.*

indult he lacks an active and a passive voice. . . ." [96] Furthermore, the suspension of a right does not necessarily imply that the right itself has been lost. It may have only the implication of a prohibition against the use of the right. The right itself remains *radicaliter.* Coronata says this in other words: "Although the rights which the transferring religious possessed in the releasing institute cannot as yet be said to have been lost, they cannot be exercised during the novitiate." [97] Because of these considerations, it seems that one can hold that the force of the words, *suspensa manent,* is at least doubtful. Furthermore, invalidating or restricting laws are to be classed among those which limit the free exercise of rights, [98] and one must follow a strict interpretation in view of the norms of canon 19.[99] Until there shall be an authentic interpretation of the law, the present writer believes that the vote would be valid, though illicit, when cast under the circumstances here considered.

With regard to the right of eligibility for office, Vermeersch in *Periodica* expressed the opinion that the election by the releasing community of a professed member already in the novitiate of another community would be valid. He based his view on the fact the religious was still a professed member of the releasing community.[100] He believed, therefore, that the religious had the option of accepting the election and returning to his community, or of refusing it. Other authors, however, prefer the view that since the rights of the religious in the releasing community have been suspended and cannot be exercised, he cannot accept the election.[101] This latter view is undoubtedly the better one. As was pointed out

[96] "Can. 639. . . . perdurante tempore indulti caret voce activa et passive. . . ."

[97] "Igitur iura quae habebat in religione *a qua* licet adhuc amissa dici nequeant, novitius transiens durante novitiatu exercere non potest"—Coronata, I, p. 850, footnote 2.

[98] Van Hove, *De Legibus Ecclesiasticis,* p. 313; Vermeersch-Creusen, *Epitome,* I, p. 118, n. 126 (98).

[99] "Can. 19. Leges quae poenam statuunt, aut liberum iurium exercitium coarctant, aut exceptionem a lege continent, strictae subsunt interpretationi."

[100] *Periodica,* XI (1923), (154).

[101] Oesterle, I, 359; Goyeneche, *De Religiosis* (Romae, 1938), p. 187, note 14; Schaefer, p. 934.

above, the Code suspends, without distinction, the rights of the religious in the releasing community, and if the law does not distinguish, the commentators ought not to distinguish either. But because of the uncertain force of the words *suspensa manent,* it is felt that one can maintain the validity of such an election if it took place.

The rights enjoyed by a member of a society of the common life would be similarly affected in the case of a transfer. His rights as possessed in the releasing society would be suspended, and he would enjoy in turn the rights accorded to other novices in the receiving society or religious institute.[102]

Article 4. The Length and the Termination of the Novitiate.

The novitiate which is required by the common law of the Code must last one complete and uninterrupted year. This is a requirement for the validity of the novitiate, and consequently for the validity of the profession and of the transfer.[103] If the constitutions of the receiving institute require a second year in the novitiate, this is obligatory for the transferring religious as well as for other aspirants.[104] It is not required for the validity of the subsequent profession, however, unless the constitutions expressly say so.[105]

The novitiate can be prolonged beyond the usual time prescribed by the Code and the constitutions. Canon 634 provides as follows:

> "Sollemniter professus aut professus a votis simplicibus perpetuis, si transierit ad aliam religionem cum votis sollemnibus vel simplicibus perpetuis, post novitiatum, praetermissa professione temporaria, de qua in can. 574, vel admittatur ad professionem sollemnem aut simplicem perpe-

[102] Cf. can. 681.

[103] "Can. 555, § 1. Praeter alia quae in can. 542 ad novitiatus validitatem enumerantur, novitiatus ut valeat, peragi debet: . . . 2° Per annum integrum et continuum. . . ."

[104] Leitner, *Das Ordensrecht,* p. 475; Berutti, III, 320.

[105] Can. 555, § 2.

> tuam vel ad pristinam redeat religionem; ius tamen est Superiori eum probandi diutius, sed non ultra annum ab expleto novitatu."

As is evident from the initial words of this canon, it is concerned only with religious who have made their final and perpetual profession of vows. When these religious transfer to another religious institute in which solemn or simple perpetual vows are taken, the superior has the right to prolong the period of probation, but not beyond one year after the completion of the novitiate. The canon does not provide for a transferring religious who is only in temporary vows, or for one who is transferring to an institute in which only temporary vows can be taken. To such a religious, therefore, one must apply canon 571, § 2, which contains the provision for the prorogation of the time of probation for novices in general:

> "Exacto novitatu, si iudicetur idoneus, novitius ad professionem admittatur, secus dimittatur; si dubium supersit sitne idoneus, potest a Superioribus maioribus probationis tempus, non tamen ultra sex menses, prorogari."

In such a case, therefore, a prorogation of no more than six months is permissible, and then only if their is a doubt concerning the requisite suitability and fitness for the life of the community.[106]

The common law does not furnish any definite norms for the computation of the period involved in a prorogation of the novitiate, for the time of the noviceship is essentially completed at the time when the prorogation begins. Consequently the validity of the subsequent profession does not depend upon the exact fulfillment of the time-period specified in the prorogation.[107] Berutti admits that the novice may be admitted to profession at any time during the extended period of probation, if all doubt concerning the candidate's fitness is dispelled.[108]

[106] Berutti, III, 320.

[107] Coronata, I, 748; Balzer, *The Computation of Time in a Canonical Novitiate*, The Catholic University of America Canon Law Studies, n. 212 (Washington, D. C.: The Catholic University of America Press, 1945), p. 193.

[108] *Institutiones Iuris Canonici*, III, 192.

Another case in which the length of the novitiate may be prolonged receives consideration in canon 556, § 2.

> "Can. 556, § 2. Si novitius ultra quindecim, sed non ultra triginta dies etiam non continuous, de Superiorum licentia vel vi coactus extra domus septa permanserit sub Superioris obedientia, ad validitatem novitiatus necesse et satis est dies hoc modo transactos supplere; si non ultra quindecim dies, supplementum potest a Superioribus praescribi, sed non est ad validitatem necessarium."

If with the permission of the superiors or when constrained by force, a novice has passed more than fifteen but not more than thirty days even interruptedly outside the precincts of the novitiate house but under the obedience of the superior, it is indeed necessary but it also suffices for the validity of the novitiate that he supply the number of days so passed outside; if the entire period did not exceed fifteen days, then the superiors may prescribe that this period be supplemented, but this is not required for validity.[109]

It is a solidly probable opinion which may be followed in practice that the days of absence from the novitiate are to be counted from midnight to midnight, in accordance with the norm of reckoning indicated in canon 32, § 1. Parts of days are not counted.[110] An act of transfer to another novitiate does not break the current novitiate, although the days spent in traveling from the one novitiate to the other must be counted as days of absence even when their combined duration does not exceed the limitation set in canon 556, § 1.[111] But the novitiate can be broken before it reaches its full term if an interruption intervenes. Canon 556, § 1, deals with the breaking of the canonical year of the novitiate. It reads as follows:

[109] Can. 556, § 2.

[110] Bouscaren-Ellis, *Canon Law* (Milwaukee: Bruce, 1946), p. 266.

[111] Pontificia Commissia Interpretationis, 13 jul. 1930—*AAS*, XXII (1930), 365.

> Novitiatus interrumpitur, ita ut denuo incipiendus ac perficiendus sit, si novitius, a Superiore dimissus, e domo exierit, aut domum sine illius licentia non reversurus deseruerit, aut extra domum, etsi reversurus, ultra triginta dies sive continuos sive non continuos permanserit quacunque ex causa, etiam de Superiorum licentia."

This canon states that the novitiate is broken (and must be begun over again): (1) if the novice leaves the novitiate house after being dismissed by the superior; (2) if he leaves of his own accord without the permission of the superior, and with the intention of not returning; and (3) if he has actually been absent from the novitiate house for a period of more than thirty days, whether continuous or interrupted, for any reason whatsoever, even with the permission of the superiors, and even if throughout that time the novice had the intention of returning.

There are then three ways in which the novitiate can be broken in consequence of an interruption: (1) dismissal; (2) abandonment of the novitiate house; and (3) absence from the novitiate for over thirty days.[112]

(1) *Dismissal.* The novitiate is broken when the novice is dismissed by the legitimate superior and departs from the house of the novitiate. Both of these conditions must be present. The moment they are verified the noviceship is broken. If the novice has been dismissed and has left the enclosure of the novices, but has not yet departed from the *house* of the novitiate, then the noviceship is not yet broken.[113] With regard to the dismissal of the novice, canon 571, § 1, indicates that he can be dismissed by the superiors or by the chapter, according as the constitutions specify, whenever a just cause exists. By analogy with canon 543, according to which it is the major superior in connection with the vote of the council or of the chapter who is authorized to admit a candidate to the

[112] For a more detailed analysis of this canon, see Balzer, *The Computation of Time in the Canonical Novitiate*, pp. 150-181.

[113] Balzer, *op. cit.*, pp. 155-156.

novitiate or to first profession, the superior in this instance is the major superior.[114]

(2) *Abandonment of the novitiate house.* The novitiate is also broken if the novice abandons the novitiate house with the intention of not returning. The moment these conditions are fulfilled the novitiate is broken. The intention must of course be manifest in the external forum, either through an express declaration or from other external signs.[115]

(3) *Absence from the novitiate for over thirty days.* The final instance of a definitive breaking of the novitiate occurs when the novice is absent from the novitiate house for over thirty days. If a novice has left the house, even with the intention of returning, but has remained away over thirty days for any reason whatsoever, even with the superior's permission, and even though the time was not a period of continuous duration, the novitiate year is broken.[116]

There is nothing in the common law which deals with the breaking or with the interruption of the added year of the novitiate which some constitutions require, or of the period of prorogation which receives mention in canons 634 and 571, § 2. As Balzer points out, "both the common law and the authors definitely avoid any specific enumeration of detailed norms as governing the integrity and continuity of the second year of noviceship. This silence is understandable in consideration of the fact that such regulations for the constitutional novitiate lie wholly within the province of the constitutions themselves to determine." He seems to indicate that prolonged absences from the house where the novice is stationed should be avoided, that they can be permitted only for just and grave reasons, but that they would not break the novitiate.[117]

One can say, however, that at any time during the added year of the novitiate or during the period of prorogation the novice is free to depart from the institute, just as the institute is also free to dismiss him.[118]

[114] Balzer, *op. cit.*, p. 156.
[115] Cf. Balzer, *op. cit.*, pp. 158, 159.
[116] Balzer, *op. cit.*, pp. 159-160.
[117] *Op. cit.*, p. 188.
[118] Cf. can. 571, § 3.

Nothing is stated in the Code concerning the necessity of a novitiate in societies of the common life. The specification of that matter is left to their own constitutions. The length of the probationary period, therefore, is to be judged from that which is prescribed by the constitutions of each society. It will be the same as that of other aspirants, unless there is an explicit provision to the contrary in the constitutions themselves.

ARTICLE 5. THE OBLIGATION TO RETURN TO THE RELEASING INSTITUTE

> **"Can. 633, § 2. Si in religione ad quam transiit, professionem non edat, ad pristinam religionem redire debet, nisi interim votorum tempus expiraverit."**

Canon 633, § 2, provides that, if the religious who is transferring to another religious institute does not make his profession in the new community, he must return to the former institute, unless the time of his vows has run out in the meantime. If, therefore, the novitiate is terminated in any of the ways indicated in article 4, it seems that immediately there arises the obligation to return to the releasing community. This obligation will, with reference to the religious who is still bound by his vows, arise in the following instances:

1. When the novice leaves the community or is dismissed from it at the end of the canonical or of the second year of the novitiate.

2. When the novice leaves the community or is dismissed from it in the course of the period of prorogation of the novitiate or at the end of it.

3. When, in the course of the canonical year of the novitiate, the novitiate has been broken in any of the ways mentioned in canon 556, § 1, i.e., by dismissal, by abandonment of the novitiate house, or by an absence of over thirty days under the circumstances described by this canon.

It is hardly necessary to point out that this obligation arises immediately from the very nature of the case, and that the religious has no right to delay in returning to his former community. Since his rights and particular obligations in that community have been suspended by canon 633, § 1, only for the duration of the novitiate, it is evident that at the end of the novitiate these obligations will immediately revive. Only a termination of the novitiate by profession in the new community will impede this revival of former rights and particular obligations.

A question may be raised whether *the attempt to transfer* is necessarily terminated by the third interruption contemplated in canon 556, § 1, namely, by an absence of over thirty days, when this absence is due to a just reason, is made with the superior's permission, and with the intention to return to the novitiate. An example of this would be an absence of over thirty days when occasioned by illness on the part of the novice. It seems to the present writer that in this case one can presume that the permission to transfer has not ceased, and that it will be possible to begin the novitiate over again without the securing of a new indult. There should, however, be no delay in beginning the new year of the canonical novitiate. This interpretation supposes that the Holy See does not intend to oblige the parties to seek a new indult when the use of the original permission has become temporarily frustrated against the will of the parties involved.

None of the authors who have been consulted by this writer has touched on the question of the cessation of the indult to transfer when upon the termination of the novitiate no profession is made in the new community. It seems that two views are possible. The first is that the indult will cease with the termination of the novitiate, with the possible exception of an interruption due to an involuntary absence of over thirty days from the novitiate. A new indult will be required if the religious wishes to make another attempt to transfer to the same (or to another) community.

The reasons for this view are as follows: 1. Canon 633, § 2, commands a return to the releasing community if the novitiate is not terminated by profession in the new community. 2. The indult must be strictly interpreted, since it is opposed to the acquired right which the original institute has to the services of the religious.[118a]

[118a] See canon 50.

3. The indult which grants the permission to *transfer* seems to imply the permission to *begin a transfer,* that is, by entrance into the novitiate of the new community. The indult, therefore, has achieved its purpose once the novitiate has been duly begun. This is confirmed by the wording of canon 633, § 2, which declares: "If he does not make profession in the institute to which he *has transferred,* he must return to the former institute" ("Si in religione ad quam *transiit,* professionem non edat, ad pristinam religionem redire debet"). The verb *transfer* is here found in the perfect tense, and therefore implies that the indult which has been granted for the *transfer* has achieved its end; it has been used, and cannot be used again. 4. It would be against the requirements of good order if an indult to transfer to another religious community should be interpreted as a permission to make an indefinite number of attempts to transfer, with an indefinite number of transfers back and forth between the one and the other community.

It is not impossible, however, that some may prefer another opinion that an indult to transfer means an indult to *transfer* in its ordinary, that is, in its complete and perfect sense, and that therefore the indult does not cease until the transfer is completed by profession in the new community. It may also be argued that in case of a doubt, if there are in the indult no explicit clauses which limit to a single undertaking the attempt to transfer, the milder view could be used, in view of the legal maxim, that favorable matters are to be interpreted liberally—*favorabilia sunt amplificanda.*

The stricter view need not necessarily become obligatory, by reason of canon 50, because the community cannot be said to have an acquired right to the person of the religious, at least if the transfer is to a more rigorous community.[119] It has, in fact, been asserted that there is a natural right to transfer to a more rigorous community which no human power can take away.[120]

While the religious who is still bound by his vows is obliged to return to the former community, that community is in turn bound to receive him. It is certain that the releasing community is obliged

[119] See above, p. 118.

[120] See above, p. 121, note 144.

to readmit the returning religious, if he is still under vows.[121] This rule obtains for the simple reason that, as soon as his severance from the novitiate of the receiving community is complete, his rights and particular obligations in the releasing community revive. This is clear from canon 633, § 1, which states that the rights and particular obligations which the religious had in the former institute are suspended during the novitiate.[122] The restricting influence exercised by the status of the religious as a novice in another institute has now been removed, and he is completely reinstated, with all his previous rights and duties, as a member of the releasing institute.

The attempted transfer does not, after the return of the religious, cause any loss of rights in the former community. Thus his precedence in that community, and his other rights which are determined from the time of profession, are not lost. The time spent in the novitiate is to be computed as time spent in the institute with regard to all of the juridical effects which flow from it. An example is had in the time which a religious must have spent in a religious institute before he can be elected as a major superior, as determined by canon 504. The reason is that he continued to be a professed religious throughout the time of the novitiate.[123]

If by privilege a particular institute should have a contrary practice, there is still in force.[124] If, however, there is in the rule and constitutions a provision which prevents his reacceptance by the releasing community, this has been abrogated by the Code.[125]

There is a dispute about the return of a religious whose vows expired during the novitiate. It is certain that such a religious need not, and in fact cannot, renew his temporal profession during the novitiate.[126] He cannot renew his vows for the releasing community, since his rights and particular obligations in that community have been suspended for the duration of the novitiate.[127]

[121] Beste, p. 428; Bastien, p. 434.

[122] Goyeneche, *art. cit.—CpR,* II (1921), 148, note 20.

[123] Goyeneche, *loc. cit.*

[124] Can. 4; Goyeneche, *loc. cit.*

[125] Goyeneche, *loc. cit.*; cf. can. 489.

[126] Cf. Wernz-Vidal, III, p. 453, note 17.

[127] Can. 633, § 1.

Nor can he make temporary profession in the new community, since his novitiate is not yet complete. Furthermore, since the vows have expired, there is no doubt that he can freely return to the world, since the law gives him liberty to return to the world at will at the end of the period of temporal profession.[128] The question is, *must* he return to the world if he does not subsequently make profession in the new community. A few authors have maintained that he must do so. They believe that in order to be received back into the releasing institute he needs an apostolic indult from the impediment of profession as established in canon 542, 1°, and that he must make a new novitiate.[129]

The reason advanced is that the wording of canon 542, 1°, is universal in scope: "they are invalidly admitted to the novitiate who are bound or have been bound by the bond of religious profession." The present law is drawn from the previous law, the decree *"Ecclesia Christi,"* [130] which was also universal in scope. It is maintained that once the vows have expired, every bond of right or of obligation with the previous community has been broken. Goyeneche appeals to several post-Code canonists who all maintain that the impediment of canon 542, 1°, applies to those who have left the community after the expiration of temporary vows, and prevents their return even to their own community without an apostolic indult.[131]

Some important canonists, however, do not believe that Goyeneche's opinion is acceptable.[132] They maintain that neither a new novitiate nor an apostolic dispensation is necessary for the return of the novice to the releasing community after his vows have expired in the novitiate. Beste argues that one who is in this situation has

[128] Can. 575, § 1; can. 637.

[129] Goyeneche, "Consultationes," *CpR,* III (1922), 8-10; Pejška, p. 183; Schaefer, p. 936, n. 524; Fanfani, p. 477 (with some hesitation, however); Gerster a Zeil, p. 134.

[130] S. C. de Religiosis, decr. 7 sept. 1909—*Fontes,* n. 4396.

[131] Goyeneche, *loc. cit.*; the authors to whom he appeals are Creusen, *Religieux et Religieuses* (ed. 2), p. 61; Führich, *De Religiosis,* p. 116; Vermeersch, *Epitome,* I, p. 235, n. 531; Blat, *De Personis* (ed. 2), p. 595.

[132] Wernz-Vidal, III, 453, note 17; Beste, p. 428; Coronata, I, 851, note 5; Berutti, III, 319-320.

neither used his liberty to return to the world, nor has he definitely abandoned the releasing institute. Therefore, the ruling of canon 542, 1° does not apply to him.[133] Berutti, too, points out that he can be readmitted to profession by the releasing community without a dispensation or a new novitiate, on the ground that the juridic bond which united him to the releasing community has not as yet been fully severed.[134]

Coronata and Wernz-Vidal attempt to show that this case differs from that contemplated in canon 542, by saying that here it is a matter of readmission, not of the first admission of an aspirant.[135] But this point does not seem to be well taken, since the same authors concede elsewhere that those who were temporarily professed, and at the termination of that profession left their community, cannot be readmitted to that same institute without an apostolic dispensation.[136] It likewise cannot be urged that there is question of a return as ordered by the law, since the law orders the return only of those whose vows have not expired.[137]

Coronata sees an analogy between the present case and the one in which the vows expired while the religious was obliged to military service.[138] The Holy See provided that novices who were subject to military service should at the end of their novitiate make a temporary profession which would last only to the time of their induction in the service. During the time of the military service, so it was declared, the religious, although not bound by religious vows, continued to be a member of his religious society, under the authority of his superiors, who were to take care of him on his return after

[133] *Loc. cit.*

[134] *Loc. cit.*

[135] *Loc. cit.*

[136] Coronata, I, 711; Wernz-Vidal, III, 202.

[137] Wernz-Vidal seem to use this argument: ". . . non videtur concludenter probatum a Goyeneche . . . non posse illum recipere sine dispensatione, cum canon 542 agat de primo ingressu, et in casu nostro sit quaestio de regressu praecepto, cui subest qui nondum usus est sua libertate ad saeculum remigrandi." —III, p. 453, note 17. But can. 633, § 2, does not state this at all: "redire debet, nisi interim votorum tempus exspiraverit."

[138] Coronata, I, 851, note 5.

the manner ordered by the decree *"Inter reliquas"*.[139] He could, however, according to canon 637, freely leave the society by notifying his superiors with a statement made in writing or before witnesses. Similarly, the society could, for just and reasonable causes, declare him dismissed.[140] It must not be presumed, Coronata maintains, that the simple expiration of the vows was equivalent to a dismissal. When the vows have not been renewed by reason of forgetfulness or ignorance, for example, the renovation can be made without a dispensation from canon 542.

The present writer prefers the opinion that the religious can return to the previous community without an apostolic indult after his vows have expired, and that he need not renew the novitiate before admission to profession. This opinion can be safely followed in practice, since the invalidating law of canon 542, 1°, does not urge in a case of doubt. Indeed, it seems, as Beste points out, that in accordance with the norm of canon 637 for the dismissal of a religious at the expiration of his temporary vows, the releasing community should not refuse to readmit him in the absence of a just and a reasonable cause.[141]

This opinion does not apply to the case in which the religious has already been dismissed by the releasing community, or when he declared that he wished to abandon that community upon the expiration of his vows.[142] By analogy with the decree of the Sacred Congregation for Religious as cited by Coronata, it is urged that this declaration be made in writing.

With regard to the application of canon 633, § 2, to the transfer of members of a society of the common life to another society of the common life or to a religious institute, the obligation to return to the former society would be present if there is an obligation to persevere in that society in consequence of an existing private vow, oath, promise, or other similar bond. The obligation to return will be present only if there has not yet expired the period of time for

139 S. C. de Religiosis, decr. 1 ian. 1911, ad II—*Fontes,* n. 4408.

140 S. C. de Religiosis, 15 iul. 1919—*AAS,* IX (1919), 321-323.

141 *Introductio in Codicem,* p. 428.

142 Cf. Coronata, I, 851, note 5.

which the obligation of perseverance in the society was originally made binding.

Article 6. Admission to Profession

I. Perpetual Profession

Can. 634. Sollemniter professus aut professus a votis simplicibus perpetuis, si transierit ad aliam religionem cum votis sollemnibus vel simplicibus perpetuis, post novitiatum, praetermissa professione temporaria, de qua in can. 574, vel admittatur ad professionem sollemnem aut simplicem perpetuam vel ad pristinam redeat religionem; ius tamen est Superiori eum probandi diutius, sed non ultra annum ab expleto novitiatu.

Canon 634 provides that a religious with perpetual vows, whether solemn or simple, who has transferred to another institute having perpetual vows, whether solemn or simple, omits at the end of the novitiate the temporary profession prescribed in canon 574, and must either be admitted to the profession of perpetual vows, either solemn or simple as the case may be, in the new institute, or must return to the releasing institute. The superior, however, has the right to extend the time of probation, but not beyond one year after the completion of the novitiate.[143]

The history of this law is interesting. The Sacred Congregation of Bishops and the Regulars, on January 25, 1884, decided that a transferring religious in perpetual vows should make perpetual profession after the novitiate. This decision was contrary to the practice of the Orders, contrary to the views of eminent canonists, and contrary to previous decisions of the Roman Curia.[144] There were some

[143] The matter of this prorogation has already been considered above on pp. 163-164.

[144] *Theologisch-praktische Quartalschrift*, XXXVI (1883), 159; XXXVII (1884), 365; Hofmeister, "Der Übertritt in eine audere religiöse genassenschaft," *AKKR*, CVIII (1928), 456.

who, at the time at which the Code was being drafted, desired that temporary profession be retained at least for those who were transferring to an institute of solemn vows.[145] The legislator, however, did not yield to this desire, because he was opposed to having so great a part of the life of a religious devoted to probation, and because the religious, since they were already of mature age, were considered to be sufficiently disposed at the end of the novitiate.[146] One can suppose that the Holy See had in mind also the consequence of permitting temporal profession for those already in perpetual vows. For, if they made only temporary profession, they could voluntarily leave or be dismissed from the receiving institute before perpetual profession. This relative instability for those who had already been perpetually professed would have been undesirable.

The validity of the profession requires that the religious be admitted by the legitimate superior, according to the constitutions.[147] This right belongs to the major superiors in connection with the vote of the council or of the chapter, as directed by the particular constitutions of each institute.[148] Goyeneche, in 1921, maintained that this vote had to be of a definitive character, since the question of a transferring religious had evidently escaped the mind of the legislator when he prescribed in canon 575, § 2, that the vote of the council or of the chapter for the *first temporary profession* was of a definitive character, and that for the subsequent perpetual profession whether it was solemn or simple, was only consultative in character. He argued that the definitive vote was prescribed in canon 575 not by reason of the fact that the profession was *temporary,* for then it would have been prescribed for other temporary professions, but for the reason that it was the *first* profession in the institute. Therefore the vote of the chapter or of the council for the first profession of a transferring religious in the receiving institute should be of a definitive character, even though the profession was perpetual.[149]

145 Goyeneche, "De transitu ad aliam religionem," *CpR,* II (1921), 174.

146 Goyeneche, *loc. cit.*

147 Can. 572, § 1, n. 2.

148 Can. 543.

149 Goyeneche, *art. cit., CpR,* II (1921), 174-175; cf. also *art. cit., CpR,* I (1920), p. 217, note 8.

This opinion was confirmed one year later by the Commission for the Interpretation of the Code.[150]

It seems proper that the releasing community should be notified once profession has been made. Furthermore, if a religious in simple vows makes his profession of solemn vows in the receiving community, the pastor of baptism should be notified, so that the proper annotation may be made in the baptismal register.[151]

Canon 681 applies the ruling of canon 634 to members of societies of the common life who transfer to another society or to a religious institute, inasmuch as it can be applied fittingly and harmoniously (*congrua congruis referendo*). It accordingly seems that if a member who is bound to persevere in his society for life by an oath, a promise, or a private vow as prescribed by the constitutions of the society, transfers to another society in which there is also a perpetual obligation to persevere, he will forego the assuming of a temporary obligation, but will become incorporated in such a way that he assumes the obligation to persevere for life in the new society.

It seems solidly probable that a member of a society who was thus bound to perpetual fidelity when he received an apostolic indult for his transfer will not be obliged to make a temporary profession of vows in transferring to a congregation or an Order in which perpetual vows are taken. He could be admitted immediately to a solemn profession in an Order, or to a simple perpetual profession in a religious congregation. Vermeersch came to that conclusion. His reason was that a perpetual promise must be regarded as the equivalent of perpetual vows with respect to the case of transfer. He drew a confirmatory argument, by analogy, from a decision of the Commission for the interpretation of the Code, which held that, with regard to the dismissal of members of societies of the common life, those whose bond with the society was temporal came under the canons dealing with the dismissal of religious in temporary vows,

[150] 14 iul. 1922: "Utrum suffragium Capituli in admittendo religioso, de quo in can. 634, ad professionem sollemnem aut simplicem perpetuam, habeat vim deliberativam an tantum consultivam. Resp.: *Affirmative* ad primam partem, *negative* ad secundam."—*AAS*, XVI (1922), 528; *Periodica*, XI (1922), 166 *Jus Pontificium*, II (1922), 123.

[151] Can. 576, § 2; can. 470, § 2.

while those whose bond with their society was perpetual came under the canons dealing with the dismissal of religious in perpetual vows.[152] He pointed also to the fact that, if such a person were permitted to take only temporary vows, then there would be awarded to him the liberty to return to an entirely secular life, when in fact he had renounced it in making a promise of perpetual fidelity in the first community.[153]

II. Temporary Profession

The canons which deal explicitly with transfer state nothing concerning the kind of profession that is to be made by religious who have made profession simply of temporary vows when they transfer to another religious institute. Therefore one must look to the general prescription regarding all novices for their first profession in a religious institute. That prescription is found in canon 574:

> § 1. In quolibet Ordine tam virorum quam mulierum et in qualibet Congregatione quae vota perpetua habeat, novitius post expletum novitiatum, in ipsa novitiatus domo debet votis perpetuis, sive sollemnibus sive simplicibus, praemittere, salvo praescripto can. 634, votorum simplicium professionem ad triennium valituram, vel ad longius tempus, si aetas ad perpetuam professionem requisita longius distet, nisi constitutiones exigant annuales professiones.
>
> § 2. Hoc tempus legitimus Superior potest, renovata a religioso temporaria professione, prorogare, non tamen ultra aliud triennium.

The canon provides that in every order of men or of women and in every congregation which has perpetual vows, the novice must, after finishing his novitiate, and before making profession of perpetual vows, whether these be solemn or simple, make profes-

152 Pontificia Commisso Interpretationis, 1 mart. 1921—*AAS*, XIII (1921), 177.

153 Vermeersch, "De Transeunte ad aliam religionem," *Periodica*, XIX (1930), pp. 164, 165.

sion of simple vows, without prejudice, however, to the prescript of canon 634. These simple vows must be taken for a period of three years, or even longer if the age required for perpetual profession will not be reached at the end of the three-year period, unless the constitutions prescribe annual professions. The second section of the canon allows a prorogation of this time by the legitimate superior, after the temporal profession has been renewed, but not for more than three years.

The right to admit a transferring religious in temporary vows to this first temporal profession in the new institute belongs, according to canons 545 and 575, § 2, to the major superior in connection with the vote of the council or of the chapter as the constitutions direct. This vote is of a definitive character.[154] The vote for the subsequent perpetual profession is merely consultative in character.[155]

With regard to the period of time for which these vows should be taken, some authors state simply that the religious must take temporary vows, or that the rule of canon 574, § 2, applies to this type of profession.[156] Others, however, who become more explicit, disagree concerning the length of the time for the new profession. Some understand canon 634 to mean that the religious must make a temporary profession for only such a period as will be necessary to complete the period for which temporary vows were taken in the releasing institute.[157] All the authors cited apply this to the completion of the three-year period, and Berutti, quite logically, extends it to the case wherein the period is longer than three years, since the religious would not have reached the age of twenty-one years as required for perpetual profession at the end of the three-years. Vidal simply indicated his preference for this interpretation

154 Berutti, III, 320; cf. also Hofmeister, "Der Übertritt in eine andere religiöse Genossenschaft," *AKKR,* CVIII (1928), 455.

155 Cf. can. 575, § 2; Vermeersch, "Annotationes, VII. De professione religiosi transeuntis," *Periodica,* XI (1922), 169.

156 Beste, p. 429; Pejška, p. 183; Prümmer, I, 334; Sipos, p. 390.

157 Wernz-Vidal, III, n. 420, note 18; Berutti, III, 320; Prikryl, Übertritt in eine andere Ordensgenossenschaft," *Theologisch-praktische Quartalschrft,* XCII (1939), 123-126, esp. p. 125.

as being in better harmony with the principles of law. Other authors, to the contrary, maintain that the first temporal profession in the receiving institute should continue for a full three years.[158]

Neither group supports its respective opinion with detailed argument. It seems to the present writer that the view which requires the new temporary profession to continue for a full period of three years is the better one. Since canon 634 makes no provision for the first profession of a transferring religious with temporary vows in the new institute, one must look to the explicit provision of canon 574, §§ 1 and 2, which deals with the first profession of all novices. The legislator could have distinguished, had he wished, so as to make a different provision for a transferring religious in temporary vows. That he was mindful of the transferring religious is shown by the reference to canon 634 in canon 574, § 1. He did not, however, make any such distinction, but simply provided that in all orders and congregations of perpetual vows the perpetual profession was to be preceded by a temporary profession of vows, which were to be taken for a period of three years. This period begins after the novitiate is completed.[159] It seems, therefore, that the new temporary profession must be for three more years, first, because it must be assumed that the legislator had the transferring religious in mind when he wrote the canon, and meant to bind all not specifically excepted, and second, because he clearly demands three years in temporary vows *after* the completion of the novitiate. The vows should be taken for a longer period if the religious will not have reached the legitimate age for perpetual profession before the end of the three-year period, unless the constitutions demand annual professions.[160]

This cannot, however, be said to be entirely certain. In the case

[158] Cf. Schaefer, p. 937, n. 527; Gerster a Zeil, p. 574; Hofmeister, *art. cit., AKKR,* CVIII (1928), 455; Coronata, I, 851. Hofmeister simply remarks that this should ordinarily be the rule.

[159] ". . . novitius post expletum novitiatum, in ipsa novitiatus domo debet votis perpetuis, sive sollemnibus sive smplicibus, praemittere, salve praescripto can. 634, votorum simplicium professionem ad triennium valituram. . . ."— can. 574, § 1.

[160] Cf. can. 574, § 2.

of transferring religious, the novitiate referred to in canon 574, § 1, could mean the first novitiate of the religious, namely, that in the releasing institute. If the transferring religious has completed three years in temporary vows, it is possible that he fulfills the requirements of 574, § 1, and can be admitted to perpetual profession in the receiving community. Both views, therefore, seem to be probable and safe in practice.

If the temporary vows should expire in the course of the novitiate in the receiving community, the religious cannot be admitted to profession, either temporary or professional, before the end of the novitiate.[161] At the end of the novitiate, he may be admitted to profession. Should this profession be temporary or perpetual? The authors consulted by the writer have not explicitly adverted to this question. Had they done so, the proponents of the view that a religious needs only three years in temporary vows before his final profession even if this should be in another community than that in which he made his novitiate should conclude that he could be admitted to perpetual profession. Those who hold that there should be a new temporary profession of three years after the novitiate in the new community would extend this rule to the case of a religious whose vows expired in the course of the novitiate. The writer believes the latter opinion is the better one. First, canon 634, which exempts religious in perpetual vows from making temporary profession in the new community, seems to be an exception from the general rule of canon 574, § 1, and should therefore be strictly interpreted. This means that religious whose temporary vows have expired are not eligible for the exception, and must be admitted to another temporary profession. Second, there may often be some suspicion of instability of intention in a religious who seeks a transfer. As a matter of prudence, it would seem better to prolong the period during which he would be bound by only temporary vows rather than to shorten it.

Canon 681 does not refer to canon 574, and consequently the Code contains no rule for the type of affiliation, temporary or perpetual, which must be contracted by a member of a society of com-

[161] See above, pp. 170-171.

mon life who transfers to another such society when he has no bond obliging him to persevere in the releasing society or has only a temporary bond. In such a case, one must examine the constitutions. If the receiving society obliges aspirants to assume an obligation of perseverance for but a limited time before they assume the obligation of perpetual perseverance, then it appears that a transferring member would be included in that general provision and would be obliged to assume that temporary obligation. If such a member transferred to a congregation or to an Order in which perpetual vows are taken, he would be obliged to make a temporary profession in another religious institute.

CHAPTER V

THE EFFECTS OF TRANSFER

Article 1. The Rights and the Obligations of the Transferred Religious

Can. 635. Transeuntes ad aliud monasterium eiusdem religionis a die transitus, ad aliam vero religionem ab edita nova professione:

1°. Amittunt omnia iura et obligationes prioris religionis vel monasterii et alterius iura et officia suscipiunt . . .

Canon 635, 1°, declares that those who transfer to another monastery of the same institute will from the day of their transfer, but that those who transfer to another institute will from the day of their new profession, lose all the rights and obligations of the former institute or monastery, and assume the rights and duties of their new institute or monastery. This canon plainly indicates how completely the transferring religious is separated from the releasing community. All rights which he enjoyed in the releasing community, whether the rights were of an active or of a passive character, are lost. The original contract, in virtue of which there were mutual rights and obligations between the religious and his community, becomes entirely abrogated. If the transfer is made to another religious institute, a new profession of vows binds the religious to observe the three substantial vows of the religious life in the manner in which they are obligatory in the new community. The effects of this act are not retroactive. They begin with the very day of transfer when the latter is made to another independent monastery, of the same religious institute, but only from the day of profession in the case of a transfer made to another religious institute.[1]

[1] Goyeneche, *art. cit.*, *CpR*, II (1921), 176.

The religious, first, loses all the rights which accrued to him from the former institute or monastery. This is a universal rule, but the authors point out that certain personal prerogatives which the religious may have obtained while in the releasing institute are not lost in the transfer. Examples are the doctorate, and also the degrees of lector and master, unless they signify something proper to a particular institute.[2] This was also the teaching of the authors before the Code.[3]

The religious is also released from all the obligations which were his in the releasing institute. This includes the vows which as special vows taken in that particular institute do not form part of the three substantial vows of the religious life. Examples of such norms are the vow to redeem captives, or the vow of hospitality.[4] This was true also before the Code.[5]

There was, however, before the Code, a single exception to this rule. It was the so-called "vow of humility," a vow taken by religious of certain institutes not to accept any dignity, prelacy, or position of authority outside of their own religious institute. This vow is taken for example, by the Jesuits, the Barnabites, and by the Discalced Augustinians.[6] By reason of the Constitution *"Honorum dignitatumque"* of Pope Urban VIII (1623-1644), this vow continued to oblige even after the transfer to another religious institute.[7] This constitution must now be considered as abrogated. The reason is the universal character of canon 635, 1°, which declares that all the obligations of the former community cease to bind. This is confirmed by the provision of canon 6, 6°, which declares that those disciplinary laws which were in force until the Code but which are

[2] Cf. Goyeneche, *loc. cit.;* Beste, p. 429; Coronata, I, 852. For the effect of the novitiate on these rights see above, pp. 159-162.

[3] Cf. above, pp. 66-67.

[4] Berutti, III, 321; Coronata, I, 852; Hofmeister, "Der Übertritt in eine andere religiöse Genossenschaft," *AKKR,* CVIII (1928), 457; Schaefer, p. 938, n. 528. For the effect of the novitiate on these obligations see above, pp. 155-159.

[5] Cf. p. 66.

[6] Cf. Hofmeister, *loc. cit.*

[7] See above, p. 67.

not found restated in it either explicitly or implicitly must be regarded as having lost their force.[8]

In return for the loss of the rights and obligations of the releasing community the religious acquires the rights and obligations of the receiving community. Since canon 635, 1°, does not distinguish, it is evident that the religious acquires all the rights and obligations which belong to other members of that community. This canon abrogates the pre-Code law. Both the Council of Vienne and the Council of Trent had established certain restrictions upon the rights of a transferred religious in his new community. The former had made it impossible for a religious who transferred from a Mendicant to a non-Mendicant Order to hold any position of authority in the new community.[9] The latter ordered that all who transferred to another Order were to remain in the enclosure, and disqualified them from holding secular benefices.[10] These restrictions are no longer in force. The reason again is that canon 635, 1°, makes no distinction, but provides simply that a transferring religious assumes all the rights of the new community. Canon 6, 6°, makes it clear that by reason of the omission of the provisions of the former law the restricting provisions which it contained have become abrogated.[11]

If the religious has made only a temporary profession in the new community, or if he was only in temporary vows when he transferred to another independent monastery of the same Order, his rights and obligations will be those of other religious with temporary vows.[12] One who has made perpetual profession, on the other hand, will have the rights of other perpetually professed members of that community. If the constitutions are silent on the matter, then the time prescribed for his enjoying both an active and a passive voice

[8] Coronata, I, 852; Hofmeister, *loc. cit.*; Oesterle, I, 360; Goyeneche, *art. cit., CpR,* II (1921), 178; Schaefer, p. 938, n. 528; Creusen-Garesché-Ellis, p. 250. Oesterle seems to maintain the opposite when he cites the constitution *Honorum dignita tumque* without comment on explanation.

[9] See above, pp. 25-26.

[10] See above, pp. 26-27.

[11] Schaefer, p. 938, n. 528; Goyeneche, *art. cit., CpR,* II (1921), 178; Coronata, I, 852; Hofmeister, *art. cit., AKKR,* CVIII (1928), 457.

[12] Cf. can. 578.

in the community is to be computed from his first profession.[13] The time required for qualifying him as an eligible candidate in an election for a major superior is also to be computed from his first profession in the new community.[14] Canon 101, § 1, 1°, likewise provides that in the event of a tie in an election for office he will be the elected candidate if he possesses temporal priority in reference to the making of the first religious profession in the community.[15]

The precedence of the religious in the community will ordinarily be computed by reason of his first profession in the community. Canon 106, 5°, provides that precedence of the members of any collegiate body is to be determined by its own legitimate constitutions; if there is no provision in these, then by legitimate custom; if this too is lacking, then by the prescript of the common law. The ordinary rule for precedence in religious communities, other things being equal, is the length of time spent in the religious institute. Religious enter the institute and become religious in the first instance by means of their first profession, as is clear from canon 488, 7°.[16]

The rule that precedence is computed from the time of first profession will hold even when the first profession of one member is temporary, of the other perpetual. Temporary and perpetual, simple and solemn profession are different species of profession, not different degrees in the sense of canon 106, 3°, and hence do not lend themselves for application as a differentiating factor in the matter of precedence.[17] Therefore one temporarily professed will enjoy precedence over one who is perpetually professed, if the former was first professed; this is true, however, only if the constitutions are silent and if there is no contrary legitimate custom.

It seems apropos here to point to the words of Augustine: "Since the Code simply states that the rights and duties of the new monas-

[13] Can. 578, 3°; Berutti, III, 321; Gerster a Zeil, p. 135; Goyeneche, *art. cit., CpR,* II (1921), 179.

[14] Can. 504; Goyeneche, *loc. cit.*; Schaefer, p. 938, n. 529; Gerster a Zeil, p. 135.

[15] Schaefer, p. 939, n. 530; Goyeneche, *loc. cit.*

[16] Cf. Goyeneche, *loc. cit.*; Schaefer, *loc. cit.*; Gerster a Zeil, *loc. cit.*

[17] Goyeneche, *loc. cit.*; Schaefer, *loc. cit.*

tery are assumed, it is evident that no restrictions as to these rights can be validly made as a quasi-condition of admittance, if for instance active and passive voice should be surrendered. Besides, the Code makes no reference to rule or constitutions, and therefore should these permit such restrictions, they are simply out of force."[18]

In virtue of canon 681, those who transfer from a society of the common life to another such society will lose all their rights and obligations in the first community and assume all the rights and duties of the second on the day in which they become incorporated in the new society, whatever the means of incorporation. If they transfer to a religious institute, the same change in their status will take place on the day of their profession.

Article 2. Property Rights

I. *Property Acquired by the Community by Reason of the Religious*

A. Property Acquired Before the Completion of the Transfer.

> Can. 635, 2°. Religio vel monasterium *a quo* bona servat, quae ipsius religiosi ratione iam ei quaesita fuerunt. . . .

Canon 635, 2°, states that the releasing institute or monastery keeps the property that it has acquired by reason of the religious. In the case of a religious of simple vows, this includes whatever the religious has acquired by his industry or personal activity, or in behalf of the religious institute, since canon 580, § 2, provides that such property is acquired by the institute.[19] In the case of a religious of solemn vows, it includes, as canon 582 directs, all the property which came to the religious in any manner whatsoever after his profession, unless the Order could not acquire such property, in which case it accrued to the Holy See.[20]

[18] *A Commentary on the New Code of Canon Law,* III, 370.

[19] Bastien, p. 435; Beste, p. 429; Claeys-Bouuaert-Simenon, I, 420; Schaefer, p. 939; Berutti, III, 321; Leitner, *Das Ordensrecht,* p. 475; Sipos, p. 390.

[20] Leitner, *loc. cit.*; Claeys-Bouuaert-Simenon, *loc. cit.*; Sipos, *loc. cit.*

Under the classification of property acquired by the institute or the monastery come also donations made by the religious to the community, provided that these were legitimately made by the religious and accepted by the community.[21] Property already acquired by the community must, however, be carefully distinguished from the property which indeed was given to the community, but in such a way that the dominion would not pass to the community until the death of the testator. This is the case when the community is the beneficiary of the last will and testament.[22] In the case of a donation, the donation must have been absolute and unconditional. If a condition was attached that the donation should be the property of the community for as long as the religious remained in that community, then the donation becomes null when the religious transfers to another community.[23]

If the disposition of the revenues which a religious of simple vows must make with regard to his property named the releasing institute as the beneficiary, the institute or monastery may keep all the revenues which it has acquired while the religious was within the community.[24] This will include the revenues which accrued to it while the religious was in the novitiate of the receiving community, unless a change had been made in the disposition in accordance with canon 580, § 3.[25]

Legacies and inheritances which became the property of an institute or a monastery by reason of a religious in solemn vows also remain in its possession.[26] This does not apply to legacies and in-

[21] Augustine, III, 367; Bastien, p. 435; Beste, p. 429; Prümmer, I, 334-335; Schaefer, p. 939; Vermeersch, "Varia quaesita de religiosis, V de attributione bonorum religiosi transeuntis ad aliud Institutum," in *Periodica,* XIV (1925), (50)-(51).

[22] Cf. Vermeersch, *loc. cit.* The last will and testament, however, cannot be changed without the formality required by canon 583, 2°.

[23] Bastien, p. 435: "Enfin, si la donation est conditionnelle, c'est-a-dire, valable tant qu'on restera dans l'Institut, elle devient nulle par le fait de la sortie."

[24] Bastien, n. 613; Beste, p. 429; Berutti, III, 321. For a discussion of the disposition which is to be made of the revenues of the property which belongs to religious of simple vows, see below, pp. 222-231.

[25] See below, pp. 229-230.

[26] Cf. Augustine, III, 367; Beste, p. 429.

herited property which were acquired while the religious was in the novitiate of the receiving institute. Most probably such acquisitions will become the property of the receiving institute, once the transfer has been completed by profession. If, however, in view of the conflicting interpretations of the law, the two communities have, before the transfer, come to an amicable agreement concerning the destination of such property, the agreement should be kept.[27]

Property acquired by the industry and the personal activity of the religious or in behalf of the receiving institute during the time of his novitiate in this institute will not belong to the releasing institute.[28] Whatever revenues from the dowry of women religious before the transfer to the novitiate accrued to the releasing community, and similarly whatever revenues were acquired by it through annual pensions and other periodical installments meant for the support of a particular religious, remain with the community inasmuch as they have already been legitimately acquired.[29]

Canon 681 applies the provision of canon 635, 2°, to the cases of a transfer from a society of the common life to another such society or to a religious institute. Inasmuch as the members of these societies are not necessarily bound by a vow of poverty, the Code provides that the society acquires whatever the members acquire on behalf of the society. The destination of property acquired in other ways is left to the constitutions of each society. Therefore the constitutions of each society will have to be examined if one is to discover what property was acquired by the community by reason of the transferring member before the transfer was made.

B. Property Acquired After the Completion of the Transfer.

After the completion of the transfer, the religious from another community has lost all his rights and obligations in the releasing

[27] See below, p. 198.

[28] See below, pp. 194-195.

[29] Whether the revenues which derive from the investment of the dowry and from pension payments, and fall due during the novitiate of the transferring religious in the receiving community, accrue to it or to the releasing institute is in dispute. It is maintained by the present writer that these invariably accrue in full to the receiving community. See below, pp. 213-215.

community, and, conversely, attained to all the rights and obligations belonging to other members of the receiving community. Henceforth, therefore, any property which he may acquire will accrue either to himself, to the community, or to the Holy See, according to the capacity in which he takes it, the nature of his vows, the capability of the community with regard to the acquisition of property, and the manner in which the property is acquired.[80] The ruling canons are canon 580, § 2, and canon 582.[81]

Canon 580, § 2, provides that whatever a religious in simple vows acquires by his industry and personal activity or in behalf of the institute accrues to the institute.[82] Canon 582 provides that after solemn profession all the property acquired in any way by a regular (without prejudice to special indults granted by the Apostolic See) in an Order which is capable of ownership accrues to the Order, or to the province, or to the religious house, in accordance with the constitutions; but in an Order which is not capable of ownership it accrues to the Holy See.

When a religious with solemn vows transfers from an Order to a congregation and makes a simple profession of vows, the solemnity of his vows is automatically abolished by the new profession, unless the apostolic indult expressly provides otherwise.[83] Hence he regains the ability to acquire and to own property. The question then arises: Does he regain a right to the property which he renounced before making his solemn profession? It is certain that the property which he actually owned at the time of his solemn profession, but which he was obliged to renounce according to the terms of canon 581, cannot be reclaimed. The renunciation consists in a transfer of the owner-

[80] Cf. Claeys-Bouuaert, Simenon, I, 420; Vermeersch-Creusen, *Epitome,* I, pp. 585-586, n. 792 (734).

[81] Beste, p. 429.

[82] Unless the constitutions have a provision to the contrary donations and inheritances can be acquired by the religious for himself because, in virtue of canon 580, § 1, he retains the capacity to acquire such property, though he must cede its administration to others and must make a disposition concerning its use and usufruct.

[83] Can. 636.

ship of the property to others, whether it be the institute or other persons, whom he can ordinarily designate at will.[34]

If the renunciation was neglected, his solemn profession automatically transferred the ownership of any property he held to the community in which he made profession. This property cannot later be claimed. The reason is that the abolition of the solemnity of the vows is not retroactive in its force. It does not affect acts previous to the actual moment of the new profession. These acts remain valid and good.[35] Consequently, no acquired rights with regard to the property which now belongs to the institute or to other parties will be disturbed.

Canon 581 obliges the religious to renounce any property which he *actually* holds at the time of his solemn profession. But it seems to be possible, at least in some Orders, to renounce also inheritances which will be acquired by the religious *at some future time,* provided that he already has some right to it before the law. This is true of the property which is his legal share of an inheritance, or even, probably, an inheritance which would come to him by law if his parents or relatives die intestate.[36] It does not seem possible for him, however, to renounce property which will be his by means of a legacy made in the will of a person still living, even if the will has already been made, or to renounce a donation which will be made only after his solemn profession.[37] Any property, furthermore, not renounced before solemn profession becomes automatically the property of the community when the profession takes place. If the community is not capable of ownership, it accrues to the Holy See.[38]

[34] Cf. can. 581, § 1.

[35] See below, pp. 231-234, where the canons dealing with renunciation are explained. Cf. also Vermeersch-Creusen, *Epitome,* I, p. 586, n. 792 (734).

[36] Cf. Schaefer, p. 607, n. 274, (b); Vermeersch-Creusen, *Epitome,* I, p. 535, n. 736 (685); Larraona, "Consultationes," *CpR,* I (1920), 79, 182. Larraona states that this view does not hold in regions where the renunciation of future inheritances is civilly null. It is fairly certain that wherever the father is not allowed to disinherit his son, the son will not be allowed by civil law to disinherit himself.

[37] Vermeersch-Creusen, *Epitome, loc. cit.*; Schaefer, *loc. cit.*

[38] Cf. Schaefer, p. 607, n. 274, (b). If the religious is the father of a

The question now arises: Must property which is the legal share that falls due to a religious in solemn vows from an inheritance or which will become his by law if his parents or relatives die intestate, be counted as property *acquired* by the releasing community, even though those from whom it is due have not yet died? If the answer is no, then one must say that the right to the property not yet inherited becomes transferred with the religious to the new community.

This question was disputed by the canonists before the Code. If a religious in solemn vows left an institute which was able to acquire the inheritances of its religious in order to transfer to another institute which could not, some thought that the right to the inheritance remained with the releasing institute, but others thought that the inheritance belonged to those in whose favor it had been renounced before the religious made his solemn profession, and others again thought that the right to the inheritance became transferred with him to the receiving community.[39]

This division of opinion has continued after the Code. Hofmeister believes that the right to the property which will be inherited will remain with the releasing community. His reason is that this right, provided that it is a certain one now present, is a *ius ad rem,* of which the religious was despoiled by his previous renunciation or solemn profession.[40] Vermeersch-Creusen and Wernz-Vidal, on the other hand, believed that the releasing community had not as yet acquired the property in question. If he transferred from an Order and made profession of simple vows, he recovered his ability to acquire and own such property, and hence he could claim it, even when he had renounced it in favor of someone else before he made his solemn profession.[41]

family and has not distributed to his children the legitimate part of their inheritance, this part of the property will be excepted from this rule.—Schaefer, *loc. cit.*

[39] Cf. Hofmeister, "Der Übertritt in eine andere religiöse genossenschaft," *AKKR,* CVIII (1928), 470-471.

[40] *Loc. cit.* We cannot speak of a *ius ad rem* if the right can be defeated by a testament. It is only a hope, an expectancy. In regions where a father cannot defeat his child's claim by a will there can be a *ius ad rem.* But this is not so in the United States except in one or the other State.

[41] "Bona tamen hereditatis nondum iacentis quando ista vota simplicia

The present writer favors the latter opinion. (1) It seems to be a more natural rendering of the term *acquired property* to understand it as applying to the inheritance, rather than to the right to acquire the inheritance, no matter how certain the right may be. (2) There seems to be an implicit condition in the renunciation itself: "If I persevere in the solemn profession I am about to make." (3) If a previous solemn profession in the releasing community would later restrict the right of the religious to claim his inheritance, or the right of the receiving community to claim it by reason of the incorporation of the religious in the community, this would be a restriction upon the free exercise of a right. Laws which so restrict the free exercise of rights should be strictly interpreted, as canon 19 demands. (4) The customary practice in the case of a transfer seems to favor this view, as Hofmeister himself attests.[42]

In consequence of this, the preferred view, if a religious transfers from an Order to a congregation and makes profession of simple vows, he can acquire inheritances coming to him from persons still alive at the time of this new profession, even if he renounced them before his previous solemn profession. If a religious in solemn vows transfers from an Order which cannot acquire inheritances to one which can do so, the inheritance, unless it has been renounced before profession, will be acquired by the receiving community.

A special problem is a transfer from an institute which can acquire inheritances due to a religious in solemn vows to another institute which is incapable of doing so. Before the Code, in some such Orders, the Society of Jesus, for instance, it was the law that the inheritance be divided as if the professed religious had not acquired it, and it thus accrued to those who would have received it

emissa sunt nondum censentur tali iure acquisita. Hanc ergo hereditatem adire poterit, etiam si ante suam professionem sollemnem illi in favorem cuiuspiam renuntiaverit."—Vermeersch-Creusen, *Epitome,* I, p. 586, n. 792 (734); Wernz-Vidal, III, 455, note 20; Berutti (*Institutiones Iuris Canonici,* III, 322) also seems to be of this opinion, since he holds that the renunciation of property which is not held at the time but which will certainly be acquired in the future loses its force when the religious transfers if the property has not as yet been acquired.

[42] Hofmeister, *ibid.,* p. 471.

if the religious had died.[43] Vermeersch-Creusen believed that the Code in canons 581 and 582 did not abolish such provisions.[44] A religious transferring to such an Order, consequently, would come under the provisions of its constitutions in this regard. Inheritances accruing to him after his transfer would be divided among the other heirs.

If there is no such provision in the constitutions of the receiving community, inheritances would be acquired by the Holy See, unless the religious before his profession in the institute to which the transfer was made had renounced them in favor of his family, friends, charity, or for some other purpose. The ruling canon here is canon 581.

Personal pensions will also follow the religious to the new community.[45] This will be true even when they were renounced in someone else's favor before solemn profession was made in the releasing community. The reason, Berutti states that the renunciation of property which is not held at the time of the renunciation but which will certainly be acquired in the future loses its force when the religious transfers, on condition that the property has not been acquired in the meantime.[46]

Any property, however, which was actually possessed at the time at which the renunciation was made, cannot according to canon 581, § 1, be reclaimed.[47]

A member of a society of the common life, in case of his transfer to another such society or to a religious institute, will from the time of the completion of the transfer by aggregation or profession acquire property for himself or for the new community according to the title on which it was received and to the norms of the new community. The Code determines only that the property acquired by him in behalf of the society of which he is a member (*intuitu societatis*) belongs to the society, and leaves any further determination as to the acquisition of property to the constitutions of each

[43] Vermeersch-Creusen, *Epitome,* I, p. 535, n. 736 (685).
[44] *Loc. cit.*
[45] Wernz-Vidal, III, 455; see below, pp. 209-215.
[46] Berutti, III, 322.
[47] Berutti, *loc. cit.*; Pejška, p. 183.

society.[48] In the event of his transfer to a religious institute he will be subject to the norms of the Code and of the constitutions as conditioned by the kind of profession he will make and by the nature of the institute.

C. Property Acquired During the Novitiate

First, there can be no question concerning the allocation of property acquired by the religious in behalf of his new institute, ***intuitu religionis***, that is, when the specific destination of the property is the institute itself. Such property will belong to the new institute.[49] Furthermore, the religious is under no obligation to accept property given him in behalf of the releasing institute, since canon 633, § 1, suspends his particular obligations to that community for the duration of the novitiate.[50]

Secondly, with regard to the property acquired by the religious through his own personal industry or activity, such as through the saying of Mass, through preaching, etc., it seems that this too belongs to the receiving community.[51] The authors give no reason for this opinion, but it seems to be founded on the provision of

48 Can. 676, § 3.

49 Berutti, III, 319.

50 See above, p. 155.

51 Goyeneche, *art. cit.*, *CpR*, II (1921), 143; Schaefer, p. 934, n. 521; Berutti, III, 322. Hofmeister, without treating this question explicitly, seems to assume that Mass stipends received by a priest religious who has transferred to another community belong to this new community.—*Art. cit.*, *AKKR*, CVIII (1928), 480. It may not be out of place to indicate here that it is difficult to see how a novice could secure emoluments from preaching, mentioned by the authors just cited, since this function is incompatible with the limitations placed upon the activities of the novice by canon 565, § 3. The canon states that novices are not to be employed in preaching, the hearing of confessions or in the external works of the institute. This limitation affects the first and canonical year of the novitiate. During the second year of novitiate which the constitutions of a particular community may require or during a period during which the novitiate is prorogated this canon does not apply. During this period, however, the novices are to take only a *subordinate* part in the works of the institute, according to an instruction of the Sacred Congregation for Religious—3 Nov. 1921, *AAS*, XIII (1921), 539.

canon 633, § 1, which suspends the particular obligations of the religious to his former community for the duration of the novitiate. A parallel may be drawn here between the effects of the vow of poverty and the effects of the vow of obedience. The Code, with regard to the vow of obedience, explicitly changes its external reference. The religious is bound to obey, even in virtue of his vow, not the superior of the former community, but the superior and the master of novices of the new. Similarly, a transferring religious is bound, in virtue of the vow of poverty, to transmit the property acquired by his industry, not to the former community, but to the new. This solution seems to be in accord with canonical equity, in that it is only fair that the community which is supporting the religious should profit from his activity.

Lastly, there is question of the pertinence of the property acquired by the religious by way of personal gift or inheritance. This question was disputed by pre-Code canonists.[52] They did not agree on whether gifts or inheritances acquired by a transferring religious (of solemn vows) belonged to the former or to the new institute. The solution given by each side depended on the judgment regarding which bond was the stronger—that which bound the religious to the releasing community, or that which bound him to the receiving institute. This controversy has continued after the Code.

The dispute is indeed not concerned with religious who have only simple vows. These religious are still capable of acquiring dominion over property. Donations or inheritances would, therefore, be acquired by these religious personally, unless the constitutions of the institute have provisions to the contrary.[53] They would however be obliged to cede the administration of this property, and make disposition concerning the use and usufruct of income.[54] But the dispute does concern those who while in solemn

[52] Cf. Goyeneche, *art. cit.*, *CpR*, II (1921), 143; Schaefer, p. 934, n. 521; see above, pp. 70-71.

[53] Can. 580, § 1; Wernz-Vidal, III, 455. The writer holds that the constitutions of the new and not of the releasing institute here apply—see above, p. 154.

[54] The cession and disposition spoken of here will be treated in detail be-

vows transfer to another institute, whether it be one in which solemn or simple vows are taken. The reason is that all property which may come to these religious in any manner whatsoever after their solemn profession accrues to the Order, province, or house, according to the constitutions, if the Order can acquire or own such property.[55]

Several authors after the Code maintain, at least in theory, the opinion of Passerini (1595-1677) and Sanchez (1550-1610) that the property should accrue to the releasing community.[56] Hofmeister, in fact, states without qualification that, whereas the pre-Code authors who favored the receiving community based their opinion on the principle that the transferring religious was more truly a member of the receiving than of the releasing community (*"proxime accingendus pro accincto habetur"*), the Code on the contrary takes the position that the transferring novice is completely and entirely a member of the releasing community, and that anything acquired during the novitiate belongs to this institute.[57]

It is true that the religious remains a member of the community of his profession in the sense that he must return to it if he leaves the novitiate, at least if his vows have not expired. On the other hand, his particular obligations to that community are suspended during the novitiate.[58] It seems that the obligation to transmit such property to the releasing community can be considered as forming such a particular obligation, whose binding force has accordingly become suspended. This is the view of Coronata, who believes that any property acquired during the novitiate by gift or inheritance by a religious in solemn vows accrues to the receiving institute.[59] He

low, pp. 222-231. Cf. canon 569, §§ 1, 2; Wernz-Vidal, III, 455; Berutti, III, 322.

55 Can. 582.

56 Chelodi, p. 446, note 2; Beste, pp. 429-430. Hofmeister, *art. cit.*, *AKKR*, CVIII (1928), 479.

57 *Loc. cit.*

58 Can. 633, § 1.

59 "Transiens ad aliam religionem durante novitiatu, si est votis sollemnibus ligatus, videtur quae acquirit acquirere religioni ad quam transit; Codex enim eum ab obligationibus erga religionem *a qua*, durante novitiatu, solvit."—*Institutiones Iuris Canonici*, I, 850.

admits, however, that the matter is not entirely plain.[60] Furthermore, one could raise several difficulties as deriving from the consequences of this view. If the religious transfers from an Order to a congregation, Coronata would have to say that the congregation acquired such property, though it could not do this in the case of other novices or even of religious who have been fully and completely incorporated into it. Moreover, it does not seem to be entirely equitable that an inheritance, which may perhaps be of considerable value, should accrue to a community in which the religious is not yet incorporated. This is particularly true if the religious should change his mind, or be dismissed from the novitiate, and should then return to the releasing community.

Perhaps these and similar considerations have led a group of canonists to maintain a third opinion. They, too, like Coronata, believe that the obligation, in virtue of which property acquired by gift or inheritance by a religious of solemn vows accrues to the releasing community, is suspended during the novitiate by the law of canon 633, § 1. But they interpret the effect of this suspension in a different way. It does not mean that the property acquired by the religious accrues to the releasing community. It means that the acquisition of the property is held in suspension, so that the ultimate effect will be achieved only upon the termination of the novitiate. If the religious is dismissed from the novitiate, or voluntarily returns to the releasing institute, the property will accrue to that institute. If the religious makes profession in the new institute, the property will then accrue to the new Order.[61] This seems to the present writer to be the most acceptable view of the three. However, it is not entirely certain. There seems to be no ground in the text of the law for a distinction between the interpretation of the suspension of the obligations of the religious with regard to the property which is acquired by gift or inheritance and

[60] *Ibid.*, note 11.

[61] Goyeneche, *art. cit., CpR*, II (1921), 143, 144; Wernz-Vidal, III, 456; Berutti, III, 322. Cf. canons 633, § 1, and 635, 1°. If the transfer is made from an Order to a congregation, the religious, after his simple profession, resumes his capacity for ownership. Such gifts and inheritances would then accrue to his personal patrimony.

property which is acquired by the novice *industria sua*. Yet, some of the same canonists maintain that property acquired *industria sua* is acquired by the receiving institute.[62]

In view of the uncertainty, therefore, which attaches to all of the three mentioned opinions, it is recommended that before the transfer is made the two religious communities agree as to the destination of such property if it should be acquired by the religious during his novitiate in the new community.[63] This suggestion is in accord with the practice of the Sacred Congregation of Religious just at the turn of the century, before the promulgation of the Code of Canon Law. At that time, as was previously seen, it was the practice to leave the question of a settlement with regard to temporal goods to an amicable arrangement between the superiors of the two institutes.[64]

Members of societies of the common life do not take public vows of poverty.[65] Whatever property of any kind the members receive because they are members, on behalf of their society, is acquired for the society. The members may retain, acquire and administer other property according to the constitutions of their society.[66] When such a member transfers to another society or to a religious institute, it seems, first, that during his period of novitiate or probation he is under no obligation to gain acquisition on behalf of the society from which he has transferred. Furthermore, any obligations to the releasing community beyond this, inasmuch as they arise from the constitutions, seem to be in suspension in virtue of canons 633, § 1, and 681. Therefore, any property he acquires will belong to him, unless he has made a private vow, a promissory oath, or a promise of poverty, which still perdures, after the man-

[62] See above, p. 275. There may be an equitable reason for the distinction, however. The receiving community must provide the food, medicine, lodging, and recreation that enable the religious to earn, unless these expenses are taken care of by revenues from the dowry or by a special charge.

[63] Biederlack-Führich, *De Religiosis* (Oeniponte, 1919), n. 89; Schaefer, p. 934, n. 521; Beste, pp. 429-430.

[64] See above, p. 71.

[65] Cf. can. 673, § 1.

[66] Can. 676, § 3.

ner of the public vow of poverty taken by a religious.[67] If there be such a restriction on the right of the transferring member to acquire property for himself, any property he will acquire by his personal industry or activity will belong to the new institute. The reason is that his case is parallel to that of a religious who is bound by vows.

II. The Dowry and Other Personal Property

Can. 635, 2° . . . quod spectat ad dotem eiusve fructus et alia bona personalia, si qua habeat religiosus, servandum praescriptum can. 551, § 2 . . .

Can. 551, § 2. Si vero religiosa professa ad aliam religionem ex apostolico indulto transeat, durante novitiatu, fructus, salvo praescripto can. 570, § 1; emissa vero nova professione, dos ipsa huic religioni debentur; si ad aliud eiusdem Ordinis monasterium, huic debeteur ipsa dos a die transitus.

Can. 635, 2°, provides that in the case of those who transfer to another institute, with regard to the dowry and its interest, and any other personal property of the religious, if he has any, the prescription of canon 551, § 2, is to be observed. Canon 551, § 2, provides that if, by virtue of an apostolic indult, a professed woman religious transfers to another institute, then, without prejudice to the prescription of canon 570, § 1, the interest on the dowry as accruing during her novitiate, and the dowry itself once she has made her profession, must be given to the latter institute. If the woman religious transfers to another monastery the dowry is transferred with her on the day on which she makes her formal juridical transfer to the new community. Canon 570, § 1, provides that, unless the constitutions or a formal agreement require the payment of a certain sum for food and clothing during the postulancy or the novitiate, nothing can be exacted in defrayment of the expenses connected with the postulancy or the novitiate.[68]

[67] See above, pp. 154-155.

[68] Canon 570, § 1.—Nisi pro alimentis et habitu religioso in constitutionibus

The conjunction of these three canons in the Code has given rise to serious doubts of law and much discussion among canonists. For the sake of order, two distinct points will be treated here, namely, A. the dowry; B. other personal property. The discussion of the expenses of the novitiate will be reserved, insofar at least as it is not involved in the arguments concerning the interest of the dowry, for Section III of the present article.[69]

A. The Dowry

During the novitiate the interest on the dowry should go to the new institute. This ruling as drawn from canon 551, § 2, seems to be perfectly self-evident, except for the fact that the same canon adds, "without prejudice to the prescription of canon 570, § 1." The latter canon in turn provides that nothing should be charged for the expenses of the support of the novice or the religious habit unless there is a special agreement or a provision for such payment in the constitutions. The modifying clause has been diversely interpreted by canonists with regard to its effect on the payment of the interest on the dowry. There are three different opinions.

(a) A few canonists have advanced the following opinion. The receiving community has a right both to the interest on the dowry and to the payment of a charge for food and clothing during the novitiate, if the charge was formally agreed upon or if the constitutions require it.[70] This opinion does not seem to be well founded. It is contrary to the true concept of the dowry, which is destined for the support of the religious. It, therefore, implies a useless reduplication. For, according to this opinion, even if the interest of the dowry were sufficient to cover the expenses of the novitiate, another sum would be required by law for the same purpose.[71] Besides, the phrase, "without prejudice to the prescription of canon 570, § 1" (*salvo praescripto can. 570, § 1*), need not mean that

vel expressa conventione aliquid in postulatu vel novitiatu ineundo solvendum caveatur, nihil pro impensis postulatus vel novitiatus exigi potest.

69 See below, pp. 239-240.

70 Leitner, *Des Ordensrecht*, p. 476; Oesterle, I, 302-303.

71 Goyeneche, *art. cit.*, *CpR*, II (1921), 121.

the expenses must be paid *in addition to* the interest of the dowry. This type of formula (*salvo* . . .) was often added in the last schema or in the promulgated edition of the Code in indication of nothing more than that there was no contradiction between the two canons and that in the interpretation of the one the other should not be overlooked.[72] In order to save canon 570, § 1, it is not necessary to give the receiving community both the interest of the dowry and a payment for the novitiate.

(b) A second group of authors, and by far the largest, believes that the interest on the dowry should never accrue to the new community, unless the constitutions or a formal agreement require the payment of a charge for food and clothing during the novitiate.[73] Several of these authors modify this opinion slightly. They believe that the interest on the dowry should go to the new community in proportion to the expenses. That is, if the interest is insufficient, the new community receives the entire interest, and can ask the religious to make a further contribution for the expenses of the novitiate. If the expenses are less than the interest on the dowry, the remainder accrues to the releasing community.[74] A few authors believe that the releasing community must add this surplus to the capital of the dowry.[75]

[72] "Hae formulae *salvificae* ("*salvo* . . .") fuerunt pluries additae in ultimo schemate vel in editione promulgata Codicis, et nihil aliud dicere volunt nisi hoc: *non esse contradictionem inter duos canones et in interpretatione unius alium salvandum esse.*"—Larraona, "Commentarium Codicis," uses this argument against the opinion cited—*CpR*, XXI (1940), p. 214, note 809; also *ibid.*, p. 212.

[73] Bastien, p. 308; Berutti, III, 322; Blat, II, 530; Cappello, II, 166, 167; Chelodi, p. 419; Cocchi, *Commentarium in Codicem Iuris Canonici*, Lib. II, Pars II, *De Religiosis* (3. ed., Taurinorum Augustae: Marietti, 1932), p. 224 (hereafter to be cited as *De Religiosis*); Coronata, I, 728; De Meester, *Juris Canonici et Juris Canonico-civilis Compendium* (3 vols. in 4, Brugis, 1921-1928), II, p. 437, n. 995 (hereafter to be cited as De Meester); Jansen, *Ordensrecht* (Paderborn, 1920), p. 207; Papi, *Religious in Church Law*, p. 100; Schaefer, pp. 508, 509, n. 231; Vermeersch-Creusen, *Epitome*, I, p. 499, n. 700 (652); Wernz-Vidal, III, 225; Kealy, *Dowry of Women Religious*, pp. 122-125.

[74] Berutti, *loc. cit.*; Cappello, *loc. cit.*; Gerster a Zeil, p. 135; Jansen, *loc. cit.*; Kealy, *op. cit.*, p. 124.

[75] Fanfani, p. 192; Schaefer, p. 508, n. 231.

The arguments for this opinion are presented in detail by Goyeneche. It is asserted, first, that this view agrees best both with canon 570, § 1, and with canon 551, § 2; the former emphasizes that *nothing* is to be charged for the expenses of the novitiate unless certain conditions are fulfilled; the latter states that its provisions intend no prejudice to the prescription of canon 570, § 1. It is claimed, secondly, that this opinion is in better accord with the pre-Code law, which was opposed to any donations for the support of aspirants in the novitiate; only the poorer monasteries, so it is stated, received the indult to charge anything for the expenses of the novitiate. It is averred, thirdly, that the current discipline likewise favors the procedure that the expenses of the novitiate be borne by the institute itself (can. 570, § 1). It is maintained, fourthly, that just as the legislator, when he prescribes that the dowry is due to the new community after the new profession, assumes that the dowry is required in the new community, so that, if it were not required, it would not be due [*sic*], so also when he orders that the interest of the dowry belongs to the new institute during the novitiate, he assumes that something is demanded there for clothing and food, so that, if nothing were demanded, then the interest would not have to be handed over.

Goyeneche draws the following practical conclusions from his opinion: (1) when something is charged for the expenses of the novitiate, this must first be taken from the dowry; (2) so much of the interest must be given as will suffice to cover the expenses for food and clothing; (3) if the interest is not sufficient to cover the charge which is being made, the remainder must be met by the religious herself from her own property, if she has any, or by her parents. In no case need it be supplied by the releasing community; and (4) if the religious leaves the novitiate before its completion, the interest need only be given for the time she actually spent in the novitiate.[76]

(c) There is however a third opinion. It contends that the interest on the dowry must always, during the novitiate, go to the new institute, and that it is the primary source to be used for de-

[76] Goyeneche, *art. cit.*, *CpR,* II (1921), 122, 123.

fraying the expenses of the novitiate. This is maintained by serious authors with weighty arguments. Their arguments, indeed, appear more convincing than the arguments employed for the other opinions.[77] Attention will now be given, first to the arguments alleged in behalf of the third opinion, and then to a refutation of the doctrine adduced by Goyeneche for the second opinion.

(1) The text of canon 551, § 2, and its historical antecedents seem to prove that the interest on the dowry should always accrue to the new community. For the canon itself, to leave aside the reference to canon 570, § 1, gives no hint that the interest should not always go to the new community. It seems to be speaking absolutely when it states simply that during the novitiate the interest of the dowry, and after the new profession the dowry itself, accrues to the new community. The phrase, "without prejudice to the prescription of canon 570, § 1," was not found in the preliminary schemata of the Code in the years 1912 and 1914; it was added only in the schema of 1916 and in the final and promulgated version. The first intention of the legislator, then, was that the interest should always go to the new community. He added the modifying phrase simply with a view to indicating that there was no conflict between the two canons, and that in the interpretation of canon 551, § 2, one should not overlook the fact that under certain conditions the receiving community had a right to make a charge for the food and clothing of the novice. This was necessary inasmuch as frequently it happened that a transferring religious

[77] Beste, p. 368; Biederlack-Führich, *De Religiosis,* pp. 131, 132; Hofmeister, *art. cit., AKKR,* CVIII (1928), pp. 467, 468; Larraona, "Commentarium Codicis," *CpR,* XXI (1940), 211-216; Sipos, p. 359; Vermeersch, "Varia Quaesita de Religiosis, c. v. De Attributisne Bonorum Religiosi Transeuntis ad alium Institutum," *Periodica,* XIV (1925), (49)-(50). Vermeersch defended this third opinion with an acute and closely reasoned argumentation in *Periodica* in 1925, but never adopted it in the *Epitome.* The latest edition (1937) follows the second opinion explained above without giving any reasons for it. Goyeneche himself admitted the third opinion as probable (1921), and his colleague, Larraona, in 1940 came to its defense in most vigorous terms as the best of the three opinions. Schaefer, p. 940, n. 533, rejects the second opinion in favor of the third, and then, apparently without realizing it, quotes with approval Goyeneche's practical conclusions, which presuppose the second opinion considered above.

had either no dowry at all, or one that proved insufficient for the support of the religious.[78]

(2) This interpretation is confirmed by canon 634, 2°, where the legislator makes a very clear distinction between the interest on the dowry and the expenses for the novitiate. Canon 635, 2°, reads as follows: ". . . as to the dowry and its interest, and other personal property of the religious, if he has such, the prescription of canon 551, § 2, is to be observed; the new institute is entitled to demand for the time of the novitiate a just compensation, if this be not opposed to the terms of canon 570, ° 1." This text is a very clear indication that the primary intention in the mind of the legislator when he introduced the phrase, "without prejudice to the prescription of canon 570, § 1," was not that ordinarily *nothing* should be charged for the expenses of the novitiate. On the contrary, he thought primarily of safeguarding the right of the new community to a just compensation for the expenses of the novitiate, since the interest on the dowry would often be insufficient or nonexistent.[79]

(3) It is the purpose of the dowry to support the religious. This is admitted by all. It would then be very strange if during the novitiate of a professed religious in another community the dowry should be diverted from its primary purpose during the life of the religious. One would then see that the dowry is being used instead for the benefit of the releasing community. It must not be forgotten that the transferring religious is not a mere novice, but a professed religious as well. A primary principle in the interpretation should be that the interest from the dowry should go to the institute in which the religious is actually abiding. Even Goyeneche admits that it would not be fully equitable for the former community to take possession of the fruits of the dowry, which ought to be used for the support of the religious, when her support is no longer a burden on that community.[80]

Consideration may now be given to the arguments proposed by

[78] Cf. Larraona, *ibid.*, pp. 213, 214; p. 214, note 809; Goyeneche, *art. cit.*, *CpR,* II (1921), 121, note 1; Vermeersch, *ibid.*, p. (49).

[79] Cf. Larraona, *loc. cit.*; Vermeersch, *ibid.*, p. (50).

[80] Larraona, *loc. cit.*; Goyeneche, *loc. cit.*; Vermeersch, *loc. cit.*

Goyeneche for the second opinion. (1) It is asserted that this opinion agrees best with the ruling of canon 570, § 1. This is conceded. But while this canon's primary intention is to deal with novices in general, it is canon 635, 2°, which deals with the novice who is a transferring religious. The emphasis which canon 635, 2°, places on the right to a just retribution accordingly takes precedence over the ruling of canon 570, § 1. The question is not that novices in general, but of the special and exceptional case of a religious who happens to be a novice as well because of the transfer. *Generi per speciem dorogatur.*[81] Furthermore, it cannot be denied that canon 551, § 2, considered in itself, seems to favor the impression that the interest always goes to the new community.

(2) It is true that both the pre-Code legislation and the Code itself are opposed to donations for the support of religious in the novitiate except under certain restrictions. But again, this is true of novices in general, and cannot be accepted as equally applicable in the matter of the dowry of a transferring professed religious. Such a novice presents a special case, in which the ruling norm must be drawn from the canons which deal specifically with the matter of a transfer, and from the purpose of the legislation concerning the dowry. Now, the whole tendency of the jurisprudence preceding the promulgation of the Code of canon law was to abandon the earlier concept of the dowry, which regarded it as a fund for the support of a poor monastery, for the concept which likened it to the dowry of wives in Roman law, on which concept it had originally been based. This is to say, the tendency became to regard the dowry as a fund to be used for the support of the person in whose behalf it had been established. This tendency was confirmed by the Code, which provided that the dowry of a transferring religious would pass with her to the new community. That the interest of the dowry should then pass to the new community during the time of the novitiate is entirely in accord with the spirit and purpose of the law.[82]

[81] Reg. 34, R.J. in VI°.

[82] Cf. Hofmeister, "Der Übertritt in eine andere religiöse Genossenschaft," *AKKR*, CVIII (1928), 467, 468; see also above, p. 78.

(3) Goyeneche draws a parallel between the dowry itself and the interest. He asserts that the legislator, in prescribing that the dowry is due to the new community, presupposes that a dowry is there required. If no dowry is required, the dowry is not due. In like manner, he asserts, the interest on the dowry during the novitiate will pass to the new community if a charge is made there for expenses of food and clothing. If no charge is made, so he states, the interest remains with the former community. But it may be countered that this argument proceeds on a false assumption. It is not true that a dowry does not pass to the new community if no dowry is there required. The Code declares quite simply and unequivocally that "after the new profession, the dowry itself must be given to the latter institute." [83]

It is a rule of law that when the law does not make any distinction the interpreter of the law should not make any distinction either. *"Ubi lex non distinguit, nec nos distingere debemus."* Not a single author whom this writer has been able to consult expresses the belief that the dowry remains with the releasing community if a dowry is not required by the receiving community. Goyeneche's *obiter dictum* must therefore be regarded as intrinsically improbable. Larraona states categorically that in the law of today the retention of the dowry by the releasing institute cannot be vindicated by a single argument. The dowry is acquired by the institute only upon the death of the religious. During her life it follows her wherever she is. Goyeneche's opinion is, therefore, improbable, and should not be followed in practice.[84] This argument as prepared for the second opinion must therefore be regarded as without foundation.

The third opinion, which seems the most acceptable of the three inasmuch as it appears to reflect the most natural interpretation of the text, may be restated thus: The interest on the dowry will always accrue to the receiving institute during the novitiate of

[83] Can. 551, § 2. Si vero religiosa professa ad aliam religionem ex apostolico indulto transeat, durante novitatu, fructus, salvo praescripto can. 570, § 1; emissa vero nova professione, dos ipsa huic religioni debentur.

[84] Cf. cans. 548-551, § 1; Larraona, *art. cit., CpR,* XXI (1940), p. 216, note 818.

the transferring religious. If with regard to the question of a charge for the expenses of the novitiate no provision is made in the constitutions of that institute, and if no formal agreement is made for the payment of these expenses, then no added obligation arises with reference to the covering of the expenses.

If a dowry was required by the releasing community, but no dowry at all or only a smaller dowry is required by the receiving community, then it seems that upon the making of profession the entire dowry must be given to the new community by reason of canon 551, § 2.[85] This is not necessary, however, if the releasing community itself has provided the dowry by reason of the inability of the aspirant to do so. It seems that in such a case the releasing community would have a right to keep it, just as it has the right to keep a similarly furnished dowry in the event that a religious has obtained and utilized an indult of secularization.[86]

There is no difficulty with regard to the effect of the completion of transfer upon the dowry, since the law is perfectly clear in itself. If a professed religious transfers to another religious institute, the dowry belongs to the receiving institute when the new profession has been made; if she transfers to another monastery of the same Order, the dowry is due to that monastery from the day of the transfer. The one question that could arise is this: What is to be done if the requirements of the releasing community as to the dowry differ from those of the receiving community? The following possibilities can be mentioned: (1) the same dowry may be required in both communities; (2) the dowry as required in the releasing community may be larger than the one required by the receiving community, or a dowry may be required in the releasing community when none was required in the receiving community; and (3) the dowry required in the releasing community may be smaller than that which is required in the receiving community, or no dowry at all is required by the releasing community while one is required in the receiving community.

(1) If the same dowry is required in both communities, there is no problem.

[85] See above, p. 206.

[86] Cf. Coronata, I, p. 728, n. 577.

(2) If the dowry in the releasing community is larger than that required by the receiving community, or if a dowry is required by the releasing but none is required by the receiving community, then it seems that in every event the whole dowry is to become transferred with the religious.[87]

If the receiving institute does not require a dowry, or should not wish to accept that part of it which exceeds the amount specified in the constitution, it seems to the writer that the following course will be open: if the religious will make a profession of simple vows, the property which constitutes the dowry would revert to the patrimonial estate of the religious; she should, before profession, make a cession of its administration and disposition of its use and usufruct as required by canon 569, §§ 1, 2. If she will make profession of solemn vows at the end of the novitiate, she should renounce the property which the receiving community will not accept in accordance with the norms of canon 581.

(3) If a dowry is required in the receiving community, and either no dowry at all or only a smaller dowry is required in the releasing community, then it seems that the lack of the dowry or its deficit should be supplied in the ways suggested in Section III of the present article for the payment of the expenses of the novitiate.[88] The needed funds could be derived: (1.) from pensions and similar personal revenues belonging to the religious or passing along with her from the releasing to the receiving community; (2) from the personal property of a religious of simple vows, or from the revenues accruing from such property; (3) through the parents or benefactors of the religious; and (4) through the releasing community itself if it be willing to donate the corresponding sum, for this community is not in justice bound to do so.[89]

In the event that the personal property, or accruing revenues are to be utilized for this purpose, then the permission as normally

[87] A great number of authors state that superiors can accept a dowry larger than that fixed by the constitutions (cf. Coronata, I, pp. 724-725). Mothon, however, disagrees, and says that they cannot (*op. cit.*, n. 398, note 547).

[88] Below, pp. 239-240.

[89] See below, pp. 239-240.

required by canon 580, § 3 will not have to be secured.[90] If the money is to be taken from the capital sum, then it likewise seems that no apostolic dispensation from canon 582, 1°, which canon forbids a religious in simple vows to alienate the ownership of her goods by gift, will be needed. The dowry, if taken from the personal belongings of the religious, is not a pure gift to the community. Rather it serves as an equitable recompense to the community for the latter's assumed duty to furnish for the religious what is needed for her support and sustenance.

If a member of a society of the common life should have a dowry when she transfers to another such society or to a religious institute, then the law of canons 635, 2°, and 551, § 2, applies to her in the same way as it applies to a religious who transfers to another religious institute.

B. Other Personal Property

The norm which canon 551, § 2, establishes with reference to the dowry is also to be applied with reference to other personal property in virtue of canon 635, 2°. There is some disagreement among canonists as to the precise extension of the expression, "other personal property." There are three general types of property which have been designated as personal property by the authors: (1) income, similar to revenue from the dowry, meant for the support of a religious, such as life pensions, military pensions, and similar periodic payments; (2) manuscripts, artistic productions, relics and clothing belonging to the religious; and (3) property which remains basically within the ownership of religious professed with simple vows. This last type will be discussed in Section C. The other two types will be discussed here.

1. A number of authors include under the expression, *other personal property*, as used in canon 635, 2°, funds, pensions, life incomes, annuities, and other periodic payments which are due to the institute indeed, but only in consideration of the person of the

[90] In virtue of this canon, a change of a notable part of this income in favor of the community would require the permission of the Holy See.

religious.[91] Personal property, in this sense, has been defined by Father Lopez as "property which accrues through the person of the religious" . . . "which belongs to the community by reason (of the religious)." [92]

This places the notion of personal property on a plane with the concept of the dowry and its revenues. This is entirely in accord with the sense of canon 635, 2°, which speaks of "the dowry, or its revenues, and other personal goods." One would expect, from the very phrasing of the canon, that the "other personal property" would be something similar to the dowry or to its revenues. Actually, this type of property has a striking similarity to the dowry or its revenues, in that its primary purpose is the support of the religious, and it is strange that many of the authors who have treated this question have not mentioned this type of property at all, or only in a secondary place. Yet it seems to be the type of property which was primarily in the mind of the legislator when he wrote the law.

There can be question of this type of property even if the religious is in solemn vows, but in that case every appearance of its being treated as a species of *peculium* must be avoided. So a religious in solemn vows cannot administer it under the direction of his superiors, or apply it to licit uses. He has no dominion over it, for this would be incompatible with his solemn vow of poverty. But this property can be administered, together with other property which belongs to a community which is capable of ownership, by the procurator of the community. It can be spent, in accordance with the prudent judgment of the superiors, in the first place for the

[91] Wernz-Vidal, III, 455; Schaefer, p. 940, n. 532; Goyeneche, "De transitu ad aliam religionem"—*CpR,* II (1921), 124; "Consultationes,"—*CpR,* XXI (1940), pp. 38-40; Hofmeister, "Der Übertritt in eine andere religiöse Genossenschaft," *AKKR,* CVIII (1928), 463; Oesterle, I, 360; Sipos, p. 390; Beste, p. 429. Beste admits this only for religious in temporary vows; Oesterle, only for those in simple vows.

[92] "Quinam debeatur legatum annui reditus monacho relictum ipso post solemnem professionem in aliud monasterium definitive translato," *CpR,* IX (1928), 234; "Bona ex persona religiosi obvenientia . . . quae communitati competunt ratione (religiosi)." Cf. Sipos, p. 390, who gives a similar definition: "Bona a religione vel monasterio intuitu personae cum votis sollemnibus vel simplicibus acquisita, e. gr. legatum annui reditus religiosi relictum."

necessities of the religious himself, but then also for the use of the entire community.[93]

In the case of a religious professed with simple vows, such pensions, life rents, etc., ordinarily form part of their patrimony. They would then not correspond to the definition given by Lopez and Sipos. But it is not impossible that such pensions should be acquired by the community in consideration of the person of the religious, just as is the case with a religious in solemn vows.[94] In fact, a decision of the Sacred Congregation for Religious plainly indicated one such case. The decision was an answer to the question whether an annual pension given because of mutilation, or in consideration of a broken health suffered in the war, to a religious professed with simple vows, or to a member of a society of the common life, or finally to one whose vows or promises are suspended, belonged to the religious society concerned. The reply was that, in the case of a religious who during his military service was bound by vows, it belongs to the institute or the society; in the case of others, that it belongs to the person himself, who however is bound to turn it over to the society as long as he remains in it.[95] As another example, it is conceivable that a provision might be made by a father in his will in behalf of his son in simple vows, turning over to the community an annual pension destined for the support of the person concerned. Hofmeister includes under the terms *census vitalitii* the pensions of private and of civil employees, pensions due to those who have been disabled in the line of duty, and foundations and gifts for the support of religious.[95a]

In the earlier law it was the universal opinion of the canonists who considered the matter of periodical payments of this sort that

[93] "Huiusmodi census, in quos ipsis regularibus votorum *solemnium* nullum ius proprietatis competere potest, bonis ipsius conventus vel ordinis religiosi alias capaci incorporati ab oeconomis administrandi et a Superioribus prudenti arbitrio expendendi sunt imprimis pro necessitatibus illius religiosi et in usum totius conventus."—Wernz-Vidal, III, 355. Beste and Oesterle deny that there can be question of such property in the case of religious in solemn vows. See above, p. 210, footnote 91.

[94] Hofmeister, *art. cit., AKKR,* CVIII (1928), 477.

[95] S. C. de Religiosis, 16 mart. 1922, ad V—*AAS,* XIV (1919), 196.

[95a] Loc. cit.

they accrued to the new community after the final transfer of a religious.[96] Their reason for believing that this property accrued to the community along with the transfer of the religious, as Lopez and Hofmeister point out, was that this type of property had a particularly personal character.[97] This gives rise to the presumption that the terminology of the Code, rooted as it is in the earlier law, follows the doctrine of the pre-Code commentators. This is confirmed by an examination of the history of the evolution of canon 635, 2°, in the preparatory schemata of the Code. In 1912 the following form of the canon was proposed:

> "2° . . . pensiones autem et reditus personales, si quos habeat, professum in altera religione sequunter a die professionis."

In 1914 the text was even clearer:

> ". . . pensiones autem et reditus personales, si quos habeat, religiosum in altera religione vel monasterio sequuntur a die professionis vel transitus."

Nothing could more clearly demonstrate what the brief formula, *bona personalia,* is intended to express.[98]

A look at canon 635, 2°, confirms the logic of this opinion. It is in perfect accord with the text and context of the words *bona personalia.* The canon states that "as to the dowry and its revenues and other personal goods of the religious, if he has such, the prescription of canon 551, § 2, is to be observed."[99] The words "other

[96] See above, p. 76.

[97] Lopez, *art. cit., CpR,* IX (1928), 234. Hofmeister, *ibid.,* p. 473. Goyeneche says that it had a most personal character (*"characterum personalissimam"*) and followed the religious as a shadow follows a body—"Consultationes"—*CpRM,* XXI (1940), 38-40. Hofmeister cites many of the older authors who taught that these goods were given in consideration of the person (of the religious), *"intuitu personae,"* and that they were therefore purely personal goods, "mere personalia."

[98] Lopez, *loc. cit.*

[99] ". . . quod spectat ad dotem eiusve fructus et alia bona personalia, si qua habeat religiosus, servandum praescriptum can. 551, § 2."

personal goods" are in apposition with the words "its revenues."[100] Therefore, like the revenues of the dowry, these goods are due the receiving community during the novitiate. But since, unlike the revenues of the dowry, they do not derive from property which is necessarily in the hands of the releasing community, this latter cannot be said always to pass to the new community after profession. But the pension will continue to accrue to the receiving community.

The authors do not enter upon the question of the relation of the income from the dowry to expenses for the novitiate in such a manner as specifically to apply their doctrine to the type of income which has been considered here.[101] But it seems perfectly consistent to conclude that the same divergence of opinion would exist among the authors if they had considered this point in sufficient detail. The present writer maintains it as the most probable opinion that in every case the pensions, like the interest of the dowry, must be ceded *in toto* to the new community during the novitiate.

An interesting application of this general principle with regard to pensions, etc., is given by Hofmeister. A soldier who has become a religious with solemn vows receives a lump sum in lieu of a life pension for an injury suffered in war. Thereafter he transfers to another institute. Since the lump sum had the character of an income for the support of the religious, it must be used for the purpose for which it was given. A proportional part of it must be given to the new community.[102]

Another unusual case is that of a religious who before his solemn profession has indeed renounced his property in favor of the institute, but with the stipulation that in the event of his transfer to

[100] It is plain that Larraona accepts this grammatical (and canonical) interpretation of canon 635, 2°: "Durante novitatu et novitiatus annali prorogatione a can. 634 permissa, *dotis fructus* (cc. 551, § 2; 635, n. 2) et *alia bona personalia* (can. 635, n. 2), si quae habeat, secumfert religiosa. Dos e contra, id est dotis sors, remanet in religione *a qua* usque dum perdurat novitiatus et vota emissa in religione originis."

[101] Only Hofmeister (p. 480 of the cited article) says explicitly that if the releasing institute has been given property for the support of the religious, it must pay the expenses of the novitiate.

[102] Hofmeister, *ibid.*, p. 475.

another community it is to pass with him to the new community. This, Hofmeister maintains, is a contract which must be honored. He warns, however, that whatever stipulations are made must not militate against the nature of solemn profession, which deprives the religious of the capacity for ownership.[103]

Pensions and similar income due to a religious with solemn vows will belong to the receiving community not only during the novitiate, but also after the transfer has been completed, provided that the new profession will also be solemn. The religious must, however, renounce it in favor of someone else before making his new profession, if this is demanded by the rule and constitutions of the new community.[104] The Holy See has decided that pensions given because of mutilation, or in view of broken health suffered in the war, to a religious who was under the obligation of simple vows at the time he was in the service belong to his institute. The payments due under this type of pension, therefore, must be given to the new institute after the transfer has been completed.[105]

The Holy See has also decided that if such a pension was earned by a religious whose simple vows were during the time of his service held in suspension, then the pension belongs to the religious, who is, however, obliged to turn it over to the institute as long as he is in it. Such a pension, *a fortiori*, must be turned over to the new institute after his transfer. If, however, a trust fund was set up to benefit the institute directly and the religious only indirectly, the intention of the donor clearly distinguishes the fund and its revenues from the pensions which have been discussed. Such income would not be personal in character, and consequently it would not follow the religious in the event of his transfer to another community.

A pension due to members of societies of the common life because of injuries or infirmities suffered in war likewise belongs to the members, but must be turned over to the society as long as they are in it. This also is a decision of the Holy See.[106] In virtue of

[103] Hofmeister, *ibid.*, p. 472.
[104] Wernz-Vidal, III, 455.
[105] See above, p. 211.
[106] S. C. de Religiosis, 16 mart. 1922, ad V—*AAS*, XIV (1922), 196, 197.

canon 681, therefore, this type of income in the matter of its due accrual will follow the rule for the pensions belonging to religious of simple vows, so that in the event of a transfer the pension will yield to the new community.

2. Manuscripts, works of art, devotional articles, relics—According to Augustine, "personal belongings are manuscripts, works of art, devotional articles, clothing. These go with the person." In his opinion, therefore, all these will pass with the religious to the new community.[107] This statement does not make a sufficient distinction relative to the various articles here to be considered. These various types of belongings must here be briefly discussed. It seems highly doubtful that devotional articles are personal property in the sense of canon 635, 2°. They are part of the remote matter of the vow of poverty.[108] As such, in the case of religious professed with solemn vows, they belong to the institute, and hence the religious can take them with him to the new institute only when the releasing institute has given them outright to the transferring religious. In the case of religious professed with simple vows, they could of course be in his ownership so that accordingly they would pass with him to the new community. Even religious in simple vows are normally not to use their own property. They could do so, of course, with the permission of the superior.

Relics, on the other hand, are not part of the matter of the vow of poverty. Therefore the religious can take them with him to the new community. But the same rule does not apply with reference to the reliquaries in which they are contained, especially if these are made of precious materials.[109]

If an outsider procured the materials used for a work of art produced by a religious, for example, a painting or a sculpture, then the art product belongs to the person who procured the materials for it.[110] If the institute furnished the materials, it is only fair to say that the work of art belongs to the institute. It cannot be taken along by the religious without the permission of the supe-

[107] *A Commentary on the New Code of Canon Law,* III, 367.

[108] Schaefer, p. 684, n. 327, 328.

[109] Cf. Schaefer, p. 484, n. 327.

[110] Schaefer, p. 484, n. 327; Bastien, p. 379, n. 537.

riors of the institute. This is especially true if the work has money value, for then it is the fruit of the industry of the religious, and as such belongs to the institute.[111]

In practice there should hardly be any difficulty, since the institute can easily settle all problems by giving the transferring religious whatever personal belongings it will be useful, necessary, and practicable for him to take along. An amicable settlement will be the best solution.

Manuscripts, however, present a special problem. As was seen in the historical section of this dissertation, authors were not in agreement on the question whether manuscripts were part of the remote matter of the vow of poverty. This disagreement naturally results in a difference of doctrine with regard to the right of a transferring religious to take manuscripts with him to the new community. If manuscripts are subject to exclusive ownership by the religious, then it is obvious that he can take them with him to the new institute; on the other hand, if the institute alone has the complete rights of ownership, the manuscripts must be left behind; finally, if the institute has indeed the right of ownership, but the religious has the irrevocable right of use, the manuscript can be taken along, but it cannot be sold or given away; after his death it must be restored to the original community.[112]

As was pointed out in the same section of the historical synopsis, the decision of the Sacred Congregation of Religious which prevented the religious, whether of solemn or of simple vows, from alienating or giving away his manuscripts, did not settle the controversy. It was still uncertain whether the religious had the ownership of his manuscripts, for it was possible that not the ownership, but only the right to exercise the prerogative of ownership through an act of the right alienation or donation, had been disavowed by the decision. It was likewise not settled by the decision whether the

[111] Cans. 580, § 2; 582. Coronata, I, 588. Vermeersch simply stated that a work of art is matter of the vow of poverty—*Theologia Moralis* (3. ed., 4 vols., Roma: Università Gregoriana, 1933-1937; Vol. III, Reimpressio, 1945), III, n. 117.

[112] See above, pp. 71-75.

religious could or could not take his manuscripts with him to the new community.[113]

The Code did not settle the problems either. The present state of the question can be summarized as follows:

(1) There seems to be no question about purely personal notes which have no money value, such as classroom notes, points for preaching, outlines of matter studied or read, spiritual notes from retreats, etc. There is no doubt that these are not a part of the remote matter of the vow of poverty. The religious therefore can take them with him when he transfers.[114]

(2) There is still a controversy with regard to manuscripts which have a money value. Some authors maintain that the ownership of manuscripts remains with the religious, though the right to exercise this ownership has been limited, so that the religious cannot donate or alienate his manuscripts without permission.[115] As a consequence of this view all manuscripts could pass with the religious to the new community. Another group of authors maintains absolutely that manuscripts are part of the remote matter of the vow of poverty, and as such belong to the community within which they were written.[116] The third view is that the religious retains the right to the use of his manuscripts, but that the right of ownership remains with the community itself. This seems to

[113] Above, pp. 74-75.

[114] Choupin, *Nature et Obligation de l'Etat Religieux-Discipline Actuelle* (Paris: Beauchesne, 1923), pp. 321, 322; Wernz-Vidal, III, 349, note 54; Lehmkuhl, I, n. 523; Goyeneche, "De transitu ad aliam religionem"—*CpR,* II (1921), 141; Arregui, *Summarium Theologiae Moralis,* p. 318, n. 500.

[115] Coronata, I, 764, 788; Sabetti-Barrett, *Compendium Theologiae Moralis* (13. ed., Neo-Eboraci: Pusted, 1939), pp. 536-537; Vermeersch, *Theologia Moralis,* III, n. 117 (who stated that manuscripts are not part of the remote matter of the vow of poverty as long as they are in the possession of the religious); Augustine, III, 305; Turner, p. 96; for other authors who hold this view, cf. Goyeneche, *art. cit., CpR,* II (1921), 142, note 9.

[116] Biederlack-Führich, p. 185; Fanfani, n. 223; Arndt, *Die kirchlichen und weltlichen Rechtsbestimmungen für Orden und Kongregationen* (Paderborn, 1919), p. 50; Voltas, "Consultationes," *CpR,* I (1920), 278; Oesterle, I, 360; Bastien, p. 379, note 2; Gennari, "Annotazioni," *Il Monitore Ecclesiastico,* 3rd Series, Vol. V (1913), p. 265. Voltas and Gennari maintained that manuscripts are products of the industry of the religious and as such belong to the institute.

imply that the religious can take the manuscripts with him when he leaves the community, but that they must be restored to it after his death.[117]

The constitutions by regulating the extension of the vow of poverty in any particular community could settle this issue. If they include manuscripts as part of the remote matter of the vow, then the consequence of that declaration must be observed, so that the manuscripts belong exclusively to the community.[118] If they do not, then some kind of agreement should be reached by the two communities. It seems to the present writer that the last of the three opinions above summarized proves the most acceptable. Accordingly the religious always retains the right to the personal use of his manuscripts. Inasmuch as these have a money value, however, they should be regarded as belonging to the community within which they were written, as products of the personal activity and industry of a religious belonging to the community. This means that sales' rights should remain with the releasing community.

A number of authors state that it is absolutely certain that the dominion over manuscripts which have been produced by religious commissioned for the work, or with special expense on the part of the community, must be attributed to the community.[119]

Finally, if a work has already been published, the sales' rights undoubtedly belong to the releasing community. The religious cannot without its permission issue further editions of the same work after his transfer to another community.[120] The profits should be distributed on a *pro rata* share between the two communities. The receiving community should receive a share proportionate to the value of the work done by the religious in preparing the new edition.

[117] Cf. Beste, p. 393; Choupin, *Nature et Obligation de l'Etat Religieux*, pp. 321, 322.

[118] Wernz-Vidal, III, 350-351.

[119] Jone, *Moral Theology*, tr. by U. Adelman (2. ed., Westminster, Newman Bookshop, 1946), n. 411; Arregui, p. 318; Goyeneche, *art. cit.*, *CpR*, II (1921), 141; Wernz-Vidal, III, 350; Ferreres, "Annotaciones," *Razón y Fe*, XXXVII (1913), 244; Ciravegna, *De Paupertate Societatis Iesu*, n. 158 (cited by Wernz-Vidal, *loc. cit.*).

[120] Goyeneche, *ibid.*, p. 142; Schaefer, p. 935, n. 523.

Similarly, a transferring religious does not have any rights with regard to an invention which has already been patented.

In the case of members of a society of the common life, the constitutions of the society will have to be consulted concerning the ownership rights of patented inventions and manuscripts which have a sale value. If these rights belong to the individual, he can take the products and the manuscripts with him to the new community.

C. The Property of Religious of Simple Vows

1. The Dominion of Religious in Simple Vows

A number of canonists apply the expression *other personal property* as it occurs in canon 635, 2°, to property which is owned by religious of simple vows.[121] Some of the authors who are of this opinion interpret canons 635, 2°, and 551, § 2, to mean that during the novitiate the revenues from this property, but, after the profession, the dominion itself, passes to the receiving institute.[122] They liken the property of religious of simple vows in this matter to the dowry, and apply to it the rule for the dowry and its revenues as given in canon 551, § 2.

This latter view is inadmissible. When examined closely, this type of property is very different from the dowry and its revenues.

121 Gerster a Zeil, p. 135; Hofmeister, *art. cit., AKKR,* CVIII (1928), 476-477; Jansen, *Ordensrecht,* p. 208; Schaefer, p. 939, n. 531, note 70. Others who seem to hold this view, without expressing themselves too clearly, are: Beste, p. 429—"Bona personalia habere possunt professi a votis temporariis, quatenus proprietatem bonorum servant, nisi eam excludant constitutiones; ex adverso, professi votorum sollemnium regulariter bona personalia possidere nequeunt, quia capacitate possidendi spoliantur, salvis peculiaribus indultis pontificiis"; Pejška, p. 183—"Bona personalia simpliciter professi cum ipso ad religionem secundam transeunt (can. 635, n. 2)"; Cocchi, *De Religiosis,* 243—"cetera bona personalia ipsius religiosi, si qua habeat, *vel* ipse sibi servat, *vel* ad novam religionem transeunt, *vel* a S. Sede acquiruntur, iuxta naturam novae professionis."

122 Gerster a Zeil, p. 135—"Si religiosus votorum simplicium bona possidet propria et in aliam religionem transit, nova religio a die transitus usumfructum et a die professionis etiam bona ipsa possidet"; Biederlack-Führich, *De Religiosis,* p. 288, n. 164; cf. Hofmeister, *ibid.,* p. 476.

The dowry has as its fundamental purpose the support of women religious in their religious institute. Property in the dominion of religious of simple vows does not. This is clear from the fact that the Code (leaving room for constitutions which may have contrary provisions) leaves religious free, before their first profession, to dispose of the use and usufruct of their property in favor of whomever they please. They are not therefore obliged, ordinarily, to give the revenues of their property to the religious institute. The Code also permits them to cede the administration of this property to whomever they wish, without any limitation, while the dowry must always be administered by the community.[123]

The analogy breaks down on another very important point. The dowry is not in the dominion of the religious, though it must be restored to them if for any reason they leave the institute, while the property of religious in simple vows is truly in their dominion.[124] When, therefore, the dowry is transferred from the one institute to the other, there is no decided change in the economic rights of the religious. There would be a most decided change, however, if the dominion which the religious in simple vows has over his patrimony would automatically be transferred to the new community. The receiving community would become the owner of property which was his while a member of the releasing community. This is inadmissible. It is utterly opposed to the great care exercised by the legislator to safeguard the basic power of ownership on the part of religious in simple vows over their property: they cannot validly renounce their property in the novitiate; [125] they are forbidden, once they have made profession of simple vows, to alienate their property by a voluntary conveyance, that is, by gift; in fact, if their vows are a preparation for solemn profession, they cannot do so validly.[126]

This opinion would, in fact, place these transferring religious in even a less favorable condition than religious who are about to take solemn vows. The latter must, within sixty days before their

[123] Cf. can. 569, §§ 1, 2; can. 547, § 2; can. 549; can. 550, § 1.

[124] Cf. canons 548-551; 580, § 1.

[125] Can. 568.

[126] Can. 583, 1°; can. 581.

solemn profession, renounce all the property which they possess, on condition of their future profession. But they are left free to abdicate their property in favor of anyone they wish, unless their freedom to so dispose of it has become qualified in some other way in consequence of a special indult that rules otherwise granted to the community by the Holy See.[127] The property of the transferring religious who are professed with simple vows would, on the contrary, pass automatically and necessarily to the receiving institute. The opinion seems entirely unsustainable if one recalls that they may be in temporary vows, and would, in the event that they left the new institute or were dismissed from it, return to the world without the property with which they entered the religious life, which is precisely what the law is so careful to prevent, even in the case of religious who have made a perpetual profession of simple vows.

The present writer is in full agreement with the doctrine of Father Benedict Lopez, as expressed in the following manner:

> "Nothing can be found that proves more contrary to the letter and to the spirit of the Code than that a religious when professed with simple vows, should be despoiled of his right of ownership over his property in consequence simply of his act of transferring to another religious institute. Indeed, a new exegetical method would be introduced if this passage in canon law, which at first sight seems so obscure, and in which the matter is touched upon only in passing, should be used as a foundation for overturning what is so lucidly established in canons which deal explicitly with these matters." [128]

This opinion certainly cannot be followed in practice. It is a question of the limitation of the free exercise of rights, and therefore the law must be rigorously interpreted.[129] This means that

[127] Can. 581, § 1.

[128] Lopez, "Cuinam debeatur legatum annui reditus monacho relictum ipso post solemnem professionem in aliud monasterium definitive translato," *CpR,* IX (1928), 217-234, p. 234. Hofmeister also believes it to be certain that a religious who is professed with simple vows does not in consequence of his transfer forfeit his previously held ownership.—"Der Übertritt in eine andere religiöse Genossenschaft," *AKKR,* CVIII (1928), 476.

[129] Cf. can. 19.

canon 635, 2°, will not cause a transferring religious who is professed with simple vows to lose the ownership of his property. Similarly, a member of a society of the common life will not lose the property which he owns when he transfers to another such society or to a religious institute.

2. The Cession of the Administration of Property and the Disposition Concerning Its Revenues.

What effect does a transfer have on the cession of the administration of his property and the disposition concerning its revenue which was made by the religious before his profession of simple vows in the releasing community? It is not clear whether the Code contains provisions which regulate this matter. It is also doubtful whether the transferring religious is to remain subject to the restrictions upon his freedom to change such a cession or disposition which are placed upon religious by canon 580, § 3, or whether he should, with the other novices, make a new cession and disposition before his new profession in virtue of his condition as a novice. For this reason there has been considerable difference of opinion among the canonists.

The canons which regulate for religious with simple vows the cession and disposition of which mention has been made are canons 569, §§ 1, 2, and canon 580, § 3. Canon 569 requires that before making profession of simple vows the novice must cede to anyone whom he wishes the administration of his property. This cession must extend to the entire period during which he will be bound by his simple vows. He is also required, while still a novice, to dispose of the use and usufruct of his property. He is free to determine the beneficiary in his disposition, unless the constitutions of his institute deprive him of this right or in any way restrict or circumscribe it.[130] If the fulfillment of this obligation should have been omitted for any reason, or if any property came into the possession of the religious after the original act of cession and disposition, the

[130] Cf. can. 569, § 1; Pontificia Commissio Interpretationis, 16 oct. 1919, ad 9—*AAS*, XI (1919), 478.

cession and disposition must be supplied or renewed, even after the simple profession has been made.[131]

Canon 580, § 3, contains prescriptions which regulate changes which the religious may desire to make in his original cession of administration or disposition of use and usufruct of his property. Changes in the cession and disposition cannot be effected at will, but require the permission of the superior-general of the institute. If the religious is a nun, it requires also the permission of the local ordinary, or, if the monastery is subject to regulars, of both the local ordinary and the regular superior. A change affecting a notable part of the property or of its use and usufruct in favor of the institute requires an apostolic indult. It is possible for the constitutions to permit the religious to make a change, exclusive of one that requires an apostolic indult, at his own will and without permission.[132]

It is not clear whether the Code contains provisions specifically intended to regulate the effect which a transfer will have on this cession of administration and disposition concerning the revenues of property belonging to a religious with simple vows.

1. One group of authors believe the matter is regulated by the general provision of canon 635, 2°, which states that the prescription of canon 551, § 2, concerning the dowry applies to any other personal property of the religious, if he has any. Canon 551, § 2, in turn provides that during the novitiate the income from the dowry, but after profession the dowry itself is due to the new community.[133] Consequently they maintain that during the novitiate in the receiving community the revenue of property belonging to religious with simple vows is due to the new community, provided that the original disposition of the revenues was made in favor of the releasing institute. The new community is simply substituted for the old, if the new community consents to the change. This change becomes permanent after the new profession.[134]

[131] Can. 569, § 2; cf. Schaefer, p. 554.

[132] For an extensive commentary on the relation of canon 580, § 3, to canon 569, §§ 1, 2, cf. Schaefer, pp. 595-598; Larraona, "Consultationes," *CpR*, I (1920), 371-372.

[133] See above, pp. 191 ff.

[134] Dieselben Bestimmungen gelten in Bezug auf das persönliche Vermögen

A slight variation of this opinion is held by Hofmeister himself. He too believes that the expression *other personal property* as occurring in canon 635, 2°, refers to the property of a religious professed with simple vows. He rejects, however, the notion that during the novitiate the revenues go to the new community, on the ground that, if the legislator had intended that they should, canon 635, 2°, should read as follows: quod spectat ad dotem et alia bona personalia, si qua habeat religiosus, eorumve fructus. . . ."[134a]

Hofmeister points out the serious difficulties that attend the interpretation which the proposed opinion suggests.[135] It necessitates a highly peculiar rendering of the word *debentur* in canon 551, § 2. The expression "are due" properly renders the meaning of this verbal form. It relates to the dowry and its revenues in canon 551, § 2, and, in canon 635, 2°, to other personal goods as well. With regard to the dowry and its revenues, it means that these are due to the receiving community in the sense that they will come into its possession. The revenues are indeed acquired absolutely, but the dowry itself is acquired solely on condition that the religious does not leave the community before her death.[136]

The word would have an entirely different meaning, if this opinion is right, when applied to personal property. This property would "be due" in the sense that the administration of the property is transferred to the new community. This is a highly artificial and forced interpretation, and stretches the meaning of this word beyond its natural reach.[137] It is highly unlikely that it should

des betreffenden Religiösen, wenn er den Nutz und den Bezug der jeweiligen Zinsen seiner bisherigen Genossenschaft zugewandt hatte, nämlich schon während des neuen Noviziates kommen diese der neuen Genossenschaft zu."—Jansen, *Ordensrecht*, p. 208; Mothon, p. 849; other authors who according to Hofmeister hold this view are Brandys, *Kirchliches Rechtshandbuch für die religiösen Laiengenossenschaften* (Paderborn, 1918), p. 89; Biederlack-Führich, p. 288, n. 164—Hofmeister, *art. cit.*, *AKKR*, CVIII (1928), 476. This view seems to imply that there would be no change if the cession and disposition had named someone other than the religious institute of which he was a member.

134a Hofmeister, *loc. cit.*

135 *Ibid.*, pp. 476-477.

136 Cans. 548-551.

137 Cf. other canons in which the same word is used: in can. 1017, § 3,

be used in such diverse senses with regard to the dowry and with regard to the other personal belongings, whatever they may be.

Again, it seems odd that the freedom which canon 569, § 1, gives to a religious with regard to the choice of an administrator for his property should be limited in the case of a transferring religious, without any apparent reason, so as to provide for a change in administrators *ex dispositione legis*.[138] The present writer wishes to point out that canon 635, 2°, if interpreted in this way, would clearly be constituted as a law which restricts the free exercise of rights, and therefore would have to be interpreted strictly. Therefore, even in that assumption it would not clearly exist as a binding law, and accordingly would remain unenforceable in practice. Hofmeister himself, moved most likely by this consideration, has modified the opinion by making its use optional. His opinion may be summarized as follows:

Canon 635, 2° (despite its obscurity), gives the professed religious *the right* (italics the present writer's) to change the cession, disposition and last will and testament made before his first profession, so that in all cases, if he had named as his beneficiary the monastery from which he transferred, a substitution which favors the new monastery should be made. The Code itself, in canon 635, 2°, gives the required apostolic permission for this procedure.[139]

2. Another group of authors hold that the cession and disposition which were made by the religious with simple vows before his

damages are spoken of as being due—"datur tamen (actio) ad reparationem damnorum, si qua debeatur"; in can. 1301, § 2, the word is used with reference to the person to whom the belongings of a cardinal are due—"cui debentur, remittat"; in can. 1909, § 1, it refers to what parties in a trial owe for judicial expenses—"quid partes debeant pro expensis iudicialibus."

138 Hofmeister, *loc. cit.*

139 Trotz dieser Schwierigkeiten glauben wir den Sinn der oben genannten Stelle (c. 635, n. 2) richtig wiederzugeben, wenn wir behaupten, dass der Professe in all den Fällen, in denen er das Kloster *a quo* bedacht hat, nach erfolgtem Übertritt berechtigt is, seiner vor der ersten Profess getroffenen Verfügung, einschliesslich der testamentarischen, einen Nachtrag beizufügen, des Inhalts, dass nunmehr an die Stelle der Genossenschaft *a qua* jene *ad quam* zu treten habe. Zu dieser Änderung ist unseres Erachtens die apostolische Erlaubnis durch den Kodex selbst gegeben."—Hofmeister, *art. cit.*, *AKKR*, CVIII (1928), 477.

profession in the releasing institute must be repeated or confirmed before profession in the receiving institute in virtue of canon 569, § 1. They believe that they find in the text of this canon a provision which applies it to religious who transfer from one institute to another.[140] Canon 569, § 1, reads as follows: "Ante professionem votorum simplicium sive temporariorum sive perpetuorum novitius debet, ad totum tempus quo simplicibus votis adstringetur, bonorum suorum administrationem cedere cui maluerit et, nisi constitutiones aliud ferant, de eorundem usu et usufructu libere disponere." Prümmer maintained that the words *sive perpetuorum* refer to the perpetual profession made by perpetually professed religious when they transfer to a religious congregation.

This view is not improbable,[141] but weighty objections can be raised against it. Larraona argues that the transferring religious is a religious in an absolute sense, a novice only in a relative sense. Therefore the rule to apply is to be taken from canon 580, § 3, which treats of the departure of a religious from his institute, rather than from canon 569, § 1, which treats of the reception of a novice into an institute. He points out that the words *sive perpetuorum* had been added in one of the preparatory schemata of the Code which did not impose on all religious institutes alike the requirement of a temporary profession before the final profession, which requirement is now made in canon 574 in the promulgated version of the Code. In that schema it was quite logical to include this phrase, so as to make provision for the institutes in which final profession was made immediately after the novitiate. At present these words refer to those who, by privilege, still make final profession after the novitiate. This is true of the Jesuits and of the Sisters of the Sacred Heart.[142] Larraona is followed in this interpretation of canon 569, § 1, by several other canonists.[143]

140 Prümmer, I, 279-280.

141 Larraona, "Studia Canonica de Paupertate Simplici," *CpR,* I (1920), 333-340; Goyeneche, "De transitu ad aliam religionem," *CpR,* II (1921), 145.

142 Larraona, *loc. cit.*

143 Coronata, I, p. 744, n. 587, note 8; Jansen, *Ordensrecht,* p. 116; Schaefer, pp. 549, 550, 597, 935. Prümmer, I, pp. 279-280, admits the probability of this opinion.

3. A third opinion contends that the religious must repeat or confirm the cession and disposition inasmuch as canon 580, § 3, provides that the cession and disposition lose their force if the religious leaves the institute.[144] This view appeals to the present writer, since a transfer really implies a departure from the institute—*discessus a religione.* To depart from the institute it is not necessary to leave the religious state entirely as in the case of secularization. *Departure* is a general word, and it would seem to be logically correct to assume that transfer to another institute is one of the particular kinds of departure which is comprehended by the general term.

Some objections, however, have been raised against the conclusive force of the argument from the final words of canon 580, § 3. First, the concept of transfer is designated with a special term (*transitus*) in the Code, and it is doubtful (so it is argued) that the word *discessus* includes that notion. Secondly, it is wrong to require a repetition of the cession and disposition *before* the profession in the receiving institute, since only an act of departure can make the original act of cession and disposition lose its force. But the act of departure (in this case the act of transfer) is not complete until the profession has been made. In consequence of this the act of profession must precede.[145]

4. In the light of these various difficulties, it is maintained by several well-known canonists that in practice a religious *can* make a new cession and disposition of his property before his profession in the new community, but is not *bound* to do so.[146]

[144] Can. 580, § 2. ". . . per discessum autem a religione eiusmodi cessio ac dispositio habere vim desinit." Cf. Berutti, III, 322; Claeys-Bouuaert-Simenon, I, p. 421, n. 695; Beste, p. 429.

[145] Goyeneche, *art. cit.*, *CpR*, II (1921), 145, 146. To the mind of the present writer, these arguments are not well founded. The second, particularly, is sophistical, since the cession and disposition need not become effective till the moment of profession.

[146] Goyeneche, *loc. cit.*; Schaefer, p. 935; Coronata, I, 850-851. Bastien (*Directoire canonique à l'usage des congregations à voeux simples*, p. 436, n. 613) stated simply that the transfer does not render null the cession and the disposition of his property which the religious made in the releasing community. As was seen above, Hofmeister suggested a slight adaptation regarding

Two restrictions are placed on the use of this opinion. A new disposition and cession of property *must* be made if the original cession and disposition are contrary to the provisions of the rule and the constitutions of the receiving institute. An example is the case in which the religious was free to make the disposition as he wished in the former community, but is restricted in this same freedom by the rule and the constitutions of the new institute.[147] Secondly, a religious who has made simple perpetual profession and transfers to an Order where he will make solemn profession cannot renew the cession and disposition of his property, but must renounce his ownership before the profession in accordance with the provisions of canon 580, § 1.[148]

The conclusion that a new cession and disposition *may* be made, if desired, but that it is not necessary to make them if they are not desired except in the cases mentioned above, seems to be a safe one in practice. First, it is not certain that there is any explicit provision in the law which was intended to regulate the effect a transfer will have on the cession and disposition concerning the property of religious with simple vows. Secondly, it is not certain that the previous cession and disposition lose their obliging force when the transfer is completed by the profession in the receiving institute. Thirdly, it is not certain that the canons require that a new cession and disposition which will become effective at the moment of the new profession. Fourthly, it seems very doubtful that the legislator intended to substitute an automatic substitution of the receiving for the releasing community in every case where

this opinion, which makes its application a little narrower in scope than the application which follows from Goyeneche's and Schaefer's opinion. He believes that in virtue of can. 635, n. 2°, the religious is given the right to change the cession and disposition of his property *after* the profession so as to substitute the new community for the releasing community, if the latter had been given the administration or had been named as the beneficiary of the use and usufruct of the property. Goyeneche and Schaefer give the religious the right to change the cession and disposition *in toto*.

147 Goyeneche, *loc. cit.*; Schaefer, *loc. cit.* This is the case when the first community used the formula of the *Normae* of 1901, art. 115, but the latter the so-called Bizzarrian formula.

148 Cf. Beste, p. 429.

the releasing community was the administrator of the property belonging to a religious with simple vows or the beneficiary of the revenues of that property.

If a new cession and disposition have been made in preparation for the new profession, then they will become binding at the moment of profession. If, on the other hand, no new cession and disposition have been made, then any changes desired after profession are subject to the restrictions found in the provisions of canon 580, § 3.[149]

A word may be added regarding the effect of the new novitiate on the cession and the disposition made in the former community. During the novitiate the religious will remain bound by this cession and disposition concerning his property and its revenues. The opinion above cited, namely, that there is an automatic change in the cession and disposition in favor of the new institute, cannot be followed in practice because it implies a restriction of the free exercise of rights which according to the legal principle as enunciated in canon 19 is not warranted.[150]

According to Goyeneche, acts of administration, of use and of usufruct cannot be exercised by the religious in the novitiate except in so far as they were permitted under his earlier profession of vows, and only within the limits set by the rule and the constitutions in the former institute.[151] This is a logical consequence of his views regarding the obligations as deriving from the vow of poverty after the transfer of the religious to the new community. Goyeneche believes that the vow obliges according to the rule and the constitutions of the releasing community.

The present writer disagrees with this view, and holds that the vow does not oblige beyond the limits of the rule and the constitutions of the receiving community.[152] It is therefore maintained that the religious can exercise acts of administration, of use and of usufruct in accordance with the rule and the constitutions of the new community. If the rule and the constitutions are more rigorous

149 See above, p. 223.
150 See above, p. 225.
151 *Art. cit., CpR,* II (1921), 120.
152 See above, pp. 152-154.

on this point than those of the releasing institute, the religious will be bound to obey them. To the extent, however, that the requirements go beyond the limits of the rule and the constitutions of the releasing community, he will not be bound to obey them in virtue of his vow, but in virtue of the law enacted in canon 561, § 2.[153]

If there is question during the novitiate of a change (exclusive of a change made as a preparation for profession in the receiving community shortly before the profession) in the cession of administration and in the disposition regarding the revenues, permission must be secured from the superiors of the receiving institute. The superiors empowered to give such permission are designated by canon 580, § 3, and by the constitutions of the institute. The reason is that in virtue of canon 633, § 1, the religious upon his transfer is subject to these, and not to his former superiors.[154]

If the religious acquires any new property not provided for by his original cession and disposition during his novitiate in the new community, he will be obliged in virtue of canon 569, § 2, to cede its administration and to dispose of its use and usufruct immediately.[155] This cession and disposition should be made in accordance with the requirements of the rule and the constitutions of the receiving institute.

A member of a society of the common life who transfers to another such society or to a religious institute would be bound during his novitiate or probation in the receiving community by the

[153] That the religious is not bound by the rule and the constitutions of his former community in this matter seems to be in accordance with the views of Larraona, who supports the opinion that the superior who can give permission for a change in the cession and disposition is the superior of the receiving community by the following consideration: "Hoc probabilius valet etsi constitutiones anterioris Religionis permitterent, proprio arbitrio, mutationem cessionis vel dispositionis facere (c. 580, § 3). Et ratio est in promptu, quia constitutionibus anterioris Religionis nec ligatur nec fruitur (c. 633, § 1)."—"Studia Canonica de Paupertate Simplici," *CpR*, I (1920), 336.

[154] Goyeneche, "De transitu ad aliam religionem," *CpR*, II (1921), 121; Berutti, III, 319. Larraona, *art. cit.*, *CpR*, I (1920), 335. Larraona regards this as at least the more probable opinion. He also points out that in the case of a nun canon 583, § 3, requires also the permission of the local ordinary.

[155] Berutti, III, 322; Goyeneche, *art. cit.*, *CpR*, II (1921), 144; Wernz-Vidal, III, 455; Bastien, p. 436; Schaefer, p. 935, n. 522.

cession and disposition made concerning his property, if such was required in the first community by reason of a private vow, a promissory oath, or a simple promise of poverty. For in this case the cession and disposition appear to be obligations which arise from something similar to the vow of poverty made by religious. Canon 633, § 1, indicates that the vows remain during the novitiate, and canon 681 applies the legal prescript of this canon to the case of a transfer made from a society of the common life to another such society or to a religious institute. Furthermore, it seems equivalent to a violation of sound juridical principle to relieve a member of such a society of these obligations, so as to give him perfect freedom in the administration, the use and the usufruct of his property, just as though he had not made a promise, or taken a private vow, or rendered a promissory oath of poverty. As is the case with a transferring religious, the permissions required for the making of a change in the cession and disposition concerning the property would have to be sought from the superiors of the new community.

If a cession and disposition are required of all novices or aspirants in the receiving community, the member of a society of common life who transfers to such an institute or a society could either make a disposition or omit making it, as is the case with religious who transfer to another religious institute.[156] Such a member must always make such cession and disposition if he has never made them and if they are required by the law or by the constitutions in the new community.

3. *The Renunciation of Property in the Novitiate.*

Under pain of invalidity canon 568 forbids novices to abdicate their goods. Canon 583, 1°, however, merely forbids those who are professed with simple vows to abdicate the ownership of their property by means of a voluntary deed of conveyance, that is, by way of gift or donation. These two canons deal expressly and respectively with novices in the one case, but with religious of simple profession in the other. They do not say anything explicitly of the

156 See above, pp. 227-229.

peculiar condition of a religious who passes from one institute to the other, that is, of one who is at one and the same time both a novice and a religious professed with simple vows. The question therefore arises as to which of the two canons affects the abdication of property on the part of a transferring religious. Would such an abdication or renunciation be only illicit (canon 583, 1°), or also invalid (canon 568)?

Coronata states that the admissibility of a valid renunciation of his property on the part of a transferred religious during his novitiate is not a certainly established fact in the law.[157] Goyeneche, on the other hand, believes that it is not improbable that he can do so validly.[158] Schaefer simply states that, if the religious should renounce his property during the novitiate, he would be acting illicitly, inasmuch as the ruling, not of canon 568, but of canon 583, 1°, applies to this case.[159]

The reasons advanced for the opinion that the renunciation would not be invalid are: (1) a transferring religious is a religious in an absolute sense, but a novice only in a relative sense, for canon 633, § 1, states that the vows remain during the novitiate; [160] (2) the purpose of the law which invalidates a renunciation when made by a novice is to safeguard the liberty of the novice to return to the world.[161] This is unnecessary in the case of a transferring religious who normally has but the freedom of returning to the institute in which he was professed; (3) a conveyance of property does not change the condition of the professed religious any more when he is in the new novitiate than it would have done before he entered it, and (4) it is a rule of law that he who bears a burden should also enjoy whatever prerogative is connected with it.[162] Since the trans-

[157] ". . . si professus ad aliam religionem transeat utrum, durante novitiatu, valide renuntiare possit res non plane constat; obstat conditio novitiatus, favet validae renuntiationi conditio professi."—Coronata, I, 850.

[158] "De transitu ad aliam religionem," *CpR,* II (1921), 119.

[159] Schaefer, p. 933, n. 518.

[160] Schaefer, *loc. cit.*; Goyeneche, *loc. cit.*

[161] Cf. Conc. Trident., sess. XXV, *de regularibus,* c. 16; Suarez, *De Religione,* tract. VI, lib. V, cap. 16, n. 10; Schmalzgrueber, III, tit. 31, n. 6.

[162] "Qui sentit onus sentire debet commodum, et e contra."—Reg. 55, R.J., in VI°.

ferring religious is truly a religious, he should therefore be given the benefit of the less rigorous law as applicable specifically to religious.[163] In view of the doubt of law arising from these considerations, the present writer holds that a renunciation would in practice be at most illicit, and not also invalid, since canon 568 is a law which limits the free exercise of rights and correspondingly calls for a strict interpretation of its restrictive enactment.[164]

One exception must be noted. A religious professed with simple vows who is later to make a solemn profession of vows cannot validly renounce his property until sixty days before his solemn profession. He must do it then, but on condition that he will make the profession.[165] This applies without doubt to all religious who when they are perpetually professed in simple vows transfer to another institute where they will make a profession of solemn vows at the end of the novitiate. Here, both canon 581, § 1, which affects him as a simply professed religious, and canon 568, which affects him as a novice, declare the invalidity of an abdication, until 60 days before profession. At that time, the provision of canon 581, 1°, that a religious who will make a solemn profession must renounce his property, will clearly prevail over the provision of canon 568 which forbids such a renunciation in the case of a novice. The renunciation of his personal property is a privilege which the law gives the religious, since without such renunciation his profession would automatically transfer the title of ownership to the community in which the solemn profession is made. To solve a doubt here by forbidding the religious to make a renunciation on the ground that it is forbidden by canon 568 would be a restriction of the free exercise of a right, and as such would not be warranted in view of the legal principle enunciated by canon 19. Canon 581, § 1, is clearly the ruling norm which is an obligatory one in practice.

Transferred religious, who then, have made only a simple profession and who are to make a solemn profession at the end of their

[163] Goyeneche, *loc. cit.*

[164] Cf. cans. 15 and 19.

[165] Can. 581, § 1; Schaefer, p. 594; Larraona, "Commentarium Codicis," *CpR,* II (1921), 202-205; Coronata, I, 763; Bouscaren-Ellis, p. 275. Cf. also Wernz-Vidal, III, n. 420, III.

novitiate must, within sixty days before that profession, renounce all the property which they actually possess (without prejudice to special indults granted by the Holy See) in favor of anyone they please. This renunciation is to become effective solely on the condition that the solemn profession is subsequenty made.[166]

The renunciation of property by members of or aspirants to societies of the common life is not governed by the Code; it is regulated by the constitutions of each society.[167] Consequently, in such cases there does not arise any problem concerning the validity of a renunciation of property made by a transferring religious during the time of his novitiate, since the enactments contained in canons 568 and 583, 1°, do not then apply.

If a member of such a society enters the novitiate of a religious institute, and then must make a renunciation of his property before his solemn profession, this renunciation will be governed by the canons that regulate the case of a religious who, when professed with simple vows at the time of his transfer, is later to make his solemn profession in the new community. If he will make only a simple profession, he cannot renounce his property under pain of the invalidity of his act during the novitiate.

4. *The Last Will and Testament.*

The canons of the Code which deal explicitly with the transfer of religious have no provision which indicates what effect, if any, the transfer will have on the last will and testament which the religious should have made before his profession of temporary vows.[168]

Hofmeister, indeed, believes that a provision which determines the effect which the transfer will have on the last will and testament of the religious is found in the following passage of canon 635, 2°: "quod spectat ad dotem eiusve fructus et alia bona personalia, si qua habeat religiosus, servandum praescriptum canon 551, § 2."

[166] Goyeneche, "De transitu ad aliam religionem," *CpR*, II (1921), 119; Berutti, III, 321, 322; Pejška, p. 183; Beste, p. 429; Coronata, I, 850; Schaefer, p. 933, n. 518.

[167] Cf. canons 676, § 3; 677.

[168] Can. 569, § 3.—Novitius in Congregatione religiosa ante professionem votorum temporariorum testamentum de bonis praesentibus vel forte obventuris libere condat.

Canon 551, § 2, in turn, provides that if a professed woman religious transfers to another religious institute the revenue of the dowry belongs to the receiving institute during her novitiate, and the dowry itself after she has made her new profession.[169] Hofmeister suggests that the phrase, "other personal property" (*alia bona personalia*) refers to the property of religious with simple vows, and gives the transferring religious the right, after his profession in the new community, to substitute the new community for the releasing institute in his last will and testament whenever the releasing institute was mentioned as his beneficiary.[170] To read into this general provision a norm regulating the effect which a transfer will have on the last will and testament made before first profession in the releasing institute seems rather far fetched. No other canonist, to this writer's knowledge, has maintained a similar opinion.

When recourse is had to the canons which deal with the last will and testament without reference to a transferring religious, a doubt arises, since two separate prescriptions of the law will come into conflict in the case of a transferring religious in virtue of the fact that he is both a novice and a professed religious. Canon 569, § 3, prescribes that a novice in a religious institute whose members are professed with simple vows must, before his profession of temporary vows, make a will regarding the goods which he possesses, or which later perchance may accrue to his estate. Canon 583, 2°, on the other hand, forbids any change in this last will and testament without permission of the Holy See. In urgent cases the major superior, or, if recourse cannot be made to him, the local superior may authorize him to change his will.[171] Which of these prescriptions is to prevail?

It is the opinion of Goyeneche that canon 583, 2°, forbids a change in the last will and testament even in the case of a transferring religious except with the permissions prescribed by this canon.[172] This seems to the writer to be the better view. It is

[169] For the commentary on canon 551, § 2, see above, pp. 200-209.

[170] Hofmeister, *art. cit.*, *AKKR*, CVIII (1928), 476, 477; see above, pp. 224-225.

[171] Can. 583, 2°. Testamentum, conditum ad normam can. 569, § 3, mutare sine licentia Sanctae Sedis, vel, si res urgeat nec tempus suppetat ad eam recurrendi, sine licentia Superioris maioris aut, si nec ille adiri possit, localis.

[172] Goyeneche, "De transitu ad aliam religionem," *CpR*, II (1921), 146.

not entirely certain, however. Schaefer is of the opinion that a transferring religious who will make profession of temporary vows in the receiving congregation at the expiration of his novitiate will come within the scope of canon 569, § 3. He would therefore permit the religious to make a new last will and testament.[173] This ligious is truly a novice and therefore comes within the scope of canon 569, § 3, despite the fact that a previous last will and testament was made.

The present writer believes that an even further extension of the scope of canon 569, § 3, is possible, in the case of transferring religious, so as to include those also who will make a perpetual profession at the termination of the novitiate. The reason is that canon 569, § 3, obviously is speaking of *first* profession when it speaks of the obligation to make a last will and testament for novices who will make a profession of temporary vows in a religious congregation.[174] It is not unreasonable to maintain that canon 569, § 3 requires the last will and testament before *temporary* profession in a congregation not because it is a *temporary* profession but because it is the *first* profession of simple vows in that institute by a religious who will be under the obligations arising from such vows throughout the whole of his religious life in that community. For a transferring religious with perpetual vows, his profession of perpetual vows at the end of the novitiate will be his *first* profession in the new community.

In a similar difficulty, the Commission for the Interpretation of the Code of Canon Law has extended a requirement of the Code for the admission of novices to the first profession of *temporary* vows, so as to make it apply to the admission of transferring religious to the *first* profession in the new community, even though it be a profession of *perpetual* vows. It was decided that the definitive vote of the council or chapter required by canon 575, § 2, for the admission of a novice to the first temporary profession is required also, in the case of transferring religious, for their admission to per-

[173] "Pro transitu valet can. 569, § 3, solummodo in casu, quo professus a votis temporariis ad novam Congregationem permeat"—*De Religiosis*, p. 556.

view cannot be said to lack probability, since the transferring re-

[174] Cf. can. 574, § 1.

petual profession at the end of their novitiate in the receiving community.[175]

It is here maintain that the broad interpretation of the meaning of canon 569, § 3, has sufficient probability to give the religious who transfers to another congregation and who will make perpetual profession at the end of the novitiate in the receiving community the right to make a last will and testament. The restriction which canon 580, 2°, places on the right of the religious to change his last will and testament must be regarded as a law which restricts the free exercise of a right and which therefore must receive a strict interpretation according to the norm of canon 19 of the Code. The opinion in favor of the liberty of the transferring religious to make a new last will and testament would also seem to be in accord with canonical equity, since it may easily happen that the releasing community is the beneficiary of the will made by the religious before his first profession. It would seem strange to require that a change in favor of either the new institute or of some other person would require the permission of the Holy See.

If, however, the opinion of Goyeneche that no change is possible except with the permissions required by canon 583, 2°, should be followed, the superiors who in an emergency would be empowered to give the religious the right to change his last will and testament, either while he is in the novitiate [176] or after his profession, will be the superiors of the receiving institute.

It is possible that a transferring religious who will make profession in a congregation has not made a last will and testament, either because he did not obey the prescript of canon 569, or because he comes from an Order whose members are not obliged to make a last will and testament, or because he had, after the original will and testament, acquired property not contemplated by any clause in that document.[177] Must such a religious make a last will

[175] 14 iul. 1922, *AAS*, XVI (1922), 528. See above, pp. 175-176.

[176] Cf. can. 633, § 1.

[177] Goyeneche, *art. cit.*, *CpR*, II (1921), 146.

and testament before his reception of vows in the receiving congregation?

If the making of the last will and testament was omitted before the first profession in the releasing institute, then a religious who has taken perpetual vows will not be strictly obliged to make a will on the occasion of his new perpetual profession in a congregation. The reason is that canon 569, § 3, if interpreted strictly and literally, comprehends only those who will make a temporary profession in a congregation. It would, however, be better for the religious to make the will, lest he die intestate. A religious who transferred when he was in temporary vows must make a new temporary profession. He therefore will come within the scope of canon 569, § 3, and will have to make a will if he did not make it at the time of his first profession.[178]

Conclusion

As a survey of this section will indicate, innumerable difficulties arise in every case in which one has to relate the expression *other personal property,* as used in canon 635, 2°, to the property of a religious who is professed with simple vows. This is true if one tries to apply the provision of canon 635, 2°, to the problem of the effect of transfer on the ownership of property on the part of a religious with simple vows, to the cession of its administration and to the disposition of its use and usufruct as made before the first profession, or to his last will and testament. On the other hand, a perfectly consistent and coherent definition of the expression *other personal property* has been furnished. This definition points to a foundation or some periodic income for the support of a particular religious which is similar to the dowry or to its revenues. In view of these considerations, the present writer has come to the conclusion that the legislator did not intend to have the expression *other personal property* applied to the property of a religious with simple vows. The ruling canons for the effect which a transfer will have on this type of property rights should accordingly in every case be sought by recourse to other sections of the Code.

[178] Schaefer, p. 933; Goyeneche, *loc. cit.*; Coronata, I, 851.

III. The Expenses of the Novitiate.

Canon 635, 2°.—. . . demum nova religio ius habet pro novitiatus tempore ad iustam retributionem, si eidem locus sit ad normam can. 570, § 1.

Canon 570, § 1.—Nisi pro alimentis et habitu religioso in constitutionibus vel expressa conventione aliquid in postulatu vel novitatu ineundo solvendum caveatur, nihil pro impensis postulatus vel novitiatus exigi potest.

Canon 635, 2°, provides that when a religious transfers to another institute the new community is entitled to demand for the time of the novitiate a just compensation, if such an arrangement is not contrary to the ruling of canon 570, § 1. This canon in turn provides that, unless the constitutions or a formal agreement require the payment of a certain sum for food and clothing during the novitiate, nothing can be exacted in defrayment of the expenses of the novitiate. In virtue of canon 681 these provisions will apply to a transfer from a society of the common life to another such society or to a religious institute. The Code does not, however, determine precisely the source from which these expenses are to be met.

There are five possible sources suggested by the authors. (1) The revenues of the dowry of women religious; [179] (2) pensions and other similar personal revenues (previously defined in the preceding section as identifiable with the *"alia bona personalia"* mentioned in canon 635, 2°); [180] (3) revenues from personal property which is owned by the religious who is professed with simple vows; [181] (4) funds offered by the parents and benefactors of the religious; [182] and (5) funds supplied by the releasing community.

179 Oesterle, I, 303; Gerster a Zeil, pp. 135-136. See above, pp. 206-207.

180 Larraona, "Commentarium Codicis," *CpRM,* XXI (1940), 215.

181 Oesterle, I, 303; Berutti, III, 321; Hofmeister, "Der Übertritt in eine andere religiöse Genossenschaft," *AKKR,* CVIII (1928), 479. It is to be remarked that this will require a change in the disposition with reference to the revenues of this property. This change will have to be made in accordance with the ruling canon 580, § 3.

182 Oesterle, I, 303; Gerster a Zeil, 135-136; Hofmeister, *loc. cit.*

Gerster a Zeil takes exception to the last mentioned category,[183] but Hofmeister indicates that in his opinion the releasing community should do this if it furnished cause for the transfer, or if the religious transferred to a more rigorous community, or if he transferred on account of illness.[184] Berutti indicates that if the religious had no property of his own, it would be most equitable that the releasing community should pay these expenses, especially if this institute had acquired much property by way of inheritances and legacies that fell due to the religious, by way of his personal industry and activity, by way of personal donations made by him to the community, and so forth.[185] This certainly seems to be the fair and equitable procedure.

It is here maintained that one should not follow in practice the opinion of those who maintain that the meaning of canon 551, § 2, in conjunction with canons 570, § 1, and 635, 2°, is to be so interpreted that the expenses must be paid to the new community in full, even if the community receives the revenues from the dowry and all personal pensions during the novitiate of the religious. This interpretation of the law would occasion inequitable burdens. Moreover, since the obligatory character of the law as thus interpreted can be called into doubt, it remains unenforceable in practice. *Odiosa sunt restringenda.*[186] An agreement, however, between the two communities which provides that the releasing institute will convey not only the interest of the dowry but also a sum equivalent to the expenses of the novitiate to the receiving community would not be invalid. It would be a free agreement which goes beyond the requirements of the law.

[183] *Loc. cit.* He says it should be the receiving community. But it is here supposed that the constitutions or an explicit agreement have ruled out this possibility by providing that the expenses must be paid from another source.

[184] *Loc. cit.* Hofmeister asserts that if the releasing institute has been given property for the support of the religious, it must pay the expenses of the novitiate. It is, however, the opinion of the present writer that the entire revenues from such property accrue in every case to the receiving community during the novitiate—see above, pp. 209-215.

[185] Berutti, III, 321; cf. also Hofmeister, *loc. cit.*

[186] See above, pp. 200-201.

ARTICLE 3. THE EFFECT OF THE COMPLETION OF THE TRANSFER ON THE VOWS.

If the transfer is made to another monastery of the same Order there is no substantial difference in the vows; they therefore remain unaffected through the transfer of the religious. In the case of those who transfer to another institute, however, the necessity of making a new profession inevitably effects a change in the vows of the religious if he is still bound by any at the end of the novitiate. Profession consists in two inseparable elements: first, the contract between the religious and the institute, consisting in his giving of himself to the institute, and in his acceptance by the institute; second, the taking of the religious vows.[187]

Neither the canons nor the commentators define the precise nature of the change which through the new profession is effected in the vows of the religious. It may perhaps be considered to be a commutation of the vows taken in the former institute, or perhaps one may believe that the former vows are abolished and are completely and entirely replaced by a new set of religious vows. But the end result is clear. The religious is bound by the new vows as if he had never been bound by vows in any other religious institute. This is evident from canon 635, 1°, which states that from the day of his profession a religious who has transferred to another institute loses all the rights and obligations of the former institute, and assumes the rights and duties of the new institute. Since this canon does not make any distinction, it is evident that the obligations arising from the vows are included with the rest. This is evident also from the fact that, if the religious ever leaves the receiving institute, his previous vows do not revive. He has definitively lost all the obligations which were his in the releasing community. So true is this that apart from an apostolic indult he cannot be readmitted by the community which released him.[188] Thenceforward the religious will be bound by the vows which

[187] Schaefer, p. 566, n. 263. See above, p. 82.

[188] Vermeersch-Creusen, *Epitome*, I, 586, n. 793 (735); Schaefer, p. 939, n. 524.

he has taken in the new community in accordance with the constitutions of that institute.

Canon 636 is a logical consequence of this fundamental norm, though it is quite new in the law:

> "Sollemnitas votorum in eo qui legitime secundum superiores canones vota simplicia in Congregatione religiosa nuncupat, eo ipso exstinguitur, nisi aliud in apostolico indulto expresse caveatur."

It provides that the solemnity of the vows of one who, according to the foregoing canons (canons 632 to 635), lawfully makes profession of simple vows in a religious congregation is by that fact abolished, unless an apostolic indult expressly determined otherwise. This is a new law and, in fact, quite revolutionary.[189] This means that thenceforward the vows will have the effects only of simple, and not of solemn, vows.

According to canon 579, a simple profession renders contrary acts illicit, but not invalid; solemn profession, however, renders contrary acts invalid, if the acts are such that they can be invalidated. Hence one who completes a transfer from an Order to a congregation will, once he has made the new simple profession, no longer be subject to the invalidating effects of solemn vows. His vow of chastity will no longer invalidate an attempted marriage, though of course it will exist as a prohibitive impediment, which renders the contracting of such a marriage gravely sinful. An exception, however, must be made for one who makes a simple profession in an institute in which the simple vow of chastity has, by special prescription of the Holy See, the power to invalidate marriage.[190]

Similarly, a transferring religious in solemn vows who makes profession in a congregation of simple vows will also recover his capacity to own property, which capacity he earlier had lost by

[189] Cf. Schaefer, p. 941, n. 534, note 79. St. Thomas had taught that the Church could never dispense from solemn vows. No provision was made in the pre-Code law for a transfer from an Order to a congregation.

[190] Cf. cans. 1058, 1073.

reason of his solemn vow of poverty.[191] The authors are agreed that the abolition of the solemnity of the vows through the simple profession does not have a retroactive effect. The restrictive effects of solemn profession do not cease until the moment of the new profession. No contrary acts placed before that time are validated by the change in the vows.[192]

Again, the change of his vows does not give a religious the right to recover from the Order or from others what they have already legitimately acquired in consequence of his earlier solemn profession. So, for example, he cannot recover property whose ownership has passed to others in consequence of his renouncement of the property in their favor, or goods that have been legitimately expended or donated in behalf of the releasing institute.[193]

It is the opinion of Vermeersch, however, that even if the religious had before his solemn profession renounced his inheritance rights in someone else's favor, these are recovered if the person from whom the inheritance is due has not yet died. In this case the person to be benefited by the renunciation has not as yet acquired any dominion over the property in question, and on the other hand, the religious has recovered his earlier forfeited capacity of acquiring inherited property.[194]

A question has been raised whether the solemnity of the vows is extinguished when the transfer is made to a congregation in which only temporary vows are taken. Haring (+1942) declared that the solemn vows did not become extinguished by the new temporary profession in this case.[195] Coronata, however, denies this. He states that it does not seem that any further recourse to the Holy See is necessary, and that it can be assumed that a dispensation was granted along with the permission for the transfer to that community.[196]

[191] Beste, p. 430.

[192] Beste, *loc. cit.*; Vermeersch-Creusen, *Epitome,* I, 586, n. 792 (734); Gerster a Zeil, p. 136; Schaefer, p. 941, n. 534; Wernz-Vidal, III, 454.

[193] Wernz-Vidal, *loc. cit.*; Vermeersch-Creusen, *Epitome, loc. cit.*

[194] *Epitome, loc. cit.*

[195] *Grundzüge des katholischen Kirchenrechts* (3. ed., 2 vols., Graz, 1924), II, p. 816, note 4.

[196] *Institutiones Iuris Canonici* I, p. 752, note 7.

It seems to the writer that the latter opinion is the more acceptable one. Canon 636 states that the solemnity of the vows is abolished when simple vows are taken in a religious congregation. The Code itself defines the term "congregation" in canon 488, 2°, as an institute in which only simple vows, whether perpetual or temporary, are taken. If one takes the word congregation in its proper sense as used in the Code, one quite naturally concludes that the solemnity of the previous profession is extinguished through a profession of vows in any congregation, whether it be a congregation of perpetual or of temporary vows.

Haring could have objected with greater reason, so it seems to the present writer, to the abolition of the *perpetuity* of the vows in consequence of a transfer to a congregation of only temporary vows, rather than to the abolition of their *solemnity*. It seems incongruous that a religious should automatically be freed of the perpetuity of his vows in consequence simply of his transfer to another community. This would mean that at the expiration of the temporary profession he could leave this community on his own authority. The possibility of such a transfer is not, however, absolutely excluded. It even seems to be implied by the wording of canon 634.[197] As long as the Holy See has been made duly aware of the nature of the community to which the transfer was requested, it seems that one should rather assume that the profession made by the transferring religious in the new community should be on a par with that of the other aspirants, that is to say, temporary in character like theirs.

A question not raised by the authors is the following: What will happen, in a case of transfer, to the simple vows which, by a special indult of the Holy See, have the same effects as solemn

[197] Canon 634 states that if one who is professed with solemn vows, or with simple perpetual vows, transfers to another institute of solemn vows, or of simple perpetual vows, he must make profession of solemn or of simple perpetual vows according to the institute. The condition, "if he transfers to another institute of solemn vows or of simple vows," does not close the door to the possible transfer of such a religious to a community in which only temporary vows are taken. One may be sure that such a transfer will not be granted without most serious reason, and one may assume that the Holy See will make explicit provisions for so unusual a case.

vows. If a religious with such simple vows transfers to an institute of simple perpetual vows wherein no such indult obtains, then certainly the extraordinary effects which the simple vow possessed in the releasing community are lost through the new profession. The reason is that canon 635, 1°, states that the religious loses all the rights and obligations which he had in the releasing community, and assumes the rights and obligations of the receiving community. If solemn vows become abolished through the later simple profession, then, *a fortiori*, the special effects which by apostolic indult were attached to the earlier simple vows should likewise become abolished through the later profession of vows in a community which does not have a like indult.

CONCLUSIONS

1. Transfer is the process by which a duly incorporated member a religious institute, of an independent monastery, or of a society of the common life loses the juridical bond which incorporates him in a stable way in that community and becomes subject simultaneously to a new juridical bond which incorporates him in some other community. This definition clearly distinguishes the term transfer from a process which is really distinct: namely, egress from one community followed by ingress into another. This latter is not a transfer in the strict and proper sense of the term, as it is used by canons 632 to 636 and canon 681.

2. A transfer of a religious from an independent house of a congregation to another independent house of the same institute requires apostolic permission. A new novitiate or profession are unnecessary in case of such a transfer.

3. If there is no juridical obligation to persevere in a particular society, no indult to transfer should be requested from the Holy See. It will be better to withdraw from the society and to seek entrance into a new community. This procedure is not a transfer in the sense in which the term is used in the Code.

4. If there is a juridical obligation to persevere in a society of the common life, a member who wishes to transfer must seek an apostolic indult. In the case where the local ordinary can dispense so as to permit the member to sever his relationship with the society, it will depend on the circumstances whether the person will seek an apostolic indult to transfer or will seek rather a dispensation from the ordinary to leave the society in order subsequently to seek admission into another institute. The latter procedure is not regulated by canons 632 to 635.

5. Privileges granted before the Code to certain institutes to permit their members to transfer to other institutes without recourse to the Holy See have not been revoked by canon 632, but their exercise has been impeded by canon 542, 1°.

6. Transfers from one religious institute to another without

the required apostolic permission are certainly invalid. Transfers from one independent monastery to another or from a society of common life to a religious institute without apostolic permission are not certainly invalid.

7. A religious who attempts to transfer without due permission may incur the penalty of excommunication as an apostate from his institute.

8. Though every transfer to another institute requires the permission of the Holy See, it is reasonable to conclude that permission to transfer to a more rigorous institute will be granted more readily than permission to transfer to a less rigorous one, and permission to transfer from a congregation to an Order more readily than a transfer from an Order to a congregation.

9. If the documents required by canon 544, §§ 1-4, for aspirants to religious communities are obligatory in a society of common life by reason of the constitutions of the society, members of such a society need only the document indicated by canon 544, § 5, in the event of a transfer to another society or to a religious institute.

10. Canonical impediments from which a dispensation was secured before entrance into the novitiate of the releasing community are no obstacle to reception into the receiving community.

11. A valid novitiate is necessary for the validity of the new profession and consequently for the validity of the transfer.

12. The postulancy should not be imposed on a religious who transfers to another religious institute.

13. A retreat of eight days before admission to the novitiate is not certainly obligatory for religious who transfer to another institute. It is obligatory if the constitutions prescribe it for all aspirants without exception.

14. Transferring religious are not subject to the provisions of canon 522, which obliges the superior of women religious to notify the ordinary of the coming admission of postulants to the novitiate and obliges the ordinary to conduct a canonical examination to determine their intentions, their knowledge of the religious life and their freedom.

15. If the statutes of a monastery prescribe that those who

transfer to another monastery of the same Order must undergo a period of probation they must be observed.

16. When there is no provision in the statutes for a probationary period or even for a temporary transfer between monasteries belonging to the same Order the law does not contemplate a period of probation. If, however, it is felt that it would be prudent to submit to a period of probation a religious who wishes to transfer, the Holy See should be requested to grant not only permission for the transfer but also permission to submit the transferring religious to a period of probation.

17. Transferring religious are to be admitted to the novitiate according to the norms of canon 543. If the constitutions require that the admitting major superior have the consent of the chapter or of the council and this requirement is neglected the admission to the novitiate will be invalid.

18. The superiors and the master of novices of the receiving institute cannot command, *in virtue of the vow of obedience,* that a religious who is in the novitiate do anything which is not explicitly or implicitly contained in the constitutions of the releasing institute, nor anything which goes beyond the scope of the constitutions of the receiving community.

19. A transferring religious, during the novitiate in the receiving institute, is excused from observing *in virtue of the vow of poverty* whatever, is not obligatory in the releasing community. He is not obliged in virtue of this vow to observe what goes beyond the scope of the rule and the constitutions of the new community. It must always be borne in mind, however, that his vow of poverty retains in full force the juridical limitations imposed by its nature, i. e., by the fact that it is solemn or simple, perpetual or temporary.

20. The Code does not define what is meant by the particular obligations referred to in canon 633, § 1. "Particular" is used in the Code as the contrary of "general" and to refer here to obligations which derive, not from the general law, but from the rules, constitutions or special laws enacted for the releasing institute. It seems reasonable also to assume that they include obligations which a religious has assumed toward the community in which he was professed (and toward no other) in virtue of his profession.

21. Vows which are obligatory in the releasing institute but which are other than the three substantial vows of the religious life remain suspended for the duration of the novitiate.

22. In so far as the obligations of the enclosure in the releasing institute are derived from the rule and the constitutions of that institute they are suspended during the novitiate in the receiving community.

23. A nun who transfers from a monastery in which the papal cloister is observed to a community in which the enclosure is episcopal only is bound during the novitiate to observe only the episcopal enclosure. If a nun transfers from a monastery where the papal enclosure is observed to a monastery where there is the same obligation she must observe the papal enclosure but a violation is not subject to the excommunication enacted by canon 2342, 3°.

24. A vote cast by a transferring religious in an election in the releasing institute while he is a novice in the receiving institute will be illicit but valid.

25. The right of eligibility for office is in suspension while a transferring religious is in the novitiate of another institute. If, however, he accepts an election to office in the releasing institute the act will be valid.

26. The novitiate of a religious with temporary vows transferring to another institute can be prorogated for no more than six months and only if there is a doubt concerning the requisite suitability and fitness of the candidate for the life of the receiving community.

27. The attempt to transfer to another institute need not be terminated nor a new indult sought when the novitiate of a transferring religious is broken by an absence of over thirty days when this absence is due to a just reason, is made with the permission of the superior and with the intention to return to the novitiate.

28. It is possible to find reasons to support two views concerning the cessation of the indult to transfer—the one, that with the possible exception of the case in conclusion 27 a new indult will be needed if the novitiate is broken without profession; the other, that the indult will not cease even after the termination of several attempts to transfer, until the transfer is completed by profession.

29. If the vows of a religious who has made temporary profession expire in the course of his novitiate in a new community, he does not need an apostolic indult for readmission to the community which he left nor need he make a new novitiate there, unless he either has definitively abandoned his former community or has been definitively dismissed from it after the expiration of his vows.

30. A member of a society of common life who has assumed the obligation according to the constitutions of his society to persevere in it for life need not be admitted to a temporary profession if he transfers to a religious institute, but can be admitted immediately to final profession.

31. It is not certain whether religious who transfer to another society after a temporary profession of vows must make a profession for a new three year period or whether they may make profession for a period sufficient to complete the three year period reckoned from the day of the first temporary profession in the releasing institute. The better view is that they should make a temporary profession of vows for a new period of three years, then also when the temporary vows taken in the releasing institute expired in the course of the novitiate.

32. After a religious transfers from an order to a congregation and makes profession of simple vows he can acquire inheritances coming to him from persons still alive at the time of his new profession, even if he renounced them before his previous solemn profession.

33. Property acquired by a transferring religious *industria sua* while in the novitiate of the receiving institute belongs to this institute. He need not accept gifts given *intuitu religionis* if they are intended for the releasing institute.

34. The acquisition of gifts and inheritances which come to a religious with solemn vows in the course of his novitiate in another community is held in suspension so that the ultimate effect will be achieved only upon the termination of the novitiate. This is the most acceptable view but it is not entirely certain. It is therefore recommended that before a transfer is made the two religious institutes agree as to what is to be done if such property should

be acquired by the religious during his novitiate in the new community.

35. The view that the interest accruing from the dowry during the novitiate of a transferring religious always belongs *in toto* to the receiving community and that it is the primary source for defraying a charge for the expenses of the novitiate is the most acceptable.

36. The view that the dowry becomes the property of the releasing institute if a woman religious transfers to a community that requires no dowry is inadmissible and should not be followed in practice.

37. The term "other personal property" in canon 635, 2°, refers primarily to pensions, annuities and similar periodic payments which accrue to a community by reason of the presence of a particular religious. These follow the religious to the receiving community during the novitiate and after profession. It is the belief of the present writer that during the novitiate the payments must be given *in toto* to the new community.

38. Manuscripts which have no money value, but a purely personal one, can be taken along when a religious transfers to a new community. In the case of manuscripts which have money value the sales' rights will remain with the releasing community, though the religious will have a right to them as regards their personal use.

39. It cannot be maintained that religious with simple vows, in the event of a transfer, lose dominion of their property to the receiving institute.

40. It is not clear that the Code contains specific provisions to regulate the effect which a transfer will have on the cession of administration and disposition of the use and of the usufruct of property belonging to a religious with simple vows. It is therefore maintained that in practice a religious can make a new cession and disposition before his profession in a receiving congregation, but that he is not bound to do so unless the original cession and disposition are contrary to the rule and the constitutions of the new institute.

41. If a new cession and disposition are made before profes-

sion, they become binding at the moment of profession. If, on the other hand, no new cession and disposition are made at this time, any changes which are desired after the profession in the receiving community are subject to the restrictions of canon 580, § 3.

42. If a transferring religious illegitimately renounces his property in the course of the novitiate the renunciation will be at most illicit and not also invalid. A transferring religious with simple vows, however, who will make profession of solemn vows at the end of the novitiate must, sixty days before his profession, renounce his property on condition of the future profession. A renunciation made before that time would be invalid.

43. It is probable that canon 569, § 3, gives to transferring religious the right of making a new last will and testament before the profession at the end of the novitiate in the receiving congregation, even then when it will be a profession of perpetual vows.

44. The term "other personal property" as used in canon 635, 2°, does not refer to the property of religious with simple vows.

45. If a religious with solemn vows receives apostolic permission to transfer to a congregation where only temporary vows are taken his new profession will be one of temporary vows unless the Holy See shall have provided otherwise.

46. If a religious with simple vows which by special indult have the same effects as solemn vows transfers to a congregation which does not have such an indult, the special effects which by apostolic indult were attached to the earlier simple vows become abolished through his later profession in the receiving community.

BIBLIOGRAPHY

Sources

Acta et Decreta Capituli Generalis XIX Congregationis Helveto-Americanae O.S.B. habiti diebus 26, 27, 28, 29 Septembris 1941.

Benedicti XIV Bullarium, 3 vols. in 4, Prati, 1845-1847.

Bizzarri, Andreas, *Collectanea in usum Secretariae Sacrae, Congregationis Episcoporum et Regularium edita,* 2. ed., Romae: ex Typographia Polyglotta S. C. de Propaganda Fide, 1885.

Bouscaren, T. Lincoln, *The Canon Law Digest,* 2 vols., Milwaukee: Bruce, 1934-1943.

Bruns, H. Th., *Canones Apostolorum et Conciliorum Saeculorum IV. V. VI. VII.,* 2 vols. Berolini, 1839.

Bullarum Diplomatum et Privilegiorum Sanctorum Romanorum Pontificum Taurinensis Editio, 24 tomes in 25 vols., Augustae Taurinorum-Neapoli, 1857-1872.

Codex Iuris Canonici Pii X Pontificis Maximi iussu digestus Benedicti Papae XV auctoritate promulgatus, Romae: Typis Polyglottis Vaticanis, 1917, Re-impressio, 1929.

Codicis Iuris Canonici Fontes cura Emi Petri Card. Gasparri editi, 9 vols., Romae (postea Civitate Vaticana): Typis Polyglottis Vaticanis, 1923-1939 (Vols. VII, VIII et IX ed. cura et studio Emi Iustiniani Card. Serédi).

Constitutiones Congregationis Benedictinae Bavarieae, Augustae Vindelicorum, 1922.

Constitutiones Ordinis Cisterciensium Strictioris Observantiae, Westmalli, 1925.

Constitutions of the Institute of the Religious Sisters of Mercy of the Union in the United States of America, Washington, D. C. Sisters of Mercy, General Motherhouse, 1941.

Corpus Iuris Canonici, ed. Lipsiensis secunda post Aemilii Ludovici Richter curas . . . instruxit Aemilius Friedberg, 2 vols., Lipsiae, 1879-1881.

Declarationes et Statuta sive Constitutiones Congregationis Ottiliensis O.S.B., 1925.

Declarationes in Regulam S.P.N. Benedicti et Statuta Congregationis Americo-Cassinensis, approved by the S. Cong. for Religious, Feb. 3, 1935, Atchison, Kansas.

Declarations on the Holy Rule and Constitutions of the Swiss-American Congregation, O.S.B., tr. from the Latin original by order of the general chapter, Oct., 1935, Conception: Altar and Home Press, 1938.

Decretales D. Gregorii IX una cum Glossis Restitutae, Romae, 1582.

Decretum Gratiani Emendatum et Observationibus Illustratum una cum Glossis, Gregorii XIII Pont. Max. iussu editum, 2 vols., Romae, 1582.

Hefele, Carolus-Leclercq, Henricus, *Histoire des Conciles,* 10 vols. in 19, Paris: Librairie Letouzey et Ané, 1907-1938.

Holstenius, L.-Brockie, M., *Codex regularum monasticarum et canonicarum*, 6 vols., Augustae Vindelicorum, 1759.

Jaffe, Philippus, *Regesta Pontificum Romanorum ab condita Ecclesia ad annum post Christum natum MCXCVIII*, ed. 2. correctam et auctam auspiciis Gulielmi Wattenbach curaverunt S. Loewenfeld, F. Kaltenbrunner, P. Ewald, 2 vols. in 1, Lipsiae, 1885-1888.

Magnum Bullarium Romanum, 19 vols., Luxemburgi, 1727-1758.

Mansi, Joannes Dominicus, *Sacrorum Conciliorum Nova et Amplissima Collecito*, 53 vols. in 60, Paris-Arnhem-Leipzig, 1901-1927.

Monumenta Germaniae Historica, Epistolae, Tom. I, II, ed. P. Ewald et L. M. Hartmann, Berolini, 1887-1899.

———, *Leges, sect. II, Capitularia, Tom I*, ed. A. Boretius, Hannoveriae, 1883.

Normae Secundum Quas S. Congr. Episcoporum et Regularium Procedere Solet in Approbandis Novis Institutis Votorum Simplicium, Romae: Typis S. Congr. de Prop. Fide, 1901.

Pallottini, Salvator, *Collectio Omnium Conclusionum et Resolutionum Quae in causis propositis apud Sacram Congregationem Cardinalium S. Concilii Tridentini Interpretum Prodierunt ab eius Institutione anno MDLXIV ad annum MDCCCLX, distinctis titulis alphabetico ordine per materias digesta*, 17 vols., Romae, 1868-1893.

Potthast, A., *Regesta Pontificum Romanorum inde ab Anno post Christum Natum 1198 ad Annum 1304*, 2 vols., Berolini, 1874-1875.

Sancti Benedicti Regula Monachorum, ed. by C. Butler, Friburgi Brisgoviae, 1912.

Schroeder, H. J., *Canons and Decrees of the Council of Trent*, St. Louis: Herder, 1941.

The Rule and Constitutions of the Religious called Sisters of Mercy, Dublin: Brown and Nolan, 1926.

Waddingus, L., *Annales Minorum seu Trium Ordinum a S. Francisco Institutorum*, 3. ed., 27 vols., Quaracchi, Ad Claras Aquas: 1932-1934.

Authors

Alphonsus de Liguori, St., *Theologia Moralis*, 4 vols. in 2, Augustae Taurinorum, 1825-1828.

Arndt, Augustinus, *Die kirchlichen und weltlichen Rechtsbestimmungen für Orden und Kongregationen*, Paderborn, 1919.

Arregui, Antonius M., *Summarium Theologiae Moralis*, 13. ed., Westminster, Maryland: The Newman Book Shop, 1944.

Augustine, Charles, *A Commentary on the New Code of Canon Law*, 8 vols., Vol. III, 3. ed., St. Louis: Herder, 1922.

Bachofen, Charles Augustine, *Compendium Iuris Regularium*, New York, 1903.

Balzer, Ralph F., *The Computation of Time in a Canonical Novitiate*, The Catholic University of America Canon Law Studies, n. 212, Washington, D. C.: The Catholic University of America Press, 1945.

Barry, G. F., *Violation of the Cloister,* The Catholic University of America Canon Law Studies, n. 148, Washington, D. C.: The Catholic University of America Press, 1942.

Bastien, Pierre, *Directoire canonique à l'usage des congrégations à voeux simples,* 4. ed., Bruges: Beyaert, 1933.

Benedictus XIV, *De Synodo Dioecesana,* 2. ed., 2 vols., Parmae, 1764.

Bernardus Papiensis, *Summa Decretalium,* ed. E. A. Th. Laspeyres, Ratisbon, 1860.

Berutti, Christopherus, *Institutiones Iuris Canonici,* 6 vols., Vol. III, *De Religiosis,* Taurini-Romae: Marietti, 1936.

Beste, Ulricus, *Introductio in Codicem,* 2. ed., Collegeville: St. John's Abbey Press, 1944.

Biederlack, Josephus-Führich, Maximilianus, *De Religiosis,* Oeniponte, 1919.

Blat, Albertus, *Commentarium Textus Codicis,* 6 vols., Romae, 1921-1927, Vol. II, *De Personis,* 1921.

Bouix, Dominicus, *Tractatus de Jure Regularium,* 2 vols., Parisiis, 1857.

Bouscaren, T. Lincoln-Ellis, Adam C., *Canon Law,* Milwaukee: Bruce, 1946.

Brandys, M., *Kirchliches Rechtshandbuch für die religiösen Laiengenossenschaften,* Paderborn, 1918.

Butler, Dom Cuthbert, *Benedictine Monasticism,* New York, 1919.

Cappello, Felix M., *Summa Iuris Canonici,* 3 vols., Romae: apud Aedes Universitatis Gregorianae, 1928-1936.

Cayré, F., *Manual of Patrology,* 2 vols., tr. by H. Howitt, Paris: Desclée & Co., 1936-1940.

Chelodi, J., *Ius Canonicum de Personis,* 3. ed., ed. P. Ciprotti, Trento: Libreria Moderna Editrice, 1942.

Choupin, Lucien, *Nature et Obligation de l'Etat Religieux—Actuelle Discipline,* Paris: Beauchesne, 1923.

Claeys Bouuaert, F.-Simenon, G., *Manuale Juris Canonici,* 3 vols., Vols. I et III, 5. ed., Vol. II, 3. ed., Gandae et Leodii: Apud Auctores, 1939.

Cocchi, Guidus, *Commentarium in Codicem Iuris Canonici,* 8 vols. in 5, Vol. IV (Liber II, Pars II, *De Religiosis*), 3. ed., Taurinorum Augustae: Marietti, 1932.

Coronata, Matthaeus Conte a, *Institutiones Iuris Canonici,* 5 vols., Vol. I, 2. ed., Taurini: Marietti, 1939.

Creusen, Joseph-Ellis, Adam-Garesché, Edward F., *Religious Men and Women in the Code,* 5. ed., Milwaukee: Bruce, 1940.

De Angelis, Philippus, *Praelectiones Iuris Canonici,* 2. ed., 5 vols., Romae, 1908.

Delatte, Paul, *A Commentary on the Rule of St. Benedict,* translated by Dom Justin McCann, New York: Benziger Brothers, 1921.

De Luca, Joannes Baptista, *Theatrum Veritatis et Iustitiae,* 16 vols. in 9, Coloniae Agrippinae, 1706.

De Meester, A., *Juris Canonici et Juris Canonico-civilis Compendium,* 3 vols. in 4, Brugis, 1921-1928.

Eichmann, Eduard, *Lehrbuch des Kirchenrechts,* 2. ed., Paderborn, 1926.

Fagnanus, Prosper, *Commentaria in Quinque Libros Decretalium,* 5 vols. in 3, Venetiis, 1719.

Fanfani, Ludovicus, *De Iure Religiosorum ad Normam Codicis Iuris Canonici,* 2. ed., Taurini-Romae: Marietti, 1925.

Ferraris, Lucius, *Prompta Bibliotheca Canonica, Juridica, Moralis, Theologica, necnon Ascetica, Polemica, Rubricistica, Historica,* 8 vols., Parisiis, 1860-1863.

Fine, Ed., *Iuris regularis tum communis tum particularis, quo regitur societas Jesu, declaratio,* Prati, 1909.

Gerster a Zeil, Thomas Villanova, *Ius Religiosorum in Compendium Redactum pro Iuvenibus Religiosis,* Taurini: Marietti, 1935.

Haring, Johann B., *Grundzüge des Katholischen Kirchenrechts,* 3. ed., 2 vols., Graz, 1924.

Heimbucher, Max, *Die Orden und Kongregationen der katholischen Kirche,* 2. ed., 3 vols., Paderborn, 1907-1908.

Hostiensis (Henricus de Segusio), *Commentaria in Quinque Libros Decretalium,* 5 vols. in 3, Venetiis, 1581.

Jansen, Joseph, *Ordensrecht,* Paderborn, 1920.

Joannes Andreae, *In Sex Decretalium Libros Novella Commentaria,* 6 vols. in 5, Venetiis, 1581.

Jone, Heribert-Adelman, Urban, *Moral Theology,* 2. ed., Westminster, Md.: The Newman Bookshop, 1946.

Kealy, Thomas M., *Dowry of Women Religious,* The Catholic University of America Canon Law Studies, n. 134, Washington, D. C.: The Catholic University of America Press, 1941.

Kearney, Raymond A., *The Principles of Delegation,* The Catholic University of American Canon Law Studies, n. 55, Washington, D. C.: The Catholic University of America, 1929.

Krimer, F., *Quaestiones Canonici in V libros Decretalium,* 5 vols., Augustae Vindelicorum, 1706-1709.

Lanslots, D. I., *Handbook of Canon Law for Women Religious,* 10. ed., New York, 1922.

Leage, R. W., *Roman Private Law,* 2. ed., ed. by C. H. Ziegler, London: Macmillan Book Co., Ltd., 1942.

Lehmkuhl, A., *Theologia Moralis,* 4. ed., 2 vols., Friburgi Brisgoviae, 1887.

Lessius, Leonardus, *De Iustitia et Iure Caeterisque Virtutibus Cardinalibus,* Lovanii, 1605.

Lezana, I. B., *Summa Quaestionum Regularium,* Lugduni, 1655.

Lombardi, C., *Iuris Canonici Privati Institutiones,* 2. ed., 3 vols., Romae, 1901.

Migne, J. P., *Patrologiae Cursus Completus, Series Graeca,* 161 vols., Paris, 1856-1866.

———, *Patrologiae Cursus Completus, Series Latina,* 221 vols., Paris, 1844-1864.

Monacelli, Francesco, *Formularium Legale Practicum,* 3. ed., 3 vols., Romae, 1844.

Montalembert, Comte de, *Monks of the West,* with an introduction by F. A. Gasquet, 6 vols., New York, 1897.

Mothon, Joseph Pie, *Traité sur l'État Religieux,* Paris, 1922.

Nervegna, Josephus Cardinalis, *De Jure Practico Regularium,* Romae, 1900.

Noldin, H., and Schmitt, A., *Summa Theologiae Moralis,* 27. ed., 3 vols., Oeniponte-Lipsiae: Rauch, 1940-1942.

Oesterle, Gerardus, *Praelectiones Iuris Canonici,* Vol. I, Romae: Cuore di Maria, 1931.

O'Neill, Francis Joseph, *The Dismissal of Religious in Temporary Vows,* The Catholic University of America Canon Law Studies, n. 165, Washington, D. C.: The Catholic University of America Press, 1942.

Panormitanus, Abbas (Nicolas de Tudeschis), *Commentaria in Quinque Libros Decretalium,* 5 vols. in 7, Venetiis, 1578.

Papi, Hector, *Religious in Church Law,* New York, 1924.

Passerini, Petrus, *De hominum statibus et officiis,* 3 vols., Lucae, 1732.

Pajška, Josephus, *Ius Canonicum Religiosorum,* 3. ed., Friburgi Brisgoviae: Herder, 1927.

Pellizarius, F., *Tractatio de Monialibus,* Venetiis, 1651.

Petra, Vincentius, *Commentaria ad Constitutiones Apostolicas,* 5 vols. in 2, Venetiis, 1729.

Piatus, Montensis (J. J. Laiseaux), *Praelectiones Juris Regularis,* Parisiis, 1888.

Pignatelli, I., *Consultationes Canonicae,* 11 vols. in 4, Coloniae Allobrogorum, 1700.

Pirhing, Emricus, *Ius Canonicum Nova Methodo Explicatum,* 5 vols. in 4, Dilingae, 1674-1678.

Prümmer, D. M., *Manuale Iuris Canonici,* 3. ed., 2 vols., Friburgi Brisgoviae, 1922.

———, *Manuale Iuris Ecclesiastici,* 2 vols., Friburgi Brisgoviae, 1907.

Reiffenstuel, Anacletus, *Ius Canonicum Universum,* 5 vols. in 7, Parisiis, 1864-1870.

Rotarius, Thomas, *Summa Quaestionum Regularium,* Lugduni, 1655.

———, *Theologia Moralis Regularium,* 3 vols. in 2, Venetiis, 1735.

Sabetti, Aloysius—Barrett, Timotheus—Creeden, J. B., *Compendium Theologiae Moralis,* 13. ed., Neo-Eboraci: Pustet, 1939.

Salmanticenses, *Cursus Theologiae Moralis,* 6 vols. in 4, Venetiis, 1714-1728.

Sanchez, Thomas, *Opus Morale in Praecepta Decalogi,* 2 vols., Parmae, 1723.

Santi, F.-Leitner, M., *Praelectiones Juris Canonici,* 4. ed., 5 vols. in 2, Ratisbon, 1903-1905.

Schaefer, Timotheus, *De Religiosis,* 3. ed., Romae: Herder, 1940.

Schmalzgrueber, Franciscus, *Ius Ecclesiasticum Universum,* 5 vols. in 12, Romae, 1843-1845.

Sebastianelli, Gulielmus, *Praelectiones Iuris Canonici,* 3 vols., 2. ed., Romae, 1905.

Sipos, Stephanus, *Enchiridion Iuris Canonici,* 2. ed., Pécs: Ex Typographia "Heladas R. T.," 1931.

Stanton, W. A., *De Societatibus sive Virorum sive Mulierum in Communi Viventium sine Votis,* Halifaxiae: Apud Custodiam Librariam Maioris Seminarii a Sanctissimo Corde B. V. M., 1936.

Suarez, Franciscus, *Opera Omnia,* 28 vols., Parisiis, 1856-1861.

Tamburini, A., *De Iure Abbatum,* Lugduni, 1640.

Thomas Aquinas, St., *Opera Omnia Iussu Impensaque Leonis P. M. XIII edita,* 15 vols., Romae, 1882.

Toso, Albertus, *Ad Codicem Iuris Canonici Benedicti XV Pont. Max. Auctoritate Promulgatum Commentaria Minora,* 5 vols., Vol. V, Romae: Ius Pontificium, 1927.

Turner, Sidney Joseph, *The Vow of Poverty,* The Catholic University of America Canon Law Studies, n. 54, Washington, D. C.: The Catholic University of America, 1929.

Van Hove, A., *Commentarium Lovaniense in Codicem Iuris Canonici,* 1 vol. in 5 tomes, Mechliniae-Romae: H. Dessain, 1928-1939, Tom. II, *De legibus ecclesiasticis,* 1930.

Verani, Caietanus Felix, *Iuris Canonici Universi Commentarium,* Monachii, 1705.

Vermeersch, Arthurus, *De Religiosis,* 2 vols., Brugis, 1902.

———, *Theologiae Moralis Principia-Responsa-Consilia,* 3. ed., 4 vols., Romae: Universita Gregoriana, 1933-1937, Vol. III, reprinted in 1945.

Vermeersch, A.-Creusen, J., *Epitome Iuris Canonici,* 3 vols., Vol. I, 6. ed., Mechliniae-Romae: H. Dessain, 1937.

Wernz, Franciscus, et Vidal, Petrus, *Ius Canonicum,* 7 vols. in 8, Romae, Universitas Gregoriana, 1923-1938, Vol. III, *De Religiosis,* 1933.

Williams, Watkins W., *Monastic Studies,* Historical Series n. LXXVI, Manchester: Manchester University Press, 1938.

Articles

Ferreres, J., "Annotaciones"—*Razón y Fe,* XXXVII (1913), 244-247.

Gennari, C., "Annotazioni"—*Il Monitore Ecclesiastico,* 3rd Series, Vol. V (1913), 265-266.

Goyeneche, S., "Consultationes"—*CpR,* III (1922), 8-13, 236-272; IV (1923), 120-122; V (1924), 390-393; VI (1925), 432-434; VIII (1927), 114-115; *CpRM,* XXI (1940), 38-40.

———, "De transitu ad aliam religionem"—*CpR,* I (1920), 217-226, 295-300, 359-365; II (1921), 116-124, 141-148, 173-176, 176-180.

Hofmeister, Ph., "Der Übertritt in eine andere religiöse Genossenschaft"—*Archiv für katholisches Kirchenrecht,* CVIII (1928), 419-481; CIX (1929), 452-453.

Hippolytus a S. Familia, "Annotationes"—*Analecta Ordinis Carmelitarum Excalceatorum,* I (1926), 490-491.

Krause, V., "Die Akten der Triburer Synode 895"—*Neues Archiv der Gesellschaft für ältere deutsche Geschichtskunde,* XVII (1892), 49-82, 281-326; XVIII (1893), 411-437.

La Puma, Vincentius, "Statuta a Sororibus Externis Servanda"—*CpR,* XV (1934), 3-33.

Larraona, Arcadius, "Commentarium Codicis"—*CpR,* II (1921), 202-205, 275-287; III (1922), 133-138; IV (1923), 39-41; VII (1926), 376-389; *CpRM,* XIX (1938), 252-260; XXI (1940), 211-216.

———, "Consultationes"—*CpR,* I (1920), 77-82, 177-183; III (1922), 8-10.

———, "Studia Canonica de Paupertate Simplici"—*CpR,* I (1920), 333-340.

Lopez, Benedictus, "Cuinam debeatur legatum annui reditus Monacho relictum, ipso post solemnem professionem in aliud Monasterium definitive translato" —*CpR,* IX (1928), 217-234.

Maroto, Philippus, "Consultationes"—*CpR,* II (1921), 6, 7.

Prikryl, F., "Übertritt in eine andere Ordensgenossenschaft"—*Theologisch-praktische Quartalschrift,* XCII (1939), 123-126.

Rothenhäusler, F., "Ältestes Mönchtum und klösterliche Beständigkeit"—*Benedictinische Monatschrift,* IV (1922), 89-112.

Salsmans, J., "Annotationes"—*Periodica,* VII (1914), 166-167.

Seckel, E., "Die Akten der Triburer Synode 895"—*Neues Archiv der Gesellschaft für ältere deutsche Geschichtskunde,* XVIII (1893), 322-409.

Tabera, A., "De dimissione religiosorum"—*CpR,* XII (1931), 140-148.

Teodori, J., "Commutatio Voti"—*Apollinaris,* VI (1933), 506-510.

Vermeersch, A., "De monasteriis seu domibus sui iuris"—*Periodica,* XI (1922), (7)—(9).

———, "Annotationes, VII. De professione religiosi transeuntis"—*Periodica,* XI (1922), 169-170.

———, "Annotationes"—Periodica, XV (1926), 230, 231.

———, "Varia Quaesita de Religiosis, c. V, De Attributione Bonorum Religiosi Transeuntis ad aliud Institutum"—*Periodica,* XIV (1925), (49)—(51).

———, "De Transeunte ad aliam religionem"—*Periodica,* XIX (1930), 164, 165.

Voltas, P., "Consultationes"—*CpR,* I (1920), 270-279.

Periodicals

Acta Apostolicae Sedis, Commentarium Officiale, Romae, 1909—

Analecta Ecclesiastica, Romae, 1893-1911.

Analecta Juris Pontificii, Romae, 1855-1869: Parisiis, 1872-1891.

Analecta Ordinis Carmelitarum Excalceatorum, Romae, 1926—

Apollinaris, Romae, 1928.

Archiv für katholisches Kirchenrecht, Innsbruck, 1857-1861: Mainz, 1862—

Benedictinische Monatschrift, Beuron, 1919—
Commentarium pro Religiosis (later [1935] *Commentarium pro Religiosis et Missionariis*), Romae, 1920—
Monitore Ecclesiastico, Il, Romae, 1876—
Neues Archiv der Gesellschaft für ältere deutsche Geschichtskunde, Hannover, 1876—
Nouvelle Revue Théologique, Tournai, 1869—
Periodica de Religiosis et Missionariis, 8 vols., Brugis, 1905-1919 (Vol. I: 1905, 2. ed., 1911; II and III: 1907, 2. ed., 1911; IV: 1909, 2. ed., 1913; V: 1911, 2. ed., 1913; VI: 1912; VII: 1912-1914; VIII: 1919); from 1920: *Periodica de Re Canonica et Morali utilia praesertim Religiosis et Missionariis*, 7 vols., Brugis, 1920-1927 (Vol. IX: 1920; X and XI: 1922-1923; XII: 1923-1924; XIII: 1924-1925; XIV: 1925-1926; XV: 1926-1927); from 1927: *Periodica de Re Morali, Canica, Liturgica*, Brugis (1927-1936) et Romae (1937—), Vol. XVI, 1927—
Razón y Fe, Madrid, 1901—
Theologisch-praktische Quartalschrift, Linz, 1848—

ABBREVIATIONS

AAS—*Acta Apostolicae Sedis.*
AKKR—*Archiv für katholisches Kirchenrecht.*
Bull. Rom. Taur.—*Bullarum Diplomatum . . . Taurinensis editio.*
CpR—*Commentarium pro Religiosis.*
CpRM—*Commentarium pro Religiosis et Missionariis.*
Fontes—*Codicis Juris Canonici Fontes cura . . . Gasparri editi.*
HL—Hefele-Leclercq, *Histoire des Conciles.*
JE—Jaffe, *Regeste Pontificum Romanorum* (edited by Ewald: from 590 to 882).
JK—Jaffe, *op. cit.* (edited by Kaltenbrunner: from 33 to 590).
JL—Jaffe, *op. cit.* (edited by Loewenfeld: from 882 to 1198).
Mansi—Mansi, J. D., *Sacrorum Conciliorum Nova et Amplissima Collectio.*
MGH—*Monumenta Germaniae Historica.*
MPG—*Migne, Patrologiae Cursus Completus, Series Graeca.*
MPL—*Migne, Patrologiae Cursus Completus, Series Latina.*
Periodica—*Periodica de Re Morali, Canonica, Liturgica.*
Potthast—Potthast, Augustus, *Regesta Pontificum Romanorum.*
R.J.—*Regula Juris.*
S. C. C.—*Sacra Congregatio Concilii.*
S. C. Ep. et Reg.—*Sacra Congregatio Episcoporum et Regularium.*

ALPHABETICAL INDEX

BIOGRAPHICAL NOTE

JOSEPH G. KONRAD was born August 17, 1916, in Brooklyn, New York. He attended public and parochial schools in Ichenhausen, Bavaria, Germany and in Brooklyn, New York. He graduated from St. Augustine Diocesan High School, Brooklyn, in 1935, and received the degree of Bachelor of Arts from Manhattan College, Bronx, New York in 1939. After his theological studies at the Seminary of the Immaculate Conception, Huntington, Long Island, he was ordained to the Priesthood for the Diocese of Brooklyn on April 27, 1943. He was admitted to the School of Canon Law at the Catholic University of America in 1944, and was given the degree of the Baccalaureate in Canon Law in May, 1945, and the degree of the Licentiate in Canon Law in June, 1946.

CANON LAW STUDIES *

1. FRERIKS, REV. CELESTINE A., C.PP.S., J.C.D., Religious Congregations in Their External Relations, 121 pp., 1916.
2. GALLIHER, REV. DANIEL M., O.P., J.C.D., Canonical Elections, 117 pp., 1917.
3. BORKOWSKI, REV. AURELIUS L., O.F.M., J.C.D., De Confraternitatibus Ecclesiasticis, 136 pp., 1918.
4. CASTILLO, REV. CAYO, J.C.D., Disertacion Historico-Canonica sobre la Potestad del Cabildo en Sede Vacante o Impedida del Vicario Capitular, 99 pp., 1919 (1918).
5. KUBELBECK, REV. WILLIAM J., S.T.B., J.C.D., The Sacred Penitentiaria and Its Relation to Faculties of Ordinaries and Priests, 129 pp., 1918.
6. PETROVITS, REV. JOSEPH, J.C., S.T.D., J.C.D., The New Church Law on Matrimony, X-461 pp., 1919.
7. HICKEY, REV. JOHN J., S.T.B., J.C.D., Irregularities and Simple Impediments in the New Code of Canon Law, 100 pp., 1920.
8. KLEKOTKA, REV. PETER J., S.T.B., J.C.D., Diocesan Consultors, 179 pp., 1920.
9. WANENMACHER, REV. FRANCIS, J.C.D., The Evidence in Ecclesiastical Procedure Affecting the Marriage Bond, 1920 (Printed 1935).
10. GOLDEN, REV. HENRY FRANCIS, J.C.D., Parochial Benefices in the New Code, IV-119 pp., 1921 (Printed 1925).
11. KOUDELKA, REV. CHARLES J., J.C.D., Pastors, Their Rights and Duties According to the New Code of Canon Law, 211 pp., 1921.
12. MELO, REV. ANTONIUS, O.F.M., J.C.D., De Exemptione Regularium, X-188 pp., 1921.
13. SCHAAF, REV. VALENTINE THEODORE, O.F.M., S.T.B., J.C.D., The Cloister, X-180 pp., 1921.
14. BURKE, REV. THOMAS JOSEPH, S.T.D., J.C.D., Competence in Ecclesiastical Tribunals, IV-117 pp., 1922.
15. LEECH, REV. GEORGE LEO, J.C.D., A Comparative Study of the Constitution "Apostolicae Sedis" and the "Codex Juris Canonici," 179 pp., 1922.
16. MOTRY, REV. HUBERT LOUIS, S.T.D., J.C.D., Diocesan Faculties According to the Code of Canon Law, II-167 pp., 1922.
17. MURPHY, REV. GEORGE LAWRENCE, J.C.D., Delinquencies and Penalties in the Administration and the Reception of the Sacraments, IV-121 pp., 1923.
18. O'REILLY, REV. JOHN ANTHONY, S.T.B., J.C.D., Ecclesiastical Sepulture in the New Code of Canon Law, II-129 pp., 1923.

* All published numbers are available from the Catholic University of America Press, 620 Michigan Avenue, N.E., Washington 17, D. C., except the following: Nos. 1-114 inclusive, 116, 118, 120, 121, 122, 123, 136, 153, 162, 182 and 198. But the following numbers, now reissued, are obtainable from *The Jurist*, The Catholic University of America, Washington 17, D. C., namely: Nos. 5, 7, 11, 17, 18, 19, 26, 28, 30, 31, 34, 42, 44, 51, 52 and 61.

19. MICHALICKA, REV. WENCESLAS CYRILL, O.S.B., J.C.D., Judicial Procedure in Dismissal of Clerical Exempt Religious, 107 pp., 1923.
20. DARGIN, REV. EDWARD VINCENT, S.T.B., J.C.D., Reserved Cases According to the Code of Canon Law, IV-103 pp., 1924.
21. GODFREY, REV. JOHN A., S.T.B., J.C.D., The Right of Patronage According to the Code of Canon Law, 153 pp., 1924.
22. HAGEDORN, REV. FRANCIS EDWARD, J.C.D., General Legislation on Indulgences, II-154 pp., 1924.
23. KING, REV. JAMES IGNATIUS, J.C.D., The Administration of the Sacraments to Dying Non-Catholics, V-141 pp., 1924.
24. WINSLOW, REV. FRANCIS JOSEPH, O.F.M., J.C.D., Vicars and Prefects Apostolic, IV-149 pp., 1924.
25. CORREA, REV. JOSE SERVELION, S.T.L., J.C.D., La Potestad Legislativa de la Iglesia Catolica, IV-127 pp., 1925.
26. DUGAN, REV. HENRY FRANCIS, A.M., J.C.D., The Judiciary Department of the Diocesan Curia, 87 pp., 1925.
27. KELLER, REV. CHARLES FREDERICK, S.T.B., J.C.D., Mass Stipends, 167 pp., 1925.
28. PASCHANG, REV. JOHN LINUS, J.C.D., The Sacramentals According to the Code of Canon Law, 129 pp., 1925.
29. PIONTEK, REV. CYRILLUS, O.F.M., S.T.B., J.C.D., De Indulto Exclaustrationis necnon Saecularizationis, XIII-289 pp., 1925.
30. KEARNEY, REV. RICHARD JOSEPH, S.T.B., J.C.D., Sponsors at Baptism According to the Code of Canon Law, IV-127 pp., 1925.
31. BARTLETT, REV. CHESTER JOSEPH, A.M., LL.B., J.C.D., The Tenure of Parochial Property in the United States of America, V-108 pp., 1926.
32. KILKER, REV. ADRIAN JEROME, J.C.D., Extreme Unction, V-425 pp., 1926.
33. MCCORMICK, REV. ROBERT EMMETT, J.C.D., Confessors of Religious, VIII-266 pp., 1926.
34. MILLER, REV. NEWTON THOMAS, J.C.D., Founded Masses According to the Code of Canon Law, VII-93 pp., 1926.
35. ROELKER, REV. EDWARD G., S.T.D., J.C.D., Principles of Privilege According to the Code of Canon Law, XI-166 pp., 1926.
36. BAKALARCZYK, REV. RICHARDUS, M.I.C., J.U.D., De Novitiatu, VIII-208 pp., 1927.
37. PIZZUTI, REV. LAWRENCE, O.F.M., J.U.L., De Parochis Religiosis, 1927. (Not Printed.)
38. BLILEY, REV. NICHOLAS MARTIN, O.S.B., J.C.D., Altars According to the Code of Canon Law, XIX-132 pp., 1927.
39. BROWN, MR. BRENDAN FRANCIS, A.B., LL.M., J.U.D., The Canonical Juristic Personality with Special Reference to Its Status in the United States of America, V-212 pp., 1927.
40. CAVANAUGH, REV. WILLIAM THOMAS, C.P., J.U.D., The Reservation of the Blessed Sacrament, VIII-101 pp., 1927.

41. Doheny, Rev. William J., C.S.C., A.B., J.C.D., Church Property: Modes of Acquisition, X-118 pp., 1927.
42. Feldhaus, Rev. Aloysius H., C.PP.S., J.C.D., Oratories, IX-141 pp., 1927.
43. Kelly, Rev. James Patrick, A.B., J.C.D., The Jurisdiction of the Simple Confessor, X-208 pp., 1927.
44. Neuberger, Rev. Nicholas J., J.C.D., Canon 6 or the Relation of the Codex Juris Canonici to the Preceding Legislation, V-95 pp., 1927.
45. O'Keefe, Rev. Gerald Michael, J.C.D., Matrimonial Dispensations. Powers of Bishops, Priests, and Confessors, VIII-232 pp., 1927.
46. Quigley, Rev. Joseph A. M., A.B., J.C.D., Condemned Societies, 139 pp., 1927.
47. Zaplotnik, Rev. Johannes Leo, J.C.D., De Vicariis Foraneis, X-142 pp., 1927.
48. Duskie, Rev. John Aloysius, A.B., J.C.D., The Canonical Status of the Orientals in the United States, VIII-196 pp., 1928.
49. Hyland, Rev. Francis Edward, J.C.D., Excommunication, Its Nature, Historical Development and Effects, VIII-181 pp., 1928.
50. Reinmann, Rev. Gerald Joseph, O.M.C., J.C.D., The Third Order Secular of Saint Francis, 201 pp., 1928.
51. Schenk, Rev. Francis J., J.C.D., The Matrimonial Impediments of Mixed Religion and Disparity of Cult, XVI-318 pp., 1929.
52. Coady, Rev. John Joseph, S.T.D., J.U.D., A.M., The Appointment of Pastors, VIII-150 pp., 1929.
53. Kay, Rev. Thomas Henry, J.C.D., Competence in Matrimonial Procedure, VIII-164 pp., 1929.
54. Turner, Rev. Sidney Joseph, C.P., J.U.D., The Vow of Poverty, XLIX-217 pp., 1929.
55. Kearney, Rev. Raymond A., A.B., S.T.D., J.C.D., The Principles of Delegation, VII-149 pp., 1929.
56. Conran, Rev. Edward James, A.B., J.C.D., The Interdict, V-163 pp., 1930.
57. O'Neill, Rev. William H., J.C.D., Papal Rescripts of Favor, VII-218 pp., 1930.
58. Bastnagel, Rev. Clement Vincent, J.U.D., The Appointment of Parochial Adjutants and Assistants, XV-257 pp., 1930.
59. Ferry, Rev. William A., A.B., J.C.D., Stole Fees, V-136 pp., 1930.
60. Costello, Rev. John Michael, A.B., J.C.D., Domicile and Quasi-Domicile, VII-201 pp., 1930.
61. Kremer, Rev. Michael Nicholas, A.B., S.T.B., J.C.D., Church Support in the United States, VI-136 pp., 1930.
62. Angulo, Rev. Luis, C.M., J.C.D., Legislation de la Iglesia sobre la intencion en la application de la Santa Misa, VII-104 pp., 1931.
63. Frey, Rev. Wolfgang Norbert, O.S.B., A.B., J.C.D., The Act of Religious Profession, VIII-174 pp., 1931.

64. Roberts, Rev. James Brendan, A.B., J.C.D., The Banns of Marriage, XIV-140 pp., 1931.

65. Ryder, Rev. Raymond Aloysius, A.B., J.C.D., Simony, IX-151 pp., 1931.

66. Campagna, Rev. Angelo, Ph.D., J.U.D., Il Vicario Generale del Vescovo, VII-205 pp., 1931.

67. Cox, Rev. Joseph Godfrey, A.B., J.C.D., The Administration of Seminaries, VI-124 pp., 1931.

68. Gregory, Rev. Donald J., J.U.D., The Pauline Privilege, XV-165 pp., 1931.

69. Donohue, Rev. John F., J.C.D., The Impediment of Crime, VII-110 pp., 1931.

70. Dooley, Rev. Eugene A., O.M.I., J.C.D., Church Law on Sacred Relics, IX-143 pp., 1931.

71. Orth, Rev. Clement Raymond, O.M.C., J.C.D., The Approbation of Religious Institutes, 171 pp., 1931.

72. Pernicone, Rev. Joseph M., A.B., J.C.D., The Ecclesiastical Prohibition of Books, XII-267 pp., 1932.

73. Clinton, Rev. Connell, A.B., J.C.D., The Paschal Precept, IX-108 pp., 1932.

74. Donnelly, Rev. Francis B., A.M., S.T.L., J.C.D., The Diocesan Synod, VIII-125 pp., 1932.

75. Torrente, Rev. Camilo, C.M.F., J.C.D., Las Procesiones Sagradas, V-145 pp., 1932.

76. Murphy, Rev. Edwin J., C.PP.S., J.C.D., Suspension Ex Informata Conscientia, XI-122 pp., 1932.

77. MacKenzie, Rev. Eric F., A.M., S.T.L., J.C.D., The Delict of Heresy in its Commission, Penalization, Absolution, VII-124 pp., 1932.

78. Lyons, Rev. Avitus E., S.T.B., J.C.D., The Collegiate Tribunal of First Instance, XI-147 pp., 1932.

79. Connolly, Rev. Thomas A., J.C.D., Appeals, XI-195, pp., 1932.

80. Sangmeister, Rev. Joseph V., A.B., J.C.D., Force and Fear as Precluding Matrimonial Consent, V-211 pp., 1932.

81. Jaeger, Rev. Leo A., A.B., J.C.D., The Administration of Vacant and Quasi-Vacant Episcopal Sees in the United States, IX-229 pp., 1932.

82. Rimlinger, Rev. Herbert T., J.C.D., Error Invalidating Matrimonial Consent, VII-79 pp., 1932.

83. Barrett, Rev. John D. M., S.S., J.C.D., A Comparative Study of the Councils of Baltimore and the Code of Canon Law, IX-223 pp., 1932.

84. Carberry, Rev. John J., Ph.D., S.T.D., J.C.D., The Juridical Form of Marriage, X-177 pp., 1934.

85. Dolan, Rev. John L., A.B., J.C.D., The Defensor Vinculi, XII-157 pp., 1934.

86. Hannan, Rev. Jerome D., A.M., S.T.D., LL.B., J.C.D., The Canon Law of Wills, IX-517 pp., 1934.

87. Lemieux, Rev. Delise A., A.M., J.C.D., The Sentence in Ecclesiastical Procedure, IX-131 pp., 1934.
88. O'Rourke, Rev. James J., A.B., J.C.D., Parish Registers, VII-109 pp., 1934.
89. Timlin, Rev. Bartholomew, O.F.M., A.M., J.C.D., Conditional Matrimonial Consent, X-381 pp., 1934.
90. Wahl, Rev. Francis X., A.B., J.C.D., The Matrimonial Impediments of Consanguinity and Affinity, VI-125 pp., 1934.
91. White, Rev. Robert J., A.B., LL.B., S.T.B., J.C.D., Canonical Ante-Nuptial Promises and the Civil Law, VI-152 pp., 1934.
92. Herrera, Rev. Antonio Parra, O.C.D., J.C.D., Legislacion Ecclesiastica sobra el Ayuno y la Abstinencia, XI-191 pp., 1935.
93. Kennedy, Rev. Edwin J., J.C.D., The Special Matrimonial Process in Cases of Evident Nullity, X-165 pp., 1935.
94. Manning, Rev. John J., A.B., J.C.D., Presumption of Law in Matrimonial Procedure, XI-111 pp., 1935.
95. Moeder, Rev. John M., J.C.D., The Proper Bishop for Ordination and Dismissorial Letters, VII-135 pp., 1935.
96. O'Mara, Rev. William A., A.B., J.C.D., Canonical Causes for Matrimonial Dispensations, IX-155 pp., 1935.
97. Reilly, Rev. Peter, J.C.D., Residence of Pastors, IX-81 pp., 1935.
98. Smith, Rev. Mariner T., O.P., S.T.Lr., J.C.D., The Penal Law for Religious, VIII-169 pp., 1935.
99. Whalen, Rev. Donald W., A.M., J.C.D., The Value of Testimonial Evidence in Matrimonial Procedure, XIII-297 pp., 1935.
100. Cleary, Rev. Joseph F., J.C.D., Canonical Limitations on the Alienation of Church Property, VIII-141 pp., 1936.
101. Glynn, Rev. John C., J.C.D., The Promoter of Justice, XX-337 pp., 1936.
102. Brennan, Rev. James H., S.S., M.A., S.T.B., J.C.D., The Simple Convalidation of Marriage, VI-135 pp., 1937.
103. Brunini, Rev. Joseph Bernard, J.C.D., The Clerical Obligations of Canons 139 and 142, X-121 pp., 1937.
104. Connor, Rev. Maurice, A.B., J.C.D., The Administrative Removal of Pastors, VIII-159 pp., 1937.
105. Guilfoyle, Rev. Merlin Joseph, J.C.D., Custom, XI-144 pp., 1937.
106. Hughes, Rev. James Austin, A.B., A.M., J.C.D., Witnesses in Criminal Trials of Clerics, IX-140 pp., 1937.
107. Jansen, Rev. Raymond J., A.B., S.T.L., J.C.D., Canonical Provisions for Catechetical Instruction, VII-153 pp., 1937.
108. Kealy, Rev. John James, A.B., J.C.D., The Introductory Libellus in Church Court Procedure, XI-121 pp., 1937.
109. McManus, Rev. James Edward, C.SS.R., J.C.D., The Administration of Temporal Goods in Religious Institutes, XVI-196 pp., 1937.

110. MORIARTY, REV. EUGENE JAMES, J.C.D., Oaths in Ecclesiastical Courts, X-115 pp., 1937.

111. RAINER, REV. ELIGIUS GEORGE, C.SS.R., J.C.D., Suspension of Clerics, XVII-249 pp., 1937.

112. REILLY, REV. THOMAS F., C.SS.R., J.C.D., Visitation of Religious, VI-195 pp., 1938.

113. MORIARTY, REV. FRANCIS E., C.SS.R., J.C.D., The Extraordinary Absolution from Censures, XV-334 pp., 1938.

114. CONNOLLY, REV. NICHOLAS P., J.C.D., The Canonical Erection of Parishes, X-132 pp., 1938.

115. DONOVAN, REV. JAMES JOSEPH, J.C.D., The Pastor's Obligation in Prenuptial Investigation, XII-322 pp., 1938.

116. HARRIGAN, REV. ROBERT J., M.A., S.T.B., J.C.D., The Radical Sanation of Invalid Marriages, VIII-208 pp., 1938.

117. BOFFA, REV. CONRAD HUMBERT, J.C.D., Canonical Provisions for Catholic Schools, VII-211 pp., 1939.

118. PARSONS, REV. ANSCAR JOHN, O.M.Cap., J.C.D., Canonical Elections, XII-236 pp., 1939.

119. REILLY, REV. EDWARD MICHAEL, A.B., J.C.D., The General Norms of Dispensation, XII-156 pp., 1939.

120. RYAN, REV. GERALD ALOYSIUS, A.B., J.C.D., Principles of Episcopal Jurisdiction, XII-172 pp., 1939.

121. BURTON, REV. FRANCIS JAMES, C.S.C., A.B., J.C.D., A Commentary on Canon 1125, X-222 pp., 1940.

122. MIASKIEWICZ, REV. FRANCIS SIGISMUND, J.C.D., Supplied Jurisdiction According to Canon 209, XII-340 pp., 1940.

123. RICE, REV. PATRICK WILLIAM, A.B., J.C.D., Proof of Death in Prenuptial Investigation, VIII-156 pp., 1940.

124. ANGLIN, REV. THOMAS FRANCIS, M.S., J.C.D., The Eucharistic Fast, VIII-183 pp., 1941.

125. COLEMAN, REV. JOHN JEROME, J.C.D., The Minister of Confirmation, VI-153 pp., 1941.

126. DOWNS, REV. JOHN EMMANUEL, A.B., J.C.D., The Concept of Clerical Immunity, XI-163 pp., 1941.

127. ESSWEIN, REV. ANTHONY ALBERT, J.C.D., Extrajudicial Penal Powers of Ecclesiastical Superiors, X-144 pp., 1941.

128. FARRELL, REV. BENJAMIN FRANCIS, M.A., S.T.L., J.C.D., The Rights and Duties of the Local Ordinary Regarding Congregations of Women Religious of Pontifical Approval, V-195 pp., 1941.

129. FEENEY, REV. THOMAS JOHN, A.B., S.T.L., J.C.D., Restitutio in Integrum, VI-169 pp., 1941.

130. FINDLAY, REV. STEPHEN WILLIAM, O.S.B., A.B., J.C.D., Canonical Norms Governing the Deposition and Degradation of Clerics, XVII-279 pp., 1941.

131. Goodwine, Rev. John, A.B., S.T.L., J.C.D., The Right of the Church to Acquire Property, VIII-119 pp., 1941.
132. Heston, Rev. Edward Louis, C.S.C., Ph.D., S.T.D., J.C.D., The Alienation of Church Property in the United States, XII-222 pp., 1941.
133. Hogan, Rev. James John, A.B., S.T.L., J.C.D., Judicial Advocates and Procurators, XIII-200 pp., 1941.
134. Kealy, Rev. Thomas M., A.B., Litt.B., J.C.D., Dowry of Women Religious, IX-152 pp., 1941.
135. Keene, Rev. Michael James, O.S.B., J.C.D., Religious Ordinaries and Canon 198, V-164 pp., 1941 (printed 1942).
136. Kerin, Rev. Charles A., S.S., M.A., S.T.B., J.C.D., The Privation of Christian Burial, XVI-279 pp., 1941.
137. Louis, Rev. William Francis, M.A., J.C.D., Diocesan Archives, X-101 pp., 1941.
138. McDevitt, Rev. Gilbert Joseph, A.B., J.C.D., Legitimacy and Legitimation, X-247 pp., 1941.
139. McDonough, Rev. Thomas Joseph, A.B., J.C.D., Apostolic Administrators, X-217 pp., 1941.
140. Meier, Rev. Carl Anthony, A.B., J.C.D., Penal Administrative Procedure Against Negligent Pastors, XI-240 pp., 1941.
141. Schmidt, Rev. John Rogg, A.B., J.C.D., The Principles of Authentic Interpretation in Canon 17 of the Code of Canon Law, XII-331 pp., 1941.
142. Slafkosky, Rev. Andrew Leonard, A.B., J.C.D., The Canonical Episcopal Visitation of the Diocese, X-197 pp., 1941.
143. Swoboda, Rev. Innocent Robert, O.F.M., J.C.D., Ignorance in Relation to the Imputability of Delicts, IX-271 pp., 1941.
144. Dubé, Rev. Arthur Joseph, A.B., J.C.D., The General Principles for the Reckoning of Time in Canon Law, VIII-299 pp., 1941.
145. McBride, Rev. James T., A.B., J.C.D., Incardination and Excardination of Seculars, XX-585 pp., 1941.
146. Król, Rev. John T., J.C.D., The Defendant in Ecclesiastical Trials, XII-207 pp., 1942.
147. Comyns, Rev. Joseph J., C.SS.R., A.B., J.C.D., Papal and Episcopal Administration of Church Property, XIV-155 pp., 1942.
148. Barry, Rev. Garrett Francis, O.M.I., J.C.D., Violation of the Cloister, XII-260 pp., 1942.
149. Bolduc, Rev. Gatien, C.S.V., A.B., S.T.L., J.C.D., Les Études dans les Religions Cléricales, VIII-155 pp., 1942.
150. Boyle, Rev. David John, M.A., J.C.D., The Juridic Effects of Moral Certitude on Pre-Nuptial Guarantees, XII-188 pp., 1942.
151. Canavan, Rev. Walter Joseph, M.A., Litt.D., J.C.D., The Profession of Faith, XII-143 pp., 1942.
152. Desrochers, Rev. Bruno, A.B., Ph.L., S.T.B., J.C.D., Le Premier Concile Plénier de Québec et le Code de Droit Canonique, XIV-186 pp., 1942.

153. Dillon, Rev. Robert Edward, A.B., J.C.D., Common Law Marriage, X-148 pp., 1942.

154. Dodwell, Rev. Edward John, Ph.D., S.T.B., J.C.D., The Time and Place for the Celebration of Marriage, X-156 pp., 1942.

155. Donnellan, Rev. Thomas Andrew, A.B., J.C.D., The Obligation of the Missa pro Populo, VII-131 pp., 1942.

156. Eltz, Rev. Louis Anthony, A.B., J.C.D., Cooperation in Crime, XII-208 pp., 1942.

157. Gass, Rev. Sylvester Francis, M.A., J.C.D., Ecclesiastical Pensions, XI-206 pp., 1942.

158. Guiniven, Rev. John Joseph, C.SS.R., J.C.D., The Precept of Hearing Mass, XIV-188 pp., 1942.

159. Gulczynski, Rev. John Theophilus, J.C.D., The Desecration and Violation of Churches, X-126 pp., 1942.

160. Hammill, Rev. John Leo, M.A., J.C.D., The Obligations of the Traveler According to Canon 14, VIII-204 pp., 1942.

161. Haydt, Rev. John Joseph, A.B., J.C.D., Reserved Benefices, XI-148 pp., 1942.

162. Huser, Rev. Roger John, O.F.M., A.B., J.C.D., The Crime of Abortion in Canon Law, XII-187 pp., 1942.

163. Kearney, Rev. Francis Patrick, A.B., S.T.L., J.C.D., The Principles of Canon 1127, X-162 pp., 1942.

164. Linahen, Rev. Leo James, S.T.L., J.C.D., De Absolutione Complicis in Peccato Turpi, V-114 pp., 1942.

165. McCloskey, Rev. Joseph Aloysius, A.B., J.C.D., The Subject of Ecclesiastical Law According to Canon 12, XVII-246 pp., 1942 (printed 1943).

166. O'Neill, Rev. Francis Joseph, C.SS.R., J.C.D., The Dismissal of Religious in Temporary Vows, XIII-220 pp., 1942.

167. Prince, Rev. John Edward, A.B., S.T.B., J.C.D., The Diocesan Chancellor, X-136 pp., 1942.

168. Riesner, Rev. Albert Joseph, C.SS.R., J.C.D., Apostates and Fugitives from Religious Institutes, IX-168 pp., 1942.

169. Stenger, Rev. Joseph Bernard, J.C.D., The Mortgaging of Church Property, 186 pp., 1942.

170. Waldron, Rev. Joseph Francis, A.B., J.C.D., The Minister of Baptism, XII-197 pp., 1942.

171. Willett, Rev. Robert Albert, J.C.D., The Probative Value of Documents in Ecclesiastical Trials, X-124 pp., 1942.

172. Woeber, Rev. Edward Martin, M.A., J.C.D., The Interpellations, XII-161 pp., 1942.

173. Benko, Rev. Matthew Aloysius, O.S.B., M.A., J.C.D., The Abbot *Nullius*, XVI-148 pp., 1943.

174. Christ, Rev. Joseph James, M.A., S.T.L., J.C.D., Dispensation from Vindicative Penalties, XIV-285 pp., 1943.
175. Clancy, Rev. Patrick M. J., O.P., A.B., S.T.Lr., J.C.D., The Local Religious Superior, X-229 pp., 1943.
176. Clarke, Rev. Thomas James, J.C.D., Parish Societies, XII-147 pp., 1943.
177. Connolly, Rev. John Patrick, S.T.L., J.C.D., Synodal Examiners and Parish Priest Consultors, X-223 pp., 1943.
178. Drumm, Rev. William Martin, A.B., J.C.D., Hospital Chaplains, XII-175 pp., 1943.
179. Flanagan, Rev. Bernard Joseph, A.B., S.T.L., J.C.D., The Canonical Erection of Religious Houses, X-147 pp., 1943.
180. Kelleher, Rev. Stephen Joseph, A.B., S.T.B., J.C.D., Discussions with Non-Catholics: Canonical Legislation, X-93 pp., 1943.
181. Lewis, Rev. Gordian, C.P., J.C.D., Chapters in Religious Institutes, XII-169 pp., 1943.
182. Marx, Rev. Adolph, J.C.D., The Declaration of Nullity of Marriages Contracted Outside the Church, X-151 pp., 1943.
183. Matulenas, Rev. Raymond Anthony, O.S.B., A.B., J.C.D., Communication, a Source of Privileges, XII-225 pp., 1943.
184. O'Leary, Rev. Charles Gerard, C.SS.R., J.C.D., Religious Dismissed After Perpetual Profession, X-213 pp., 1943.
185. Power, Rev. Cornelius Michael, J.C.D., The Blessing of Cemeteries, XII-231 pp., 1943.
186. Shuhler, Rev. Ralph Vincent, O.S.A., J.C.D., Privileges of Religious to Absolve and Dispense, XII-195 pp., 1943.
187. Ziolkowski, Rev. Thaddeus Stanislaus, A.B., J.C.D., The Consecration and Blessing of Churches, XII-151 pp., 1943.
188. Heneghan, Rev. John Joseph, S.T.D., J.C.D., The Marriages of Unworthy Catholics: Canons 1065 and 1066, XVI-213 pp., 1944.
189. Carroll, Rev. Coleman Francis, M.A., S.T.L., J.C.L., Charitable Institutions.
190. Ciesluk, Rev. Joseph Edward, Ph.B., S.T.L., J.C.D., National Parishes in the United States, VI-178 pp., 1944.
191. Coburn, Rev. Vincent Paul, A.B., J.C.D., Marriages of Conscience, XII-172 pp., 1944.
192. Connors, Rev. Charles Paul, C.S.Sp., A.B., J.C.D., Extra-Judicial Procurators in the Code of Canon Law, X-94 pp., 1944.
193. Coyle, Rev. Paul Raymond, A.B., J.C.D., Judicial Exceptions, X-142 pp., 1944.
194. Fair, Rev. Bartholomew Francis, A.B., S.T.L., J.C.D., The Impediment of Abduction, XII-122 pp., 1944.
195. Gallagher, Rev. Thomas Raphael, O.P., A.B., S.T.Lr., J.C.D., The Examination of the Qualities of the Ordinand, X-166 pp., 1944.

196. Gannon, Rev. John Mark, S.T.L., J.C.D., The Interstices Required for the Promotion to Orders, XII-100 pp., 1944.
197. Goldsmith, Rev. J. William, B.C.S., S.T.L., J.C.D., The Competence of Church and State Over Marriages—Disputed Points, X-128 pp., 1944.
198. Goodwine, Rev. Joseph Gerard, A.B., S.T.B., J.C.D., The Reception of Converts, XIV-326 pp., 1944.
199. Kowalski, Rev. Romuald Eugene, O.F.M., A.B., J.C.D., Sustenance of Religious Houses of Regulars, X-174 pp., 1944.
200. McCoy, Rev. Alan Edward, O.F.M., J.C.D., Force and Fear in Relation to Delictual Imputability and Penal Responsibility, XII-160 pp., 1944.
201. McDevitt, Rev. Vincent John, Ph.B., S.T.L., J.C.L., Perjury.
202. Martin, Rev. Thomas Owen, Ph.D., S.T.D., J.C.D., Adverse Possession, Prescription and Limitation of Actions: The Canonical "Praescriptio," XX-208 pp., 1944.
203. Miklosovic, Rev. Paul John, A.B., J.C.L., Attempted Marriages and Their Consequent Juridic Effects.
204. Mundy, Rev. Thomas Maurice, A.B., S.T.L., J.C.D., The Union of Parishes, X-164 pp., 1944.
205. O'Dea, Rev. John Coyle, A.B., J.C.D., The Matrimonial Impediment of Nonage, VIII-126 pp., 1944.
206. Olalia, Rev. Alexander Ayson, S.T.L., J.C.D., A Comparative Study of the Christian Constitution of States and the Constitution of the Philippine Commonwealth, XII-136 pp., 1944.
207. Poisson, Rev. Pierre-Marie, C.S.C., A.B., Ph.L., Th.L., J.C.L., Droits Patrimoniaux des Maisons et des Eglises Religieuses.
208. Stadalnikas, Rev. Casimir Joseph, M.I.C., J.C.D., Reservation of Censures, X-141 pp., 1944.
209. Sullivan, Rev. Eugene Henry, S.T.L., J.C.D., Proof of the Reception of the Sacraments, X-165 pp., 1944.
210. Vaughan, Rev. William Edward, J.C.D., Constitutions for Diocesan Courts, X-210 pp., 1944.
211. Paro, Rev. Gino, S.T.D., J.C.D., The Right of Papal Legation, X-221 pp., 1944 (printed 1947).
212. Balzer, Rev. Ralph Francis, C.P., J.C.D., The Computation of Time in a Canonical Novitiate, X-227 pp., 1945.
213. Dougherty, Rev. John Whelan, A.B., S.T.L., J.C.D., De Inquisitione Speciali, XII-195 pp., 1945.
214. Dziob, Rev. Michael Walter, J.C.D., The Sacred Congregation for the Oriental Church, XII-181 pp., 1945.
215. Eidenschink, Rev. John Albert, O.S.B., B.A., J.C.D., The Election of Bishops in the Letters of Pope Gregory the Great, VIII-200 pp., 1945.
216. Gill, Rev. Nicholas, C.P., J.C.D., The Spiritual Prefect in Clerical Religious Houses of Study, X-140 pp., 1945.

217. Hynes, Rev. Harry Gerard, S.T.L., J.C.D., The Privileges of Cardinals, XII-183 pp., 1945.
218. McDevitt, Rev. Gerald Vincent, S.T.L., J.C.D., The Renunciation of an Ecclesiastical Office, XIV-179 pp., 1945.
219. Manning, Rev. Joseph Leroy, J.C.D., The Free Conferral of Offices, VII-116 pp., 1945.
220. Meyer, Rev. Louis G., O.S.B., A.B., S.T.B., J.C.D., Alms-gathering by Religious, XII-163 pp., 1945.
221. O'Donnell, Rev. Cletus Francis, M.A., J.C.D., The Marriage of Minors, XII-268 pp., 1945.
222. Prunskis, Rev. Joseph, J.C.D., Comparative Law, Ecclesiastical and Civil, in Lithuanian Concordat, X-161 pp., 1945.
223. Sweeney, Rev. Francis Patrick, C.SS.R., J.C.D., The Reduction of Clerics to the Lay State, X-199 pp., 1945.
224. Vogelpohl, Rev. Henry John, J.C.D., The Simple Impediments to Holy Orders, XVI-190 pp., 1945.
225. Brockhaus, Rev. Thomas Aquinas, O.S.B., J.C.D., Religious who are known as *Conversi*, X-127 pp., 1945.
226. Griese, Rev. Orville Nicholas, S.T.D., J.C.D., The Marriage Contract and the Procreation of Offspring, XVI-224 pp., 1946.
227. Boudreaux, Rev. Warren Louis, J.C.D., The *"ab acatholicis nati"* of Canon 1099, § 2, XII-110 pp., 1946.
228. Bowe, Rev. Thomas Joseph, A.B., J.C.D., Religious Superioresses, VIII-206 pp., 1946.
229. Diederichs, Rev. Michael Ferdinand, S.C.J., J.C.D., The Jurisdiction of the Latin Ordinaries over their Oriental Subjects, XIV-153 pp., 1946.
230. Dingman, Rev. Maurice John, A.B., S.T.L., J.C.L., The Plaintiff in Contentious Trials.
231. Frison, Rev. Basil, C.M.F., M.Mus., J.C.D., The Retroactivity of Law, X-221 pp., 1946.
232. Galvin, Rev. William Anthony, M.A., J.C.D., The Administrative Transfer of Pastors, XII-288 pp., 1946.
233. Goracy, Rev. Joseph C., J.C.L., The Diriment Matrimonial Impediment of Major Orders.
234. Hale, Rev. Joseph Francis, M.A., S.T.L., J.C.D., The Pastor of Burial, X-247 pp., 1946 (printed 1949).
235. Henry, Rev. Joseph Arthur, A.B., J.C.D., The Mass and Holy Communion: Interritual Law, XII-138 pp., 1946.
236. Linenberger, Rev. Herbert, C.PP.S., J.C.D., The False Denunciation of an Innocent Confessor, VIII-205 pp., 1946 (printed 1949).
237. Lowry, Rev. James Martin, A.B., J.C.D., Dispensation from Private Vows, XII-266 pp., 1946.
238. Lynch, Rev. George Edward, A.B., S.T.L., J.C.D., Coadjutors and Auxiliaries of Bishops, X-107 pp., 1946 (printed 1947).

239. Lynch, Rev. Timothy, M.S.SS.T., J.C.D., Contracts between Bishops and Religious Congregations, XIII-232 pp., 1946.
240. McClunn, Rev. Justin David, A.B., S.T.L., J.C.D., Administrative Recourse, VII-142 pp., 1946.
241. Lohmuller, Rev. Martin Nicholas, A.B., J.C.D., The Promulgation of Law, XII-140 pp., 1947.
242. McGrath, Rev. James, A.B., J.C.D., The Privilege of the Canon, XII-156 pp., 1946.
243. Marbach, Rev. Joseph Francis, A.B., J.C.D., Marriage Legislation for the Catholics of the Oriental Rites in the United States and Canada, XIV-314 pp., 1946.
244. Shimkus, Rev. Bernard Aloysius, A.B., J.C.L., The Determination and Transfer of Rite.
245. Smith, Rev. Vincent Michael, A.B., S.T.L., J.C.L., Ignorance Affecting Matrimonial Consent.
246. Wachtrle, Rev. Paul Anthony, A.B., J.C.L., The Baptism of the Children of Non-Catholics.
247. Crotty, Rev. Matthew Michael, J.C.D., The Recipient of First Holy Communion, X-142 pp., 1947.
248. Eagleton, Rev. George, J.C.D., The Quinquennial Faculties, Formula IV, XIV-199 pp., 1947 (printed 1948).
249. Gibbons, Rev. Marion Leo, C.M., J.C.L., Domicile of the Wife Unlawfully Separated from Her Husband, XIV-171 pp., 1947.
250. Kelly, Rev. Bernard M., S.T.L., J.C.D., The Functions Reserved to Pastors, XII-141 pp., 1947.
251. Kilcullen, Rev. Thomas J., LL.M., J.C.D., The Collegiate Moral Person as Party Litigant, X-150 pp., 1947.
252. Lafontaine, Rev. Germaine Joseph, W.F., J.C.D., Relations Canoniques entre le Missionaire et Ses Superieurs, X-117 pp., 1947.
253. Lane, Rev. Loras Thomas, A.B., S.T.L., J.C.D., Matrimonial Procedure in the Ordinary Court of Second Instance, XVI-184 pp., 1947.
254. Lover, Rev. James Francis, C.Ss.R., J.C.D., The Master of Novices, X-168 pp., 1947.
255. McNicholas, Rev. Timothy Joseph, J.C.L., The *Septimae Manus* Witness.
256. Marositz, Rev. Joseph John, M.S.C., J.C.D., Obligations and Privileges of Religious Promoted to the Episcopal or Cardinalitial Dignities, XII-180 pp., 1947.
257. Murphy, Rev. Francis Joseph, J.C.D., Legislative Powers of the Provincial Council, XII-158 pp., 1947.
258. O'Brien, Rev. Romaeus William, O.Carm., J.C.D., The Provincial Superior in Religious Orders of Men, X-294 pp., 1947.
259. Pfaller, Rev. Benedict Anthony, O.S.B., J.C.D., *The ipso facto* Effected Dismissal of Religious, XII-225 pp., 1947.

260. Popek, Rev. Alphonse Sylvester, J.C.D., The Rights and Obligations of Metropolitans, XX-460 pp., 1947.

261. Ristuccia, Rev. Bernard Joseph, C.M., J.C.D., Quasi-Religious, XVI-318 pp., 1947 (printed 1949).

262. Sonntag, Rev. Nathaniel Louis, O.F.M.Cap., J.C.D., Censorship of Special Classes of Books, XII-147 pp., 1947.

263. Stadler, Rev. Joseph Nicholas, J.C.D., Frequent Holy Communion, X-158 pp., 1947.

264. Szal, Rev. Ignatius Joseph, J.C.D., The Communication of Catholics with Schismatics, XII-217 pp., 1947.

265. Wagner, Rev. Urban S., O.F.M. Conv., J.C.D., Parochial Substitute Vicars and Supplying Priests, IX-126 pp., 1947.

266. Quinn, Rev. Joseph, M.A., J.C.D., Documents Required for the Reception of Orders, XIV-207 pp., 1948.

267. Bennington, Rev. James Clement, A.B., J.C.L., The Recipient of Confirmation.

268. Blaher, Rev. Damian Joseph, O.F.M., A.B., J.C.L., The Ordinary Processes in Causes of Beatification and Canonization.

269. Clune, Rev. Robert Bell, B.A., J.C.L., The Judicial Interrogation of the Parties.

270. Courtemanche, Rev. Basil F., B.A., J.C.L., The Total Simulation of Matrimonial Consent.

271. Dlouhy, Rev. Maur John, O.S.B., A.B., J.C.L., The Ordination of Exempt Religious.

272. Donovan, Rev. John Thomas, Ph.B., S.T.L., J.C.D., The Clerical Obligation of Canons 138 and 140, XII-209 pp., 1948.

273. Freking, Rev. Frederick W., A.B., S.T.B., J.C.L., The Canonical Installation of Pastors.

274. Fulton, Rev. Thomas B., J.C.L., Prenuptial Investigation.

275. Godley, Rev. James P., J.C.L., Time and Place for the Celebration of Mass.

276. Kane, Rev. Thomas A., A.B., B.S., J.C.D., Jurisdiction of the Patriarchs of the Major Sees, XII-153 pp., 1948 (printed 1949).

277. Kennedy, Rev. Andrew A., J.C.L., The Annual Pastoral Report to the Local Ordinary.

278. Konrad, Rev. Joseph George, J.C.L., Transfer of Religious.

279. Kress, Rev. Alphonse, J.C.L., Contumacy in Ecclesiastical Trials.

280. McCartney, Rev. Marcellus Anthony, O.F.M., M.A., J.C.L., Faculties of Regular Confessors.

281. McCaslin, Rev. Edward Patrick, M.A., S.T.L., J.C.L., The Division of Parishes.

282. McElroy, Rev. Francis J., A.B., J.C.L., The Privileges of Bishops.

283. QUINN, REV. STEPHEN, M.S.SS.T., J.C.D., Relation Between the Local Ordinary and Religious of Diocesan Approval, XII-153 pp., 1948 (printed 1949).
284. SCHNEIDER, REV. EDELHARD LOUIS, S.D.S., B.A., J.C.D., The Status of Secularized Ex-Religious Clerics, X-155 pp., 1948.
285. THOMPSON, CHESTER J., A.B., J.C.L., The Simple Removal from Office.
286. O'BRIEN, REV. KENNETH R., A.B., J.C.D., The Nature of Support of Diocesan Priests in the United States, XVI-162 pp., 1949.
287. METZ, REV. JOHN E., S.T.L., J.C.D., The Recording Judge in the Ecclesiastical Collegiate Tribunal, X-130 pp., 1949.
288. REINHARDT, REV. MARION J., S.T.L., J.C.L., The Rogatory Commission.
289. ORTEGA UHIUK, REV. JUAN, S.J., J.C.L., De Delicto Sollicitationis.
290. CASEY, REV. JAMES V., J.C.D., A Study of Canon 2222 § 1, XII-127 pp., 1949.
291. ALLGEIER, REV. JOSEPH L., J.C.L., The Canonical Obligation of Preaching in Parish Churches.
292. CAHILL, REV. DANIEL R., J.C.L., The Custody of the Holy Eucharist.
293. CARR, REV. AIDEN, O.F.M. Conv., S.T.D., J.C.L., Vocation to the Priesthood: Its Canonical Concept.
294. KNOPKE, REV. ROCH F., O.F.M., J.C.L., Reverential Fear in Matrimonial Cases in Asiatic Countries: Rota Cases.
295. LAVELLE, REV. HOWARD D., J.C.L., The Obligation of Holding Sacred Missions in Parishes.
296. MICKELLS, REV. ANTHONY B., J.C.L., The Constitutive Elements of Parishes.
297. NOONE, REV. JOHN J., J.C.L., Nullity in Judicial Acts.
298. SHEEHAN, REV. DANIEL E., J.C.L., The Minister of Holy Communion.
299. STATKUS, REV. FRANCIS J., J.C.L., The Minister of the Last Sacraments.
300. COOK, REV. JOHN P., J.C.L., Ecclesiastical Communities and Their Ability to Induce Legal Customs.
301. FAZZALARO, REV. FRANCIS J., J.C.L., The Place for the Hearing of Confessions.
302. HANNAN, REV. PHILIP M., J.C.L., The Canonical Concept of *congrua sustentatio* for the Secular Clergy.
303. QUINN, REV. HUGH G., S.T.L., J.C.L., The Particular Penal Precept.
304. GALLAGHER, REV. JOHN F., J.C.L., The Matrimonial Impediment of Public Propriety.
305. WELSH, REV. THOMAS J., J.C.L., The Use of the Portable Altar.

www.ingramcontent.com/pod-product-compliance
Lightning Source LLC
LaVergne TN
LVHW050255080826
844660LV00012B/642
9780813224558